REMEMBRANCE
OF THINGS
PARIS

REMEMBRANCE OF THINGS PARIS

SIXTY YEARS OF WRITING
FROM *Gourmet*

Edited and with an Introduction
by Ruth Reichl

THE MODERN LIBRARY

NEW YORK

2004 Modern Library Edition

All of the essays in this work were originally published in *Gourmet*.

LIBRARY OF CONGRESS CATALOGING-IN-PUBLICATION DATA
Remembrance of things Paris: sixty years of writing from Gourmet/edited and with
an introduction by Ruth Reichl.
p. cm.
Includes bibliographical references and index.
ISBN 0-679-64309-5
1. Cooks—France—Paris. 2. Food writers. I. Reichl, Ruth. II. Gourmet.
TX649.R46 2004
641.5944'361—dc22   2003044288

Modern Library website address: www.modernlibrary.com

Printed in the United States of America on acid-free paper

2 4 6 8 9 7 5 3 1

Contents

PARISIANS

PARIS TODAY

INTRODUCTION

Ruth Reichl

For a true gourmet in the first few decades of the twentieth century, Paris was the heart's home, the place that mattered, a shrine for everyone who believed that eating well was the best revenge. It was where Hemingway's *Moveable Feast* took place, where Liebling spent his time *Between Meals,* where M.F.K. Fisher's *Gastronomical Me* was born.

But *Gourmet* came into the world in 1941, just as the United States was going to war and Paris was impossible to visit. Reading through the early issues of the war years you get a certain forlorn sense, a hole in the place where Paris should have been. Is it any wonder that the moment the war ended the magazine's editor and publisher, Earle MacAusland, immediately dispatched a correspondent to find out what was going on in the City of Light? The story that Don Dresden sent back was slightly dispiriting; rationing was still on, he reported, there was no cream, no butter, and very little meat. All over town he found chefs who were wringing their hands and doing their best.

But conditions soon improved. Within a few years the magazine was publishing stories about a Paris that had happily returned to its prewar ways. Old men left their mistresses to sit in cafés and watch the world go by, endlessly debating the important question of where dinner should be served. The great parties resumed—set pieces of high fashion and fabulous food. As the good times came back to the metropolis, *Gourmet* sent off the first of what would be an unbroken line of full-time Paris correspondents to chronicle the life of the city for its eager readers.

That first resident correspondent was Naomi Barry, who may be the most underappreciated restaurant writer of all time. Reading fifty-year-old restaurant reviews would not normally be much fun; it takes a writer of extraordinary abilities to make you care about meals that you will never be able to eat. But with each review Barry offers up such a rich slice of life that you feel you are sitting at the next table, eavesdropping on your neighbors chatting with the chef. Her reviews are like little time machines that not only allow you to taste the food she is eating, but somehow transport you back to a city that no longer exists.

For me that is the magic of this collection of essays. Each is a passport to the past, a way to watch Paris grow and change at the very moment it was happening. This is living history, vibrant and unselfconscious, and it offers an amazing opportunity to watch an entire civilization transform itself and move into what will become the present.

This would not work, of course, had the magazine not been blessed with such extraordinary writers. But after Barry came Joseph Wechsberg, a man who truly belongs in the pantheon of great food writers along with A. J. Liebling and M.F.K. Fisher. He had good taste and great talent, but more than that he had an interesting mind. The subjects that he chose to write about—a bookshop, the opening of a fashion house, the way that Parisians walk down the street—offer you an intimate portrait of a city by an accomplished watcher whose greatest joy was simply to observe the city as it strolled past his table.

But having its own correspondent in the city was never enough for *Gourmet*, whose readers had an insatiable appetite for all things Paris. Great writers have always been eager to eat there, and the magazine has always been eager for their thoughts. And so we also have Lillian Langseth-Christensen, Louis Diat, Judith and Evan Jones, Diane Johnson, Michael Lewis, Frank Prial, Paul Goldberger, and Jonathan

Gold, among others, each devouring Paris in his or her own particular fashion.

No change went unobserved. The demise of Les Halles was reported by five different people (we have included three). The magazine wrote about the new buildings, the new telephones, the new food. In the early seventies when a generation of young chefs created a whole new style of cooking, *Gourmet's* writers were thrilled; something new to write about! We follow the development of nouvelle cuisine, and as the chefs cook and the years pass we see the old city slowly disappear, fade away as if it were being erased to make way for the new. With this new food came a modern and more aggressive metropolis to take the place of Paris past.

This collection closes with the slightly bemused observation of François Simon, who wrote the finale for *Gourmet's* Paris issue at the beginning of the twenty-first century. It is not Naomi Barry's Paris, nor that of Joseph Wechsberg, but it remains a vibrant and fascinating city. And although M. Simon's city would have been almost impossible to imagine sixty years earlier, it is a reminder that, in one form or another, we will always have Paris.

REMEMBERING
PARIS

Paris in the Twenties

Irene Corbally Kuhn

The year was 1921. The month was May. The city was Paris. And I had just bought a new hat that I remember to this day: an exquisite, wide-brimmed straw hat trimmed with an enormous silk violet. I was about to start work as fashion editor, general reporter, and the only woman on the ten-member staff of the four-year-old Paris edition of the *Chicago Tribune*.

The world had passed through the long darkness of the "war to end all wars" and was more than ready for the frenzied gaiety and brief brilliance of the roaring twenties. Paris was packed with Americans—and, for the most part, the French were happy to have us. Artists, writers, composers, dilettantes, bankers, businessmen, army officers, diplomats, and journalists, we had little in common beyond a passion for Paris and tended to travel in separate circles that only occasionally intersected. The journalists were a most clannish group. We did not mix with the literati, which is to say the Americans who came to Paris to write novels. We were, however, most gregarious and mixed with everyone else, because a story could come from anywhere. And frequently it did.

The Paris *Chicago Tribune* was one of the two principal English-language daily newspapers published there through the 1920s. The other was the Paris edition of the *New York Herald Tribune*. Although their names were similar they had little else in common. The Paris *Chicago Tribune*, known as "the *Trib*," was a grubby gamin compared with that sober, prosperous burgher, the Paris *Herald Tribune*, known as "the *Herald*," and whereas the competition between the two was friendly, it was often fierce. The *Herald* had been around a long time; the *Trib* was a brash newcomer, founded to keep the troops of the American Expeditionary Forces stationed in France during World War I in touch with news from home.

The *Herald* had editorial offices; the *Trib* was put out from a single, dingy room on the upper floor of a building on the rue Lamartine— an unremarkable street running off the rue Lafayette on the Right Bank. There were no desks, merely scarred, battered plank tables to support the decrepit typewriters, of which there were never enough to go around. Rickety chairs, a Telex machine, a few telephones, and a half dozen or so naked lightbulbs dangling from a painted-tin ceiling completed the décor. A few of the bulbs were covered with makeshift shades fashioned from newsprint, alarmingly charred. This inelegant space was rented from *Le Petit Journal* as were the presses and the services of its boisterous Montmartre compositors, who spoke a baffling patois that took months to master. More significant than any of these details, however, was the fact that the building housing the *Trib*'s editorial room backed onto the same courtyard as a cheerful, rowdy bistro. Arrangements had long since been made for buckets of cool, foaming beer to be conveyed by means of a rope from the courtyard to the editorial room to speed the flow of copy on a hot summer's night.

One unique and irreplaceable advantage that the *Trib* enjoyed over the *Herald*, though, was the editorial and reportorial talents of Floyd Gibbons, who was the European manager for the Chicago Tribune Company. Gibbons was even then legendary, the quintessential foreign correspondent, a handsome man with a huge sense of adventure, unlimited daring, and great personal courage. He had become a legend for his colorful reporting from the Mexican border war of 1916 and later embellished the legend when he sailed to England in February 1917 aboard the Cunard passenger liner *Laconia*. The ship was torpedoed off the Irish coast and sank almost immediately. After a night spent in a lifeboat Gibbons and the other survivors were rescued, and half an hour after landing in Liverpool Gibbons was in a telegraph office cabling the dramatic story to his editor in Chicago. It is no wonder he was as much a hero to his fellow correspondents as he was to the public. Later he was to lose an eye while covering the battle of Belleau Wood in World War I, and the white eyepatch he wore from then on became his trademark.

Although Gibbons was off on assignment in Russia the day I showed up with a letter of introduction from my former editor in New York, we subsequently became lifelong friends. I was hired anyway by his deputy, who took me on to replace the *Trib*'s fashion editor, Rosemary Carr. She was leaving to return home to marry a promising young poet, Stephen Vincent Benét. My salary was fifteen hundred francs a month, or about ninety dollars at the then prevailing rate of exchange. It was scarcely a fortune, but Paris in those days was accommodating to the impecunious young.

———

Even though I had always loved clothes and followed fashion, *haute couture* was something I had to learn about in a hurry. But, as with many professions, I shortly found that familiarity bred assurance. Most of the great *couture* houses, eager for publicity among Americans, gave me ready access to their workrooms and showrooms, where, almost by osmosis, I learned the workings of the trade and its terminology. Some even lent me finery to wear on special assignments as when, turned out by Patou, I reported on the activities of the first week of "the season" in Deauville. Others, like Worth and Chanel, habitually gave generous discounts to fashion writers, a practice that worked no hardship on them as there were so few of us then.

My wardrobe was a matter of some moment in my general reporting as well, because one of my principal tasks was to keep track of arrivals at hotels like the Ritz, the Crillon, the George V, and the Meurice. Never mind that I lived in a garret room in a tiny Left Bank hotel myself; dressed in my designer best, I could command any of those opulent lobbies.

For sheer elegance and stylishness it's hard to imagine what could ever equal that small segment of Paris that became my regular beat and daily delight. It included the honey-colored stone colonnades of the marvelously proportioned seventeenth-century Palais-Royal, where I'd sometimes steal a few minutes to wander through the tranquil inner gardens. Next came the imposing classical façade of the Church of the Madeleine, where I one day discovered, in a niche on an outer wall, a beheaded statue of Saint Luc, a victim of the German bombardment a few years earlier. Then there was the gorgeous nineteenth-century exuberance of the Opéra; and finally the peaceful, unpretentious pleasures of the Garden of the Tuileries.

My surveillance of the grand hotels was, more often than not, an unmomentous routine devised principally to fill a column headed "Americans in Paris." But not infrequently the routine could become exciting, as when I was dispatched to interview Charlie Chaplin. Because the weather was glorious and his morning was free, we strolled the length of the Champs-Élysées together, and I caught glimpses of the shy, gentle spirit of the man who was known as the greatest comedian of his day.

It was another story when Peggy Hopkins Joyce took up residence at the Ritz while she selected her next season's wardrobe. A striking, natural blonde, Peggy was famous for being famous. She had shot to celebrity as a show girl and shortly thereafter began to enjoy a long and successful career as a courtesan. Not only diamonds but sapphires, emeralds, and rubies were *all* her best friends. And furs. And clothes. And a shrewdly chosen investment portfolio. It was the mark of a successful man to be seen in her company, and her salon was the world of the wealthy. Had she lived in Louis XV's day, she undoubtedly would have given Madame de Pompadour real competition as the royal favorite. Like Pompadour, she was intelligent, capable, discreet, and a wonderfully entertaining companion. Warm, generous, and naturally gracious, she was secure in her chosen calling and counted almost as many women as men among her friends. The French found her enchanting, as I discovered when she invited me to dine with her and her latest conquest—a French industrialist who was a regular patron of the Tour d'Argent. There, at a window table, we drank Champagne and watched the long blue twilight gently mantle the magnificent south front of Notre-Dame just opposite, a sight so achingly lovely I scarcely tasted the food.

And that was a pity because the likes of the Tour d'Argent, the Grand Véfour, and Lasserre, for example, were seldom accessible to newsmen and newswomen living from one undernourished salary check to the next. We were more likely to seek out the bistros frequented by taxi drivers (an estimably knowledgeable group about food as about much else) or the small, family-run restaurants where provincial food of every variety flourished and where one could often find a delicious locally produced wine available nowhere else. In memory, the food was sublimely and universally good, the coffee unvaryingly poisonous.

———

Then, of course, there were the cafés, some of which not only still exist but continue as centers for the same clientele. For Paris is a place where habit dominates perhaps more than in any other major metropolis. Montparnasse has been the haunt of artists forever. Now, as in my day, Le Sélect, La Coupole, and Le Dôme, all arrayed near one another along the boulevard du Montparnasse as it cuts through the short streets and hidden squares of the Left Bank, attract the young and struggling equally with the established and prosperous among artists.

The literary set favored Saint-Germain-des-Prés, and their cafés, then as now, were Le Flore and Les Deux Magots, with the brasserie Lipp a distant third. Here, if one cared to, one could find from time to time not only Hemingway and the Fitzgeralds but a range of young American literary talent one is less likely to associate with Paris in the twenties: the poets Archibald MacLeish, Hart Crane, and e. e. cummings; the novelists John Dos Passos and Glenway Westcott, to cite just a few. They, as well as the tens of dozens of others who came to Paris then "To Write" but never quite made it, belied the title "the Lost Generation." They were anything but, if diligence and a zest for life are used as the measures.

Still, most of us who were engaged in the unceasing demands of meeting deadlines for a daily newspaper saw little of our literary countrymen and regarded them as rare birds given to strange habits and mysterious enthusiasms. Our interests, we believed, were those of the real world and reflected everyday reality. This meant, among other things, that the shadow of the war often filled our consciousness, as on Memorial Day in 1921, when ceremonies were held all over France to honor Americans who had lost their lives on the battle-fields. As I traveled by train from Paris to Belleau Wood near Château-Thierry, with the American ambassador and other officials, American as well as French, it was impossible to prepare myself adequately for the sight that greeted our arrival. The day was soft and fine; May was merging into June, and the sky was an infinite blue. But the blackened ruins of abandoned villages, the charred skeletons of ancient trees, and the shell-pocked fields lying fallow stood in terrible contrast to the loveliness of the weather. Dominating everything was the endless expanse of white crosses, each grave marked by a small American flag, made even more moving by the nosegays of wildflowers set out before dawn by local farmers. As the scene impressed itself on my memory forever, I could only think of how many just my age must lie beneath those crosses.

But few of my assignments were so tinged with tragedy. Some, in fact, were marvelous fun. On one that was particularly entertaining, I was paired with a young Frenchwoman, Simone Heller, married to an American and working as a reviewer and critic for *Le Matin*. Following a carefully prepared route we spent a day shopping the rue de la Paix, the Faubourg Saint-Honoré, and the rue de Castiglione for expensive gowns, hats, and blouses; and the specialty shops along the rue Saint-Honoré for handbags, scarves, and shoes. We queried prices on rooms in hotels near the Étoile. At a cabstand near the Opéra we dickered with cabbies over the cost of a round trip to Saint-Cloud, where the French national tennis championships were about to be held. Finally at day's end we dined, ordering the same meal, wine and all, at a well-known restaurant near the Comédie-Française.

We did not travel as a team but separately, Simone speaking her lovely, liquid Parisian French, I professing no knowledge of anything but English. We took the whole day for this and kept careful notes of all prices we were quoted or, as in the case of our dinners, were charged. The point of the exercise was to discover just how outrageous *was* the constantly claimed overcharging of Americans by the "greedy French." The joke was on the cynics and complainers, for in every case the prices asked were identical. Except for one. At a small, chic milliner's I had been offered the same hat Simone had earlier tried on, but for me it was to be a few francs less. Both stories relating our adventures in comparison shopping ran in parallel columns under our bylines in the *Trib* in English and in *Le Matin* in French. The feeling of virtuousness among the shopkeepers we had visited must have been immense—and rightly so.

———

One of the appeals of journalism for those who choose it as a profession is that every day brings something new, something different, and one can confidently expect the unexpected. Certainly for me those days in Paris more than proved that adage. How else could I ever have been a guest at the wedding that was the romantic sensation of the year, that of the nineteen-year-old American heir to a vast tin-mining fortune, William B. Leeds, to the comparably youthful Princess Xenia, daughter of the Grand Duchess Marie of Russia? It was held in the gold-domed Russian Orthodox Cathédrale de Saint-Alexandre Newsky on the rue Daru. At first the panoply, the pageantry, the plethora of titled, grandly garbed guests, the candles, the symbolic crowns, the cascading organ music were enthralling. But, as quarter hours expanded into half hours and we stood and stood and stood, even such exotica began to pall.

The next assignment might be a cultural event, as when in all innocence I went to the Galérie Montaigne to report on the first exhibition of what proved to be the fortuitously short-lived craze dubbed Dadaism. Like most of the rest of the bewildered spectators who studied such works of art as a row of dozens of ready-tied neckties strung side by side, I quickly concluded that this movement would never last. And it didn't. But its natural child, surrealism, was born in Paris just a few years later. So much for prophecy in the world of art.

Surrealism aside, Janet Flanner, *The New Yorker*'s longtime Paris correspondent, once observed: "At any season, and all year long, in the evening the view of the city from the bridges was always exquisitely pictorial. One's eyes became the eyes of a painter, because the sight itself approximated art.... The Pont Neuf still looked as we had known it on the canvases of Sisley and Pissarro.... In the early twenties, when I was new there, Paris was still yesterday."

For all those who shared that time in Paris her words ring with a bittersweet truth. But Paris is also today—and tomorrow. Despite the encroachments of the startlingly new as in the Centre Pompidou or the ring of towering skyscrapers that seems to be closing in on all that has made Paris a place of unique beauty, it remains, after two thousand years, more immutable than any other capital city in the world. Perhaps that is because so many of us left our youth there. And gladly.

March 1988

After the War

Don Dresden

Returning to live in Paris again is a strange mingling of impressions: memories of prewar days when France was a soft and lovely place where everything abounded; crowding thoughts of first seeing Paris at an age when foreign capitals took on an added glamour and charm; recollections with a touch of knight-in-shining-armor feeling when returning with the invasion forces; reminiscences of the incomparable enthusiasm and joy of Parisians on their day of liberation when the capital was short of food but long on goodwill, and when old bottles hidden during the occupation were brought out in celebration.

All those thoughts of days gone by tumbled over one another when I first returned. I found myself looking for things I had remembered so fondly and discovering that more than one might normally expect were still in their places from prewar and war days. Yet Paris was a place of strange contrasts during the first winter.

Out of the fairyland dream that is Paris for so many who come just to see it and end up loving it, resolves a very real kind of being when one comes to the city to live again after several months' absence. Even the weather seems to contrive to be different from how it was remembered, and everywhere one hears the natives remark, "Well, it has never been like this before."

Most days during the winter have been rainy with a tomblike sky shrouding the city. The streets have looked black and wet from the moisture in the wood or stone blocks, and footsteps were muffled in the damp air. There have been bright days when the thin winter sun with its lemon rays burned off the nighttime mist, and the spires of churches and the outlines of the classical architecture slowly lifted as though they were being pushed up and out by an invisible hand for everyone to see. Waves of cold have hit the capital. The Siberian blasts have frozen the pavement, turned the dark streets white and sparkling. The heels of pedestrians clicked in a high, hollow sound as people hurried to warm themselves in the nearest heated place, a search not always fruitful. On such days and nights, the people who always have looked less cold and forlorn than the average person seemed unchanged: the news vendors, the roasters of chestnuts, the ticket collectors on the buses. But their apparent acclimatization had nothing to do with avoiding the penetrating kind of cold that seeped into every cell of the softened American and made him want to run for copious libations of hot grog. Luckily there were days when the temperature lifted, and snow fell softly as though designed for a city with lovely lines on which to shed its grace. People were happy, for *le grand froid* was temporarily at an end; children romped in *la neige* that for them is a rarity. All these meteorological variations have been striking.

So it has been with gastronomy—stark contrasts.

Disregarding such exigencies, it is possible to find a sound and most pleasant meal, provided one is well heeled and knows his way around. As has always been the case, refreshing one's gastronomical lore about this center of eating is a pleasant process. It is possible that one might contract gout in searching for new taste sensations or in trying to recapture old ones, but the odds are that he won't. Moreover, there is a better than even chance that the waistline will go down.

Before starting on a tour of the city's restaurants, one must prepare for changes, the first and most important of which is monetary. Without mixing finances and gastronomy too much, the franc today is worth about eight tenths of a cent in contrast to about three cents just before the war. A bistro meal without anything to drink, an unsatisfactory way to eat, costs about 120 francs or $1 today. Before the war it was common to find the equivalent for a tenth that price, *vin compris.* At the other end of the scale, the average check at Maxim's is about 2,000 francs or $16. Between those extremes are many small restaurants where prices range from 350 to 700 francs ($2.80 to $5.60) with a moderately good half-bottle of wine.

The next most striking change from prewar days is the lack of butter and other dairy products. This scarcity makes cooking with butter a rarity, a cream sauce practically unheard of, and also keeps one from bulging out at the middle. Chefs in some of the more *bon ton* spots refuse to have anything to do with substitutes for the real products with which they practice their craft. Like artists who don't have the proper paint with which to do a scene, they refuse to attempt dishes that were common in happier days when there was plenty of everything.

There is still another change. Good drinking has always been a part of good eating in France. It has meant the effervescent joy of Champagne, the light white wines of Alsace kept in their long-necked bottles and served in long-stemmed glasses, the deep body and bouquet of a fine Burgundy, the delicate color and lovely aftertaste of an excellent Bordeaux. It has also meant the honest *vin rouge* and *vin blanc ordinaire* served for free in carafes with meals all over the nation. As this article is being written, the ration for two months ago has not yet been distributed; there have been scandals in many departments of distribution, including wine.

A reasonable amount of good wine can be found in most restaurants, but often it is young and unmarked except for the region of its birth. The price is approximately ten times as high as it was before the war. Famous cellars such as Maxim's which were moved to the country just before the green wave hit Paris in June 1940 have been retained intact with their magnificent selections. The value of such stocks has jumped many times over; the owners are unwilling to predict what prices might be for their bottles several months hence. In a nation where prices have gone up at least ten times over prewar levels, it is understandable that dealers, distributors, and patrons should want to hang on to their tangibles (in this case potables) as they see their balance of francs diminish in value.

Throughout this past winter, during the seemingly endless crises in the distribution of meat, it was common to find much more of the insides of the animal on the menu, such as heart, liver, brains, and sweetbreads, than the steaks and chops and roasts, which had been sold in the black market or were being held under the counter in reserve for regular customers.

Restaurants that before the war would have offered seven or eight entrées could muster only two or three, and often the choicest items were quickly exhausted by hungry and wise patrons who came early.

Lastly, there are many little things that one misses in the cuisine, such as the variety of cakes and tarts now restricted because of flour and sugar shortages and the scarcity of lemons that always were linked with oysters, *bis,* and a good glass of *vin blanc.* It is possible to find the lemon at times, the *bis* at others, but rarely both together. Real coffee is scarce; the *café national* is a mélange of real coffee with a high percentage of some strange roasted thing.

Lest all these changes give the impression that dining out in Paris is so different that it is no longer enjoyable, the returnee to this land of the table can be assured that he will get full measure for his time and money. One of the best indications of the restaurant situation is the fact that a mess for newspaper correspondents and businessmen closed because members found other places to eat more interesting and not too expensive.

My gastronomical wandering started from the rue Cassette, which is on the Left Bank in the Sixth Arrondissement. I walked along the rue de Vaugirard that skirts the Luxembourg Gardens, somber in winter, gay in spring and summer, past the rue Servandoni, which tilts and winds and where the houses for centuries have leaned out and bulged over the street like portly gentlemen in suits made for them long before they have partaken so heartily of the table. My path took me past the Senate, where nearby Foyot stood for years as a landmark of excellent food and service. I was headed for the Place de l'Odéon where one can always find a good restaurant open, for hard by each other are the Mediterranée and the Restaurant Voltaire, while Au Cochon de Lait in the rue Corneille is nearby—no suckling pig at the last visit, but promised soon.

The oyster boxes with their bits of green seaweed bursting from the covers were stacked in front of nearly every place, but especially the Mediterranée, which specializes in seafood and has, among many delightful dishes, a fine *soupe aux poissons,* a kind of bouillabaisse. I remembered the Restaurant Voltaire particularly from the days following the liberation of Paris, for it was there that I had my first meal outside an army mess. That day ended with much celebration in nearby haunts of the *Résistance.* The first time I went back this winter it looked just the same; the precise waiter who had served me three years ago and demanded ration tickets repeated himself. This time I had the tickets. The food was excellent: *fine de claire* oysters, cold and filled with juice, a tender *poulet rôti cresson* with french-fried potatoes, tiny peas, a *tarte aux cerises,* all helped down with refreshing Riesling and topped with passable coffee. The atmosphere was as French as the tricolor: the polite yet not obsequious waiter, the center serving table on which the oyster sauces and cheese are kept, the hissing of steam through coffee as it was freshly prepared, the view toward the columns of the old Odéon Théâtre through the falling rain.

After that first lunch, I wandered about a great deal renewing acquaintances with big and little places on the Left Bank. The Restaurant Polidor at 40, rue Monsieur le Prince seemed the same; so did the genial patron and his kitchen-handy wife whose combined arts have apparently meant a prosperous business, for there is little modernization compared to the days when the restaurant was largely a hangout at mealtime for ex–French Forces of the Interior. It provides honest food and drink for a relatively small price to habitués of the *quartier.* The Restaurant des Arts in the rue de Seine is operating under normal management and provides its usual inexpensive fare. About halfway down the serpentine rue Saint-André-des-Arts is Chez Vincent, long known to most Left-Bankers, and others too, as one of the soundest establishments where one can satisfy an appetite for excellent cuisine. It hasn't changed, luckily.

Eventually one gets around to those places he remembers among the first he saw years ago. For me the Coupole on the boulevard du Montparnasse was one, for it was there that I was taken for an introduction to the Left Bank, and especially to French oysters. I remem-

ber how frightened I was of *la Portugaise verte,* the green oyster, un-
adorned except for a dash of lemon juice, I who had been brought up
on the standard tomato ketchup sauce with oysters in America. Later
I became a devotee of French oysters and longed for them when I was
away from France.

The Coupole is a disarming establishment, for outwardly it isn't
the kind of place in which one would expect to find such excellent
cooking. It is a large, airy place with something of the mood of the
Left Bank; an artist with long flowing hair is often seated at a table
sketching a client; M. Lop, the perennial and strange candidate for
the presidency, pops in to make a quick and fiery speech. But most of
the customers are interested mainly in food. They are ably cared for
under the personal direction of Messrs. Fraux and Lafon, who keep a
very close watch on their establishment during lunch and dinner.

Oysters come to the Coupole directly from Brittany, the wines are
purchased directly from the producers. Beer has always been famed
here: Today French, Danish, and the renowned Pilsen from Czecho-
slovakia are on draft; it must be admitted that the latter is not up
to its prewar standard. English stout and ale used to be additional
choices.

On the other side of the river at the rue Royale is one of the restaurants best known all over the world for years—Maxim's. Going there
today is like turning the clock back for as many years as one can remember, for outwardly it seems to have changed so little.

At first the restaurant seems to be closed, for the steel shutters are
down and only a tiny light shows through the doors, like an imperfect
wartime blackout. Inside, Albert the maître d'hôtel stands Buddha-like
at the entry to greet the clientele, just as he has stood for years. The
deep red carpet, the polished bar out of another age, the regiment of
waiters, the faultlessly laundered linen, the flowers on the tables, the
polished glassware—everything is complete and exactly as it has been
for years. M. Vaudable, formerly at LaRue up the street, is manager
today.

Every place that has a name with a glamorous past—Maxim's has
gone through a series of lives since its birth in 1893—is certain to attract foreigners. The crop of natives who patronize it changes with the

winds. Today it is easy to distinguish many of the Americans even without their uniforms, for they can be heard across the room. The English are conspicuous more from their choice of food, for they come from an austerity country where the counterpart of a menu like Maxim's is just about unknown. There are a few of the old-guard French with sufficient cash to take the check without whimpering, although their currency has been cut to less than a twentieth of its value of a quarter of a century ago. And there are *nouveaux riches,* whose bulging billfolds can take an inordinate amount of punishment.

The most striking differences between a menu at Maxim's last winter and its counterpart of the early thirties are, first, the number of dishes, reduced by about half; second, the prices, which have gone up about ten times; and third, the complete lack of meat on the menu except young wild boar, during part of the winter of scarcities. There was plenty to eat—fish, chicken, duckling, pheasant, venison, all beautifully prepared—but to find Maxim's without meat on the menu is an indication of the times in France.

The time might come again when Maxim's will offer *truite vivante au bleu, gratin queues d'écrevisses, basrond d'agneau de Pauillac persillé pommes Maxim's, médallion de ris de veau Grand Duc, coeur de filet bordelaise,* and such things. M. Vaudable and his chef, M. Barthe, say that there is no *grande cuisine* today because of the lack of butter and cream. Until such things return one will be able to get along adequately, and the lack of such products makes unnecessary the only really efficacious waist-reducing exercise: pushing yourself away from the table.

June 1947

Chicken Demi-Deuil

George Bijur

"You must read Flaubert aloud, holding a pencil tightly clenched between your teeth," Monsieur Thibaut, professor of phonetics at l'Institut du Panthéon, had always insisted. "If you wish to learn to pronounce the most beautiful language in the world correctly, this is the only way to make move your lazy American lips."

Now that I had at last returned to Paris, seven years later, the hectic day after *la Libération,* I kept wondering if my tyrannical teacher was still alive and well; if he would still make his American pupils perform violent setting-up exercises while reciting Géraldy's *poèmes d'amour—* an ambidextrous athletics designed to remedy Western twang by making it impossible to breathe through the nose while conversing.

After lunch I stuffed my pockets with Life Savers and K rations, gifts which famished Parisians seemed to find comparable to the little gondolas of gold that Marco Polo had once proffered to Kublai Khan, pushed through the crowds of girls with berets and guys with bottles, and headed for the university district.

The Institut du Panthéon is around the corner from the Sorbonne, just behind the Café Dupont, *"où tout est bon."* Its narrow entrance is guarded by a small glass slot in the door, through which a secretary may gauge the academic fitness of visitors before inviting them to

enter. Resembling the peepholes in our erstwhile speakeasies, this re-
connaissance slot is called by the French *un vasistas,* an onomatopoeic
word satirizing the habit German soldiers had during the Franco-
Prussian War of inquiring *"Was ist das?"* when they first saw so unfa-
miliar a contrivance.

As I rang the bell, the face of the student behind *le vasistas* took on
a startled expression. A uniformed Yank, perhaps a member of the U.S.
Gestapo! *"C'est un amerloque, un 'ricain!"*

There was barely a few seconds' wait until I was ceremoniously
ushered into that inner sanctum of phonetics, the office of M. Thibaut.
The old man was sitting in the same dilapidated, overcarved armchair
that I remembered so well, wearing the same enormous shell-rimmed
spectacles that Disney might have designed for an animated owl, peer-
ing up at the same old cobwebs on the ceiling.

When he stood up, you could see that his trouser cuffs were fringed
and tattered, but his shoes, in honor presumably of the great victory,
were polished until they had become brown leather looking glasses,
worthy of a place in the newly emancipated Hall of Mirrors at Versailles. He shook hands with me as formally as General de Gaulle
would have, no doubt, if welcoming President Roosevelt, then flung
his arms around my shoulders and cried. Much later, after I had asked
about his health, his family, his vineyards in Beaujolais, and above all
the blue-ribbon snails he reared with the care of pedigreed pets, I
asked if I might not have a lesson in phonetics. He nodded, obviously
pleased, then got up and hobbled over to a huge mahogany filing cabinet, pulled open a drawer marked *B,* and all but disappeared from
sight as he dived into its cavernous depths. When he emerged, he was
triumphantly clutching a large manila envelope, deeply yellowed with
age. "Now we shall see what we shall see," he exclaimed, slitting open
the flap to unearth a two-page list of my ancient faults of phonetics,
preserved in the wood since 1937.

For nearly an hour I paraded and auditioned all the Gallic noises in
my repertoire. To an eavesdropper on the other side of the partition,
it would have seemed as if some radio actor were rehearsing barnyard
sound effects as I squealed, mooed, whined, barked, and clucked my
way through the vowels, semivowels, and nasal vowels as laid down

by *Larousse*. To squeeze out that half-explosive, half-mincing sound of *pu*, my reluctant lips would pucker to the shape of an ancient loud-speaker. For developing correct pronunciation of nasalized vowels as in *faim* and *pain*, there would be the tantalizing task of exhaling through nose and mouth at the same time, all the while bleating "ba-a-a-" like Bopeep's sheep; for short *a* as in *patte*, the effort to open one's mouth wider than Joe E. Brown's, while touching the teeth with the tongue tip, an assignment that seemed harder than Arty McGovern's old reducing exercise of touching the toes with the fingertips without bending the knees.

When at last the solemn grandfather's clock on the wall pointed to closing time, M. Thibaut shook his head sadly. "I am overjoyed," he said, "to see an old pupil once more, especially as an officer in the American Air Force, but I am desolated at the deterioration in your diphthongs."

To cheer me up, perhaps, after this depressing news, he invited me to "Come and break a crust with us this evening. My daughter will be honored. And you must observe *her* diphthongs—they are fit to be framed!" At his home that night, we feasted on a rare Lyonese specialty, apparently chosen to symbolize the old man's conflict of emotions: *la poularde en demi-deuil*, "chicken, half in mourning." It is so named because truffles are carefully inserted just beneath the transparent skin, offsetting the golden hue of *la poularde* with flecks of somber black. A sort of culinary concerto with a split personality, it reminded you of that piano piece of Lord Bernes, "Funeral March of a Rich Aunt." In this, you remember, the left hand thumps out a dutiful bass of the mourners' procession, while the right hand goes off into irreverent trills of joyful anticipation, as a graceless young nephew imagines all the gay delights he will buy with his just-acquired legacy.

So, with *la poularde en demi-deuil*, our palates simultaneously celebrated the liberation of Paris, and mourned the death of my diphthongs. M. Thibaut's daughter, Claudine, dined with us, stuttering with excitement. Soon to be married, she wanted to fashion her wedding dress from the very Pennsylvania parachute that had borne her *Maquis* fiancé back to France, one nervous night long before D day. There was just one difficulty, and perhaps *M'sieu le Commandant* could solve that:

The white parachute silk carried heavily stenciled blue numbers which no amount of secret nocturnal scrubbing had been able to remove. Was it possible that the quartermaster of the great American Army could lend her just a tiny bottle of ink eradicator?

As her father poured glass after glass of warm Champagne, for August was hot and there was no ice in Paris, we clinked glasses and proposed toasts. We drank to General de Gaulle, General Eisenhower, and the girl next door, who had fulfilled a patriotic pledge by jumping into the Seine that morning wearing her very best clothes. We soon progressed to the drinking toasts of taxi drivers and students of the rue Sommerard. *"Derrière la cravate"* ("Down behind your necktie"). *"Faites flotter le poisson"* ("To float the fish you ate earlier"). *"Pour tuer le ver"* ("To kill the worm"). According to French bistro belief, a wicked worm lurks in every man's intestines: Unless held in check by regular applications of wine, it may grow to enormous proportions. Thus the more you drink, the more you feel the virtuous righteousness of Saint George conquering a homemade dragon.

In between sips, M. Thibaut would lecture me on snails. "A good eating snail is not soft. It is not lazy. It is not one of your stay-in-bed-all-days. *Mais non!* Snail flavor is concentrated in the muscles. That is why it is so easy to distinguish between a snail worth his weight in garlic and a snail hardly worth the pain of preparation. A champion snail has the instincts of a Percheron. You have only to place him on the kitchen table, tied to a weight, and he will leap to the challenge: He will pull and pull and pull."

You could almost picture the old man visiting his vineyards and exercising his herd of snails, making them do a hundred inches around a crawling track every morning, and perhaps perform setting-up exercises before their wine-leaf breakfast. "It is incredible," he would sigh, shaking his head, "that in a great country like America you should prefer *chiens chauds* to snails."

As we continued to "undry the throat" with a *Cognac de guerre,* Claudine suddenly interrupted. "But, Papa," she exclaimed, "something very strange has happened. It to me seems that your diphthongs have become just the least bit muddy, while those faults you referred to in *le commandant's* pronunciation have cleared away entirely."

And so toward the end of the evening we made a compact: Each year on this anniversary, no matter where we might be, I would dine, if possible, on snails and *poularde en demi-deuil* (its very name a diphthong), while he, getting the raw end of the bargain, would feast on hamburgers or hot dogs, if available. Furthermore, I promised that whatever French I might unload during the evening would be delivered with double diphthongal diligence; M. Thibaut would deliberately slur his *voyelles finales*—an act of linguistic self-sacrifice equal to the dropping of *h*'s by the Speaker of Britain's House of Lords.

It is only a few days now since the anniversary of our own private D day (D for Dinner). Others may have celebrated the occasion of *la Libération* by marching in parades, laying wreaths, or chanting the *"Marseillaise,"* but I spent the evening inflicting my irregular French verbs (and are they irregular!) upon a defenseless chef on East 56th Street. Between courses, I browsed through M. Thibaut's just-arrived letter, which ends with these interesting words: "Thanks to the help your so-noble country is sending, we may soon have a chicken, half in mourning, in every pot. Take care to remain strong, *mon ami*, for there are those who would like to dine on eagle."

August 1947

Cuisine Parisienne

Louis Diat

See Paris and die? No, see Paris and eat. That is, or should be, the intention of the thousands of visitors who will go to Paris this anniversary year. The treasures of the Louvre, the grandeur of the Arc de Triomphe, the majesty of Notre-Dame, the swank shops of the rue de la Paix, and the calm serenity of the Bois . . . all this *la Ville Lumière* offers, and more, much more. Paris provides today—as it did fifty, one hundred, and several hundred years ago—an inimitable hospitality, expressed practically and pleasantly by the superb food one can depend on finding in Paris at every turn.

Fine food is the tradition of Paris and has been since . . . I was about to say since the founding of the city, but the Gauls of Lutetia, which was the name of Paris under the Roman Empire, were no gourmets. Those gentry lived on game, fish, and fruit—raw. But for some centuries, at least, Paris has been the source and inspiration and heart of *la grande cuisine.* Now, in 1951, every menu, whether in one of the luxurious restaurants on the Place Vendôme or in a neighborhood bistro, reflects the ancient tradition. If a dish is served with one of the great sauces, it belongs to the era of Louis XIV, *le Roi Soleil*, whose reign gave France the utmost in gracious living. The mayonnaise on a contemporary menu is the same mayonnaise that Cardinal Richelieu devised early in the seventeenth century. Henry IV's *pot-au-feu* with a chicken in it, *petite marmite Henri IV,* dates back a century more.

In the time of the Louis—*quatorze, quinze,* and *seize*—Paris knew unsurpassed opulence, an endless succession of banquets notable for the quantities of food served and for the exotic and sculptured extravagancies of the kitchen artists. But when I came to Paris as a boy, fifty years ago, reform had begun. Then, it was fine shades of flavor and texture that spelled perfection; eye appeal had to depend upon natural beauty rather than upon artifice, and the food served at the Ritz, the Bristol, Prunier, Voisin, and such places was the finest in France.

The Paris of 1951 is not too different from the Paris I knew before the First World War. The Bois de Boulogne, the Champs-Élysées, Les Halles, the gently flowing Seine, and the bridges over it are all the same. The changes wrought by the years are superficial, not basic. People dress differently, more simply, with fewer furbelows; and they go about their affairs differently, moving from place to place expeditiously in taxis and buses, instead of following the old, leisurely fashions.

Food customs have followed a similar course. Fundamentally, the cuisine of the fine restaurants of Paris has not changed. The well-known hotels and restaurants still live and still serve the dishes that made their reputations. The perfectly seasoned soups and sauces made famous by great chefs are there—carefully, lovingly mixed and stirred, simmered, and stewed. But now they are less extravagant, have fewer flourishes, and the menus list more simple preparations and fewer elaborate ones than they did in my day.

I am sure, however, that some of the dishes which we laboriously prepared when I was learning to be a chef will never be served again. The cost of the raw materials is too great; the labor involved, excessive. Take, for example, *oeufs Reine Amélie.* This dish was created in honor of the Queen of Portugal and became a favorite of royal visitors to the Bristol.

I have never seen the recipe for eggs Queen Amelia in print, so I set it down here as a matter of history. Pieces of butter were cut and shaped to resemble hen's eggs. Each butter egg was rolled in flour, in beaten egg, and in fine white bread crumbs. This process was repeated to obtain two coats *à l'anglaise*. A sharp cutter cut out a small plug at the end of each egg, and the eggs were put away to be chilled thoroughly. They were then fried in deep hot fat. The heat melted the butter, which was then emptied out of the hole in the end of the egg. The simulated shells were filled with eggs scrambled to a delicate creaminess with finely chopped truffles.

In the meantime, the nests for the eggs were being made. Shoestring potatoes were used to line thickly the bottom and sides of a wire frying basket. A smaller frying basket set inside held the potatoes firmly until they were fried. When the baskets were separated, the crisp nest slipped out. The nests were apt to roll on the serving dish, so a supporting bed was made to hold them steady. This was done by forming a support from noodle dough shaped to look like part of a tree. It had to be baked in the oven right on the platter to give it sufficient rigidity to hold the nest. Then, some cooked noodles, colored green and yellow and cut in fancy shapes, were arranged on the dish.

A tasty dish, this *oeufs Reine Amélie*. Even a small party could dispose of dozens of eggs; and there was the hazard of breakage, inevitable during the preparation of this finicking dish, to consider. In New York at today's costs for food and labor, a portion could not be served for less than twenty dollars. Needless to say, *oeufs Reine Amélie* is not a menu staple nowadays.

In Paris fifty years ago, we served many dishes which similarly did not lend themselves to shortcuts. Some of them are gone. Modern kitchen equipment has made others easier. No one pounds raw meat by hand to make the fine, smooth paste required for *godiveau*, quenelles, and mousses. Good grinders have replaced strong muscles. No one blanches and dries almonds and then pounds and pounds them with sugar, when almond paste can be purchased so easily. No one whips a batch of forty or fifty egg whites with a hand whip for the biscuits *à la cuiller* to make sponge cakes and ladyfingers. And for a bisque no one crushes lobsters and crawfish—shells and all—with rice to an unbelievable fineness in a huge marble mortar with the great wooden pestle swinging from the ceiling.

Yet, the fine eating places of Paris still serve many dishes that give evidence of the painstaking cookery for which the French are famous. And there are other customs which differ from our American ways. The relaxed atmosphere is noticeable. Kitchens will not be hurried, and it will do no good to be impatient. Guests are expected to show their appreciation by eating slowly, savoring each mouthful well. In many restaurants, one ought to take the *spécialité du jour* or, at least, follow the suggestion of the waiter. The *spécialité* is usually made from the best the market offers, and consequently the chef considers that it is worth preparing properly, no matter how much time it takes.

Try soup in a Paris restaurant. Even the most reluctant soup-eater will soon be converted to soups that never disappoint. There are, too, certain niceties of serving—the tiny daintiness of pastries, for instance, that permits the diner to enjoy three, all different sorts, instead of the single pastry he would eat at home. I remember how infuriated Madame Ritz became when our pastry chef made any even a fraction larger than they should have been. Back they went to the kitchen, and a chef who thought his day's work behind him had to begin all over again.

Exacting employers like Madame Ritz were the secret of the success of the Ritz and other hotels that catered to the *haut monde*. As an apprentice chef in the kitchens of such hotels, I knew my survival—not to mention my advancement—depended upon my skill in satisfying the demands of those most sophisticated of kitchens.

Much water has gone under the bridge since I first came to Paris at the turn of the century, a wide-eyed country lad with little in my pocket but the address of a *pension* and a few francs to live on until I should find a job. I recall eating my breakfast of brioche and café au lait at the sidewalk stall on the rue de Lille, near the Pont-Neuf where the statue of Henry IV stands. It was cheaper than in a café and was no detriment to my dreams of someday becoming a great chef. My first job was in a *pâtisserie* on the Place de la Bastille—not what I wanted, but a start. Then, M. Malley—*sous-chef* at the newly opened Ritz and, fortunately for me, from *mon pays*—found me a place at the Hôtel du Rhin, the Bristol, and, finally, in his own kitchen at the Ritz. Over the years, I have watched the changes time makes in the fashions of cuisine as in other fashions, and I am happy to be able to say that one can still see Paris and eat!

The recipes that follow are the classic dishes that may be found in the Paris restaurants. They may be modified, this year, to conform with the limitations of the times, but they show how Paris cooks when the veal is white and delicate, the cream heavy and rich, the truffles fresh and fragrant, and the foie gras succulent.

SELLE DE VEAU MAINTENON
(*Saddle of Veal with Onion Purée*)

Tie up a saddle of veal securely with string and put it in a roasting pan on a bed of sliced onions and carrots. Season it with salt and spread with 2 tablespoons butter. Add some veal bones and a bouquet garni of 4 sprigs of parsley, 3 stalks of celery, a little thyme, and a piece of bay leaf. Put the pan, uncovered, in a moderately hot oven (400°F) and roast the veal, basting frequently, until the onions and carrots are brown. Add 2 cups water, cover the meat with buttered paper cut to fit the inside of the pan, and cover the pan. Reduce the oven temperature to 375°F and continue to cook the veal for 3 to 3½ hours, or until the meat detaches easily from the bones, adding more water or veal stock if needed. Remove the meat, add enough water or veal stock to the drippings in the pan to make 3 or 4 cups light veal gravy, thickening it with a little arrowroot or cornstarch, and set aside.

Meanwhile, prepare a thick *purée Soubise,* or onion purée. Cut 30 to 40 slices each of truffles and canned natural foie gras, cutting each slice about ⅛ inch thick, and mix the leftover trimmings from the truffles and foie gras with the *purée Soubise.*

With a very sharp knife cut down both sides of the center bone of the saddle of veal, leaving ½ inch of meat uncut at each end. Remove the filets from both sides, leaving intact the meat at the ends, and cut the filets into slices ¼ inch thick. Spread a little *purée Soubise* on the uncut ends of the saddle and lay on the purée a piece of truffle and foie gras and a slice of the filet. Continue to reconstruct the saddle in this manner, using about 15 to 20 slices each of truffle and foie gras on each side. Spread the re-formed saddle with *purée Soubise,* then with alternate slices of the goose liver and truffles, and finally with another coating of the purée. Cover with Mornay sauce and sprinkle with grated Parmesan.

Set the platter on a pan that contains a little warm water and reheat the veal in a moderate oven (350°F) until the sauce is golden-brown. Garnish with small glazed carrots, artichoke bottoms stuffed with tiny peas, hearts of braised celery, small potatoes *rissolées,* asparagus tips, green beans, or other vegetables in season and serve the dish with the veal gravy.

CANETON EN CHEMISE
(*Duck with Rouennaise*)

Bone a 5- to 6-pound duck and stuff it with *rouennaise* to which 1 egg has been added. Roll up the duck securely in a napkin, tying both ends with soft string. (In France we tied them in a *vessie,* made from the bladder of a hog.) Add the duck to a kettle of boiling stock, return the stock to the boil, and simmer for about 1 hour, or until tender.

Remove the duck from the kettle, discarding the napkin, and put it on a heatproof platter with a little of the stock. Brush with butter and brown in a hot oven or under the broiler flame. Arrange the duck over a clean napkin on a serving platter and garnish with slices of orange on top and with slices of lemon around the platter. Present the platter to the guests, slice through the duck and stuffing, and serve the slices with *sauce rouennaise.*

ROUENNAISE
(*Liver Paste*)

Heat thoroughly 4 tablespoons salt pork fat. Add 2 cups duck or chicken livers, a little thyme, 1 bay leaf, 1 teaspoon salt, and a little freshly ground pepper. Cook, stirring, for about 3 minutes over a hot fire and stir in 4 tablespoons Cognac or sherry. Pound the mixture in a mortar and rub it through a fine sieve.

SAUCE ROUENNAISE
(*Duck Liver Sauce*)

Put 1 cup red wine, 10 peppercorns, 1 bay leaf, ½ teaspoon thyme, and 4 shallots, chopped, in a saucepan. Bring to a boil and cook until the liquid is reduced to ⅓ its original quantity. Add 4 tablespoons brown sauce and 5 or 6 duck or chicken livers, finely chopped. Bring again to a boil, correct the seasoning, and rub the sauce through a fine sieve. Finish by stirring in 4 tablespoons Cognac.

SOLE SOUFFLÉE TANTE MARIE
(*Sole Stuffed with Fish Mousse*)

Clean and skin 2 soles, each weighing about 2 pounds. Make a pocket in each fish as follows:

Cut off the fins with sharp scissors. Starting from the head, slip a very sharp, thin knife closely along each side of the backbone, cutting down to detach the flesh but leaving uncut the underedge and the part near the tail. Sever the backbone at the head and tail with the scissors and lift the bones out.

Stuff the pocket with fish mousse and close it so that the sides meet along the back. Wrap each fish in cheesecloth and tie the ends with string. Put 4 tablespoons butter and 2 teaspoons chopped shallots in a shallow saucepan, lay the fish on this bed, and sprinkle with 1 cup white wine. Put the bones on top of the fish to give the sauce a better flavor. Bring the wine to a boil, cover the pan, and simmer on top of the range or in a moderate oven (350°F) for 18 to 20 minutes, or until the stuffing is set and the fish is cooked. Remove the soles to a serving dish, discarding the cloth.

Reduce the liquor in the pan to about 6 tablespoons and add 1 cup cream sauce. Thicken the sauce with 5 or 6 tablespoons hollandaise or with 2 egg yolks mixed with a little cream and swirl in 2 tablespoons butter, taking the pan from the fire as soon as the butter is melted. Fold in 4 tablespoons whipped cream, pour the sauce over the fish, and glaze in a very hot oven or under the broiler flame.

FISH MOUSSE

Put 1 pound of boned sole, cod, or other white fish in a mortar and pound it to a fine paste, adding ½ teaspoon salt, a little pepper, and 2 egg whites. Rub the purée through a fine sieve into a saucepan. Set the saucepan in a bowl containing cracked ice and continue to work the mixture with a wooden spoon, adding gradually about 2 cups heavy cream. The mixture has the right consistency when a rounded spoonful of it can be slipped off the spoon into a pan of hot water and will hold its shape when poached. When the mousse reaches this consistency, add ¼ cup *sauce américaine* and ½ cup mushroom duxelles.

SAUCE AMÉRICAINE

Cook 4 cups stewed tomatoes until most of the liquid has cooked away and strain through a fine sieve.

Heat 1 tablespoon olive oil and 2 tablespoons butter in a saucepan and add 2 shallots, finely chopped, 1 clove of garlic, and 1 tablespoon each chopped parsley and chervil. Add the tomato purée and simmer until the shallots are soft. Remove the clove of garlic, add 2 tablespoons brandy, and cook for a few minutes without letting the sauce boil.

MUSHROOM DUXELLES

Heat 1 tablespoon butter in a saucepan, add ¼ pound mushrooms, finely chopped, and 1 shallot, chopped, and cook until the moisture is evaporated. Stir in 1 teaspoon chopped parsley and salt to taste.

FAISAN SOUVAROV
(*Pheasant Souvaroff*)

Sauté in butter large pieces of fresh goose liver or canned natural foie gras. Add an equal quantity of whole small truffles or larger ones cut into pieces and combine with 2 tablespoons beef extract mixed with 4 tablespoons Madeira or sherry.

Clean a pheasant and stuff it with the above mixture. Truss the legs and wings close to the body and sew up the opening. Lard the breast with thin strips of fat salt pork and cover with more salt pork, securing the slices with string. Put the pheasant in a roasting pan, season with salt, and spread with good fat. Roast it in a moderately hot oven (425°F) for 15 minutes, turn, and roast it for 15 minutes on the other side, basting frequently. Remove the pheasant and put it on its back in a casserole.

Remove the excess fat from the roasting pan and to the drippings in the pan add 3 ounces Madeira or sherry, 2 or 3 tablespoons truffle juice, 2 truffles, diced, and ½ cup good gravy or brown sauce. Cook the sauce for a few minutes and pour it around the pheasant in the casserole. Put 1 tablespoon of butter on the breast, cover the casserole, and seal with a roll of dough made of flour, water, and a little fat. Bake in a moderately hot oven (425°F) for about 30 minutes, unseal, and serve.

This recipe may also be used for partridge or for any poultry.

VOL-AU-VENT EUGÉNIE

Prepare a puff-paste shell as follows: Roll out puff paste about ⅜ inch thick and from it cut a circle about 7 inches in diameter. Moisten a pastry sheet with water and on it lay the circle, turning this over so that the top side is underneath. Cut another 7-inch circle from puff paste rolled to the same thickness and cut out and reserve the center to leave a rim 1 inch wide. Moisten a 1-inch border around the first circle and on this lay the cut-out rim, reversing it so that the top side is underneath. Press the two borders firmly together and cut small scallops about ½ inch apart to make a decorative edging. Lay the reserved circle lightly inside the rim and chill the shell in the refrigerator for about 15 minutes.

Brush the top with 1 egg beaten with a little milk and bake in a hot oven (450°F) for about 10 minutes, or until the pastry is puffed and golden-brown. Reduce the oven temperature to 375°F and bake for 25 to 30 minutes longer. Remove the *vol-au-vent* from the oven and with a sharp knife gently lift out and reserve the center circle.

Prepare the filling as follows: Cut into large pieces the white meat and the second-joint meat from a poached chicken. Cut into pieces 3 sweetbreads poached until tender in salted water acidulated with lemon juice. Flute the edges of 1 dozen mushrooms and cook them for a few minutes over a hot fire in 3 to 4 tablespoons water mixed with 1 teaspoon each lemon juice and butter. Drain the mushrooms, reserving the liquor, and combine them with the chicken and sweetbreads. Add 12 small quenelles of chicken and ½ cup Madeira or sherry and heat all together.

Prepare 3 cups chicken *velouté* and add to it the reserved mushroom liquor. Stir in 2 egg yolks mixed with 1 cup heavy cream and bring the sauce to the boiling point. Add all but about 1 cup of this sauce to the chicken mixture and fill the *vol-au-vent*. Pour the reserved sauce on just before serving, garnish with a border of sliced truffles, and top with the baked pastry cover.

CHICKEN QUENELLES

Grind finely 1 pound raw chicken flesh, place it in a mortar with 1 teaspoon salt, ½ teaspoon pepper, and ¼ teaspoon nutmeg, and pound it to a paste. Add gradually the whites of 2 eggs, working the paste vigorously with a wooden spoon. Rub the forcemeat through a fine sieve, place it in a saucepan over cracked ice, and gradually work in about 2 cups heavy cream.

Form the forcemeat into small balls and poach them in chicken broth or salted water. Do not let the liquid boil or the quenelles will split.

July 1951

PARIS ONE STEP AT A TIME

Joseph Wechsberg

This seems to be my nostalgic day. Paris is losing one of its great delights, well expressed by the French verb *flâner,* "to stroll, to saunter," to which the *Larousse* adds, *"s'arrêtant souvent pour regarder."* Where in Paris is it possible now to stroll, "stopping often to look" perhaps at a few flowers, at the sun falling through the leaves of the trees (as Monet and Renoir magically painted them), or at a pretty woman? The women are still there, but they don't walk; they ride in their cars. The truth is that the automobile has ruined one of the joys of Paris—the joy of walking. Even the sacred domain of the Paris *flâneur,* the Bois de Boulogne, was recently declared off limits to the stroller after dark. The police warned innocent people not to walk in the Bois at night because quite a few not-so-innocent people pursue their dubious activities there. There have been holdups by characters who are convinced that crime *does* pay.

In recent months I made a survey of my own, asking people in Paris, "Do you still walk in the city for the pleasure of walking?" Many of them didn't know what I was talking about, so I couldn't even ask them "Where?" The young ones of course never learned to enjoy walking as we did when we were young. We had no cars, no motorcycles; we walked because we thought it was nice to walk. But even older

Parisians no longer walk. They remember that they loved to explore the hidden corners of their beautiful city, and they often discovered something they hadn't noticed before. Paris was truly made for the observant stroller.

Now the *voiture* has taken over the city. There is no place to walk aimlessly. Of course people still walk; many streets are crowded with people, but most of the walkers are going somewhere, and many are in a hurry. The classical *flâneur* never walked because he wanted to go somewhere, and he was never in a hurry. But now even the Champs-Élysées, once the rendezvous of *flâneurs* and *boulevardiers*, has become noisy and dirty. The air is full of exhaust fumes, people bump into one another, and there are construction sites and parked cars. And, and, and . . . It's all very sad.

Some people still walk on the Grands Boulevards, especially in the poorer districts, from the Opéra toward the Place de la République and the Bastille, and sometimes they sit on benches, enjoying the sunshine and watching life go by. But they are not *flâneurs*. They just cannot afford a glass of beer or a coffee in a sidewalk café. Some amusement is provided, free of charge, by street vendors and the sellers of lottery tickets. But people agree that it's not what it used to be. They look at you sadly and you understand. American tourists rarely venture into these *quartiers*. Those who do will be rewarded by a short glance into the past.

A few years ago it was nice to walk along the Seine. On the Right Bank, one passed the Jardin des Tuileries and the noble façade of the Louvre. Soon one would cross over to the Left Bank, to walk past the stalls along the Seine that offered forgotten thirdhand books, prints, magazines that are no longer published, art nouveau posters, and cheerful absurdities. But now the roads along the river have become one-way express highways noisy with automobiles.

The steady flow of traffic never stops along the *quais*. Gradually, the owners or tenants of the bookstalls have drifted away, and the stalls remain locked. I talked to one of the few people whose stalls were open. He was a *policier en retraite*, and his name was Monsieur Dupont. He had taken over the stall from an old friend because he loved the company of books. M. Dupont is a Paris phenomenon, a retired *literary* policeman. He loves the Seine and wishes there were more strollers coming to look at his books. Once in a while somebody may buy one, but it doesn't happen often. Business is so bad that he couldn't make ends meet if he didn't have his pension. Having been on both sides of the fence, as a traffic cop and as a *flâneur,* M. Dupont approaches the issue with Gallic logic.

"Who would want to stand here and leisurely browse, immersing himself in the labyrinths of French literature?" he asked rhetorically, pointing at the cars going by at high speed with much noise. "After a while even the loyal clients can't stand it anymore and go away. In summer the exhaust fumes make it impossible to breathe. *Ah, Monsieur, c'est la barbe.*"

Some limited walking can be done in the Jardin des Tuileries, which we owe to André Lenôtre, the great seventeenth-century designer of parks and gardens. There one sees *bonnes* (maids) with richly dressed infants. The onetime pleasure of walking under the arcades of the rue de Rivoli is spoiled by traffic noises and hordes of tourists trying to find bargains in the cheap souvenir stores. There are inexpensive things for sale but no bargains. The green Michelin guide, *Paris et sa banlieue,* has a section on *promenades,* meaning *promenades en voiture.* The pleasure of such a promenade is doubtful. "The Paris of Baron Haussmann had about 100,000 horse-driven coaches. Today there are over 910,000 motorcars in Paris. . . . When only 140,000 of them circulate at the same time, the 1200 kilometers of streets in Paris are jammed."

For the sturdy few who still walk because it *is* the best way to see Paris, the guide proposes a four-day promenade. For the afternoon of the third day the guide suggests a

> . . . tour of the Quartier Latin. The calm of the small streets surrounding the church of St. Séverin contrasts with the liveliness of the Boulevard St. Michel, which we follow as far as the Place Edmond-Rostand. After visiting the Panthéon we return to the Luxembourg gardens . . .

and so on. Personally, I suggest walking around the Île de la Cité, where some of the city's former charm and tranquillity has been magically preserved. I also like the quiet side streets of the Butte Montmartre, which Picasso and Utrillo discovered long before I did. Most of the old *flâneurs* were residents of this picturesque *quartier,* but they have disappeared. Some sit in front of their old houses or hide in the gardens behind them. The Parc des Buttes-Chaumont is still popular, as is the Parc du Champ de Mars. The Service des Monuments Historiques organizes daily lecture tours in Paris, mostly in French. I recently joined a tour that took a small group of bizarre spinsters, precocious children, and bored Sunday-afternoon husbands through the Hôtel Sully. Many ex-*flâneurs* seem to have escaped into the museums of Paris, especially the less well known ones.

When all is said about strolling in Paris, the fact emerges that almost everybody has a car or knows someone who has a car, which is even better. People try to get out of the city as often as possible. In some of the quiet suburbs it is still possible to stroll. A wise French gentleman who lives in an elegant western suburb walks for an hour in the morning in the nearby woods—he is eighty-seven—before he is driven to his office on the avenue Foch. In the old days he loved to walk there. But he has read that every twenty-four hours over 200,000 foolhardy drivers join the vicious circle around the Arc de Triomphe, praying to the Lord to get them out of it somehow. That bothers the old gentleman. Yes, strolling in Paris is fast becoming a memory. Soon it may be a forgotten memory.

July 1975

CITY OF LIGHT

THE OLD FLOWER MARKET

Joseph Wechsberg

The Marché aux Fleurs, the old flower market on the Île de la Cité, is much loved by the Parisians, who go there all year long to buy their flowers—from small violets and modest anemones to large plants and imposing trees for terraces and balconies. La Cité, one of the islands in the Seine, is the oldest part of Paris. Two centuries before the Christian era, fishermen from the Parisii tribe founded the Celtic settlement of Lutèce on the two islands now known as La Cité and the Île Saint-Louis. The Roman legions came there in 52 B.C. and built a small Gallo-Roman town. In A.D. 360, Julian the Apostate, a Roman prefect with great ambitions, had himself crowned emperor by the legions. About that time Lutèce changed its name and became Paris.

When Attila, king of the Huns, crossed the Rhine with his 700,000 wild soldiers in A.D. 451, panic broke out among the Parisians and many ran away. According to legend, Geneviève, a young girl from Nanterre, calmed them, promising that Paris would be saved by God. The Huns arrived, seemed to hesitate, and turned toward Orléans. Paris was saved, and Geneviève became its patron. Ten years later she saved the town again when it was besieged by the Franks and starving. Geneviève was still alive in 506 when the larger of the two islands became known as La Cité. Later the Normans appeared, and after long struggles took over the islands. They were eventually turned back by the Parisians under Eudes, Count of Paris, who was chosen king.

During the Middle Ages people began to settle on the adjacent banks of the Seine. Famous schools and institutions opened in the shadow of Notre-Dame. In the cloister of Notre-Dame a celebrated love affair began between the philosopher Abelard and Héloïse, niece of the Canon Fulbert, that has fascinated generations of Frenchmen. At the beginning of the thirteenth century there were twenty-three convents and chapels on the Cité. Various revolutions shook the tranquillity of the small island. During the Reign of Terror at the end of the eighteenth century the prisons of the Conciergerie were crowded with hopeless *citoyens.* At the Palais de Justice the revolutionary tribunal pronounced death sentences against which there was no appeal.

Near the scene of all these horrors there was a *place,* surrounded by the Tribunal de Commerce and the Préfecture de Police. In 1809 Napoleon created the peaceful enclave of the flower market there, though the merchants claim it was done much earlier by Blanche of Castile, the mother of Saint Louis, who founded the Hôtel-Dieu. Could be. The flower market was to give the place a more cheerful note.

And it still is cheerful. The cast-iron stalls look like leftovers from the Eiffel Tower, and the lovely decorations are early art nouveau. The merchants, about thirty of them, have no comforts, no heat, no electricity. Their stalls are primitive, but they love the place. There was excitement three years ago when it was rumored that the flower market might be moved to the Georges Pompidou National Art and Cultural Center, under construction on the Plateau Beaubourg. The flower people were promised comfortable, well-heated, well-lighted stalls and modern surroundings. One would think the merchants would have been delighted by the move.

Not at all. They overwhelmingly rejected the very idea. Only a couple of younger people are said to have even considered the proposal. The most stubborn merchants were those selling garden plants and bulbs at small stalls on the Quai de Corse, on the northern side of the market, where the narrow sidewalk is always crowded. But the movement in favor of *not* moving was also joined by the merchants on the Place Louis-Lépine, who sell cut flowers, *plantes vertes,* and *plantes fleuries* for apartments and terraces. They have been there "for generations" and don't care about the lack of comfort. They brought petitions before the City Council, the owner of the land. Many passersby who regularly come to the market signed the petitions. They have always bought their flowers there and hope to do so until they die. Who needs heat and electricity? They are bad for the flowers anyway, aren't they?

"Yes, but at Beaubourg you wouldn't be outside in the cold and rain," countered the center's proponents.

"It's not us that matter," a resolute woman told me. "It's the flowers, Monsieur. The flowers are happy here, and we are happy where our flowers like it." She was quite serious and so were other merchants who listened and nodded. Anyway, the petitions were accepted, and the Marché aux Fleurs stays.

Almost everybody seemed happy when I went there. It was a cold day, with north winds, and the men and women wore thick sweaters and had blue hands. Every morning they must put out their flowers and trees in the square and along the sidewalk; and every evening they put them back into their stalls, but they don't mind. They are as proud of their shabby stalls as certain dynasties are of their medieval castles. It is admitted that "these *types*"—the promoters of Beaubourg—may succeed in getting *some* flower merchants for their center. But most merchants expect their loyal clients to stay with them on La Cité. I talked to some loyal clients—women ordering plants for their apartments, a few old men buying anemones—and they agreed. They consider the Marché aux Fleurs a national monument, "almost like Notre-Dame and the Sainte-Chapelle."

No one thinks that is an exaggeration. "Take the flowers away from Paris and what have you got?" an old man asked me. "I've come here every week for forty years, and I hope to come as long as I live. These people belong here, like the *bouquinistes* along the Seine nearby who sell old books and drawings."

The Parisians love the place for its sense of continuity. In 1944, during the Liberation, many *agents de police* barricaded themselves in the Préfecture and ran up the Tricolore. The Germans began shelling the area, and one girder in the Marché aux Fleurs was hit, but then the Division Leclerc arrived and the occupiers were chased out. No one in the Marché was very surprised. The stall holders have always been there, and they're going to stay, period. One merchant has a sign, JEAN GANTER, GENDRE DE M. IMBERT. Elderly people remember Monsieur Imbert, and now they buy from his son-in-law and successor. The flower merchants understand human nature. Some have small signs stuck between their flowerpots, PRIÈRE DE TOUCHER AVEC LES YEUX. Please touch with the eyes only. MERCI.

January 1977

ALL THAT GLITTERS

Joseph Wechsberg

Last spring I spent an afternoon at Cartier, at 13, rue de la Paix, and have reluctantly revised my ideas about the V.V.R., the Very Very Rich. It was my first visit to the fabulous jeweler and it may be, I'm afraid, my last excursion into "the plush surroundings which were frequented by Kings, Highnesses, international millionaires, Russian princes, stars, the great ones of the earth." Are you properly impressed? I'm quoting from a press release by Gilberte Gautier, on the occasion of the exhibition celebrating the hundredth birthday of Louis Cartier, 1875–1942, a third-generation member of the great dynasty. The firm was founded earlier, in 1847, by Louis-François Cartier, who became the court jeweler of the Second Empire. Princess Mathilde started the vogue, other members of the nobility followed, and in no time the rich bankers and *nouveau-riche* operators were going to Cartier to get a little gift, say a nine-carat diamond, for their lady friends—maybe even for their wives. Other customers were some doubtful habitués of the nearby Café Anglais on the boulevard des Italiens. In 1872, Alfred, the son of the founder, became his father's partner and immediately pulled off a spectacular coup when he got hold of the jewels of "la Barucci, *courtisane royale*." She needed the money, having just lost her protector. Since time immemorial, famous jewelers have made fortunes by first selling expensive jewels to certain ladies (or to their admirers) and later buying the jewels back when the ladies suffered reverses. In Alfred's case, the profits to the firm were much needed, since it had had bad losses in the war of 1870–71. A few years later, Louis was born.

He became the greatest Cartier, an innovator who modernized jewelry and revolutionized the art of setting by using elements of painting, sculpture, architecture, and *haute couture*. He was called "the couturier of jewelry," and in 1898 he married Andrée-Caroline Worth, granddaughter of the great couturier Charles-Frédéric Worth. That year the firm moved to 13, rue de la Paix, and the place has been kept exactly as it was. Cartier's two hundred employees (designers, jewelers, artisans, and office and sales staff) all work in the old house. From workrooms in the rear and upstairs, which have never been open to the public, came the masterpieces that made the style of Louis Cartier world famous.

The great past becomes evident as one steps into the elegant store, with its old wood paneling. The historical jewels were exhibited in electronically protected vitrines. There were more security guards than visitors. The guards had a terrible time during the opening on May 27, when lots of people crashed the party to see the jewelry and stones, insured for seventy million dollars, and to goggle at members of *le Tout-Paris,* not insured. Everybody came, from Madame Marcel Achard to the Baronne von Zitzewitz (according to the special press release) and Madame Spirito-Santo. (I always thought that was the name of a bank in Rome.) The show was such a success that it will go to Monte Carlo and may later be seen at other branches of Cartier.

The walls are adorned with framed warrants issued by the courts of England, Spain, Greece, Italy, and Egypt. Assorted queens and highnesses ordered twenty-seven diadems for the coronation of Edward VII in 1902. His Majesty was a good customer when he wasn't busy at Maxim's, a few blocks away, where The Ladies from Maxim's paraded Cartier jewels. Louis Cartier was also popular in Saint Petersburg, where he was shown a beautiful necklace that he identified at once as one that Napoleon had given to Josephine. Princess Lobanoff, known as "the princess of jewels," was so impressed by his expertise that she ordered in her will an auction of her 280 jewels, many made by Cartier, in Lausanne under the direction of Louis Cartier. The auction is still considered one of the most important of the century. Some of the diadems and necklaces that have found their way back to Cartier in the past fifty years were displayed in the windows facing the rue de la Paix. Several passersby thought they couldn't be genuine, "because such things don't exist anymore." Oh yes, folks, they do, at Cartier.

Louis Cartier embraced orientalism as a style of jewelry and created beautiful "arabesques" in subdued shades, and under the influence of Diaghilev's Ballets Russes he created polychrome variants in brilliant hues. He was aware of cubism, naturalism, and art deco but was not overwhelmed by any style. Using combinations of diamonds, emeralds, rubies, sapphires, jade, onyx, and coral and blending platinum with enamel, lapis lazuli, and turquoise, he always showed artistic restraint. He surrounded himself with the finest artists he could find. Lalique designed for him before going off on his own, Dalí once created for the firm a heart made of rubies, and Cocteau drew sketches for Cartier jewelry. The great era of the firm was the early years of the century, when Cartier opened in London (1902) and New York (1908). In 1919 Louis Cartier designed and executed the ceremonial baton for Marshal Foch. He invented the clip and created the swords for several members of the Académie Française. Other branch offices were opened in Monte Carlo (1935), Cannes (1938), Hong Kong (1969), Geneva (1970), Munich (1971), and Tokyo (1974). Cartier always goes where the big money is. Louis Cartier died in New York in 1942. Later, only the New York and London stores were run by Pierre and Jacques Cartier. Today the Paris firm is controlled by Robert Hocq, a wealthy French industrialist, whose daughter Nathalie is *directrice* of the *haute joaillerie. Sic transit gloria* . . . even at Cartier.

The exposition shows the evolution of jewelry in the past hundred years, the symbiosis of precious materials and fine work. There are several "mysterious clocks," created by Louis Cartier and his master watchmakers. They have an invisible mechanism (often hidden in the socle) and were a favorite status symbol in royal circles around 1925; they are no longer made, being prohibitively expensive. One sees birds and butterflies made of precious stones, flowers and tiny trees, the creations of gifted Jeanne Toussaint, and there is a remarkable panther bracelet made of tiny diamonds. The panther becomes "alive" when the arm with the bracelet is moved. None of the exhibits are for sale, but the firm has received several orders for the panther and will make them up. It takes a master craftsman one year to create such a bracelet. There are other dazzling pieces of jewelry: *nécessaires* in Chinese style enriched with emeralds, coral, jade; brooches artfully composed of diamonds and sapphires; vanity cases in gold with black and white enamel; a butterfly brooch of platinum, with diamonds, turquoises, and sapphires set in gold; and an incredible piece, twenty-one centimeters long (loaned to the show by an unidentified customer), made of one thousand diamonds set in platinum. The stones weigh over a hundred carats. Among the wonders of contemporary jewelry (and thus for sale) are a necklace made of stunning emeralds (seventy-seven carats), another made of rubies, one formed of three "priceless" emeralds, and a ring with a large, fine ruby (twenty-seven carats).

No wonder the security was as tight as that in a Soviet atomic bomb center! The day of my visit the viewers were either fragile old ladies, who smiled sadly and knowingly, as though they recognized the diadems and necklaces (perhaps they had known the owners or, heaven forbid, had owned them themselves, though they did not look like former *courtisanes*), or hard-looking young women, escorted by tough characters who seemed to have made hard-currency millions recently, perhaps selling soap powder or putting up those dreadful skyscrapers that don't improve the Paris cityscape. They hardly glanced at the masterpieces of the past that were not for sale but headed straight for the air-conditioned, modern rooms in the rear, where some incredible diamonds, emeralds, sapphires, and rubies were displayed in special vitrines, dramatically lighted. There were heart-shaped diamonds as large as walnuts (would any woman wear one?). In the field of precious, very large stones the line between elegance and vulgarity is very thin. One woman asked to try on a ring with a *very* large stone.

The vitrine was opened, while four guards approached. The woman put the ring on her finger, where it didn't look much better. Nor did she. Her escort was pale; poor fellow, he might have to put up another skyscraper if she insisted on having that ring. The salesman looked at his price list, operated a small calculator that he held in his hand, and told her the price, in Swiss francs, which I thought was funny. I asked how much it would be in dollars, and he consulted his machine and said, "Approximately 625,000 American dollars," and I thanked him very politely.

There was a stone I happened to like, not too large, almost blue, and very pure. Madame Joëlle Sylvestre, the young public-relations lady who escorted me, called another salesman. He gave me a disgusted look; obviously I was not a serious prospect. He opened his price list and informed me that the stone was clean and white, *not* blue, and cost 1,943,759.40 francs. Then the salesman showed us a stone *he* liked, a magnificent sapphire from Kashmir, for over two million francs, truly extra-ordinary. He also liked a stunning ruby from Burma and a necklace made of diamonds and sapphires, which could be taken apart. He said the parts might be worn "for minor occasions" if one didn't feel like wearing the whole three-million-franc thing. They think of everything at Cartier.

I asked him—somewhat naïvely, I now realize—whether there were still customers for these things. Hadn't the customers disappeared with the kings and maharajas and the Russian Grand Duchesses of the feudal past? The salesman was very offended.

"Of course, Monsieur, there are such people," he said. "They keep us in business." He closed his price list and walked away. We walked back to one of the old salesrooms in the front. An ample elderly woman was shown a beautiful necklace selling for some three million francs. I watched in fascination as they put it around her neck. Even the guards were smiling. At another desk an attractive young woman had apparently concluded the final step of a major purchase. She took a checkbook out of her bag and with no hesitation wrote out a check for six figures, the first being an "8," which meant that the amount was over $200,000. She did this matter-of-factly, as if paying the grocer's bill.

I said good-bye to Mme. Sylvestre, who was slim and gentle and wore no jewelry whatsoever, and left the "plush surroundings," having learned something about the V.V.R.

October 1975

Haute Couture

Joseph Wechsberg

I never pretended to understand the mysteries of women's fashions. Like many other men, I had long suspected a sinister conspiracy among the important *haute couture* designers, who appeared to have secretly agreed on what the new fashions would be and thereupon issued their dictatorial edicts twice a year. How else, I wondered, was it possible that the clothes created by the various designers seemed so similar that most of us men couldn't tell them apart? Women, of course, know a thousand differences. Anyway, they would follow the dictates, sometimes reluctantly, but more often enthusiastically, and men would pay. That seemed to be the essence of the plot.

Fellow men, I've changed my way of thinking after talking to Marc Bohan. I did not expect that I would ever learn anything about couture and collections, colors and styles, but better late than never.

Marc Bohan is the artist who is Dior, who personifies the House of Christian Dior. (This sentence was written for men only, who may not know about Monsieur Bohan.) In a medium that combines the bizarre unpredictability of Monte Carlo roulette with the enigmas of feminine fancy, Bohan has shown astonishing staying power. Since 1961, when he was only thirty-five, he has designed the Christian Dior *haute couture* collections.

Marc Bohan has never resorted to tricks and gimmicks in order to *épater les femmes bourgeoises*. Even his competitors admit he has never tried to shock the masses, and they don't like to admit anything. Bohan has always believed that femininity and charm are a woman's essential assets. I agree. A woman doesn't have to be beautiful if she is a *woman*. (That will no doubt be called a male chauvinist point of view in some circles, but I couldn't care less.)

"I've always liked women who dress for men and not against other women," M. Bohan said as I sat down across from him in his small private office. Bravo! Most of us men like women who dress to please us, not to compete with their women friends. We men react to women's fashions emotionally. Women often treat the subject of clothes with cold intellect.

Bohan's office, three floors above the Dior Boutique, looks out on the rue François-1er whereas the hallowed *haute couture* salons, the paradise of the last billionairesses, face the elegant avenue Montaigne, complete with canopy and uniformed doorman wearing white gloves. One wall of the office is papered with covers and pages from fashion magazines showing Dior models wearing Bohan's dresses—an elegant pinup girl collection if ever there was one. The only nonprofessional model on the wall is Princess Caroline of Monaco, looking young and lovely, no matter what she wears. On Bohan's glass desk was a poinsettia, which reminded me briefly of southern California. On the wall across from his desk is a collagelike arrangement of scissors, hundreds of them, in clever patterns. The windows have vertical white shades to keep out the sun. It was raining though. The place is coldly functional. M. Bohan, who believes in self-discipline, doesn't like to be cozy when he is working.

He was tense and shy and sat stiffly behind his desk, facing me with undisguised reserve. On a door to his adjoining studio a sign said, IT IS FORBIDDEN TO ENTER WITHOUT FIRST RINGING. Being somewhat reserved myself, I was encouraged by his quest for privacy, which is a great luxury today. He was well dressed, with no ostentation, wearing a three-piece suit, a beautiful striped shirt with narrow cuffs, and a solid-color tie. He designs his own things. There is a boutique for men downstairs, which is very successful. For men M. Bohan believes in classic, strict lines for suits and in accessories chosen to harmonize with the individual suit. There should be no whimsy, except at home or for vacation clothes, and no compromise with style.

I had been told that Bohan doesn't like interviews, and I don't blame him. He soon relaxed when I said this was not an "interview," and he almost smiled when I assured him I didn't want to know the secrets of his prominent customers or how much he charges a billionairess for an evening dress. He wouldn't have told me anyway, so why ask him? *Haute couture* designers are as reticent as Swiss bankers and international jewelers about who pays how much for what.

I asked M. Bohan the question that interested me most: How does he manage to divine, season after season and year after year, what women will want to wear in six to twelve months not only in Paris and London and New York, but practically everywhere?

"These things cannot be explained rationally. There is the mystery or the mystique of creation. I have never tried to explain it, even to myself. I suppose it's a matter of instinct, of intuition, though. Certain things suddenly seem *démodé*. All fashion is a reflection of the current ambience of life, of social changes, of what people believe in and want at the moment. It's often thought that we couturiers force women to wear these new things. I couldn't force a woman to wear something just because I like it. A few maybe, but certainly not many. A new style will never become accepted unless one guesses correctly what women secretly long for. I must sense it well in advance; I must be sure they will accept it. That sounds simple and is terribly difficult. Timing is important, and you cannot learn timing; no one has taught it successfully, though they teach almost everything nowadays. To be too early is as bad as to be too late. When I created the Long Look in the spring collection of 1970, I was too early. By the time the Long Look had been accepted in 1971, I had lost interest in it."

Bohan impatiently denied any suggestion of "conspiring" with his fellow designers in the creation of a new trend. Apparently the great couturiers guard their inspirations as jealously as great chefs keep theirs to themselves.

"I've always wanted to *please*," said Bohan. "It is better to please than to create sensation. I want women to wear feminine clothes, made of soft, feminine materials. I could never create anything abstract. I always think of a certain woman when I create something. I like to work with the material, to have it around me, to touch it. Everything must come together—the material, the design, the woman wearing the clothes, the accessories, and the ambience in which she will wear these things. If one of the components is wrong, the whole thing will be wrong.

"Sometimes I am not sure; in fact, very often I am not sure. I don't know exactly *why* something is good or isn't. I only feel it. But then, after I see my design translated into material and see the model wearing the dress, suddenly and unfathomably I know it is good. *That* is the great satisfaction, but it doesn't happen often. It couldn't happen often."

Designing must be a very difficult métier. You must always notice changes, you must be subconsciously aware of the constant evolution, and you must be able to express that evolution so that a woman will feel in tune—because she dresses according to the place in which she lives, her mood, and the essence of her era. Often she is pleased but cannot explain why she is pleased. It is a metaphysical thing, a sort of sixth sense. Somebody either has it or doesn't have it. Marc Bohan is convinced he has it; otherwise he wouldn't be where he is today. Twice a year he retires to his country place near Fontainebleau, where "the bathrooms blend into the bedrooms" and "modern furniture is juxtaposed with wooden beams and brick walls," and there he designs the more than eighty models of the *haute couture* collections and many other things.

He doesn't begin with conscious, definitive designs. "I start drawing. Often I throw things away as fast as I draw them. Technique is important, of course; one always tries to make things better. But technique is only a means of expressing one's ideas. Technique must never be used for the sake of technique. I know I must create elegance and charm, but our ideas of elegance change all the time, and what was charming yesterday may not be thought so today. The creator cannot afford to remain in an ivory tower as some designers did twenty or thirty years ago. They would design abstract clothes and tell women to wear them."

Bohan shook his head emphatically. "I must travel, meet intelligent people, and find out what interests them. I like to talk to artists and writers. They are often ahead of other people of their time. I see shows, the ballet, movies; I look at paintings, old and avant-garde. And all the time my subconscious is working. Who can explain the secret of creation?" He gave a shrug.

"Today all fashion is alive and full of meaning. I believe the creator must be aware of the undercurrents. We are now going through a troubled epoch, like that of the 1930s. It is no accident that people try to escape into the past and become nostalgic in their thoughts and feelings and, naturally, in fashion, too, since all honest fashion reflects thoughts and feelings. This is the answer to your question whether a trend can be artificially created. Personally, I could never do it."

Very often Bohan, with his inner eye, "sees" a certain design, made of a certain material, in a certain color. He cannot explain what comes first, the design or the material or the color or, possibly, the person who is going to wear the dress. "I suppose the idea comes first. Next, I try to express the idea, but I'll be sure only when I see the dress on a person. Fashion, as you know, is a *façon de vivre*, a way of life, and that explains why we designers who perceive and anticipate evolution often have similar ideas, first each for himself and then all together—because we have similar thoughts and similar feelings about a given period. When I changed the silhouette in 1961 and again in 1970, the change was in the air. I was just lucky to sense it a little earlier."

So there goes my theory of the sinister conspiracy of the *haute couture* creators.

"People know a lot today," Bohan said. "At a time when we can see on television events happening on the other side of the globe, when the mass media intrude into our living rooms, it would be absurd to try to create abstract things. On the contrary, one must be closer to real life. Sometimes women know what they want, but often they come to me and ask me because they don't know. It is my job to tell them, to persuade them what I think is right for them. What was the secret of Coco Chanel? Very simple. She guessed correctly what women needed and liked, and she gave it to them."

Coco Chanel was the only designer Bohan mentioned by name

during our talk. Once I asked him whom he meant when he talked of designers who had created abstract things in an ivory tower. He shook his head, almost regretfully.

"You don't really expect me to answer your question, do you?"

"No, I don't."

———

Marc Bohan looks like a modern Parisian—competent, brilliant, nervous. No wonder, since he was born in Paris on August 22, 1926. Yes, under the sign of Leo the Lion, if you believe in those things. His mother was a milliner from Paris, his father, from Brittany. As long as Bohan can remember he has liked to draw and to create. He took art courses and cared about women's fashions at an age when other boys cared about soccer. When he was only nineteen he did some fashion designing for Robert Piguet (where the late Christian Dior had started). For four years he was assistant stylist with Piguet, then he was assistant to Molyneux, and in 1954 he designed the *haute couture* collections for Jean Patou. He had known Christian Dior for a long time and admired him, and Dior encouraged the young man and taught him.

Dior had met Marcel Boussac, the French industrialist, in 1945 and together they created the House of Christian Dior on December 15, 1946. In the annals of French *haute couture* February 13, 1947, remains a historic date, for on that day Christian Dior presented his first collection and his New Look became a worldwide success. The House of Dior has never lost its dominating position, even after the death of Christian Dior on October 24, 1957. In August, 1958, Marc Bohan, after a short stay in New York, was asked by the firm to handle the Christian Dior London collections. In 1960 he was placed in charge of the artistic management of the firm, and in 1961 he reached the top: He designed his first *haute couture* collections for Christian Dior Paris.

Bohan has been in charge ever since—fifteen years, which is a long time in the fast-changing fashion business. His first show presented the Slim Look, which was a great success. So was the long coat, sometimes known as the Dr. Zhivago coat, which launched the Maxi silhouette. Some of us men thought the ladies were better off without it, but men don't really count in the wonderland of feminine fashion, except a few men who *know*.

Much has changed in the wonderland since the early 1960s, but Bohan has remained the same; he is interested in creating a balance between forms and colors, in the silhouette in its entirety. The changes have not always been pleasant. The number of women who can still afford *haute couture* has shrunk dramatically. Among the different houses estimates of the number vary between one thousand and three thousand, "at the most." The *haute couture* department of Dior remains the firm's heart and symbol of prestige, but no one at Dior would claim that it makes big money. Of the thousand-odd people who work at Christian Dior—in the various buildings surrounding the headquarters and elsewhere—only two hundred are employed in the inner *haute couture* sanctum. There the finest things, the most exclusive materials are used; no shortcuts in workmanship are permitted. The pressure is high; there must be constant renewal, yet Bohan has managed to create a continuity, avoiding all style breaks between his collections. Many women admire Dior for this constantly renewed image, for the trend toward continuity; they feel that *chez* Dior, *plus ça change* it's always beautiful and feminine.

The eighty-odd *haute couture* models, designed by Marc Bohan himself, are sold only at 30, avenue Montaigne, where the atmosphere is so refined that no one would discuss the sordid subject of money aloud; perhaps some figures are whispered. Bohan also designs the more than eighty Christian Dior *prêt-à-porter* (ready-to-wear) models, which are sold at the Dior Boutiques at prices from a thousand francs upward. These clothes are made for what is called "limited retail distribution" in fine materials (though not the finest, which remain reserved for the *haute couture* models) and offer a carefully planned line and the possibility of being fitted. The boutique at 28, avenue Montaigne, and the new boutique, at 12, rue Boissy-d'Anglas (opened last year "because Dior must be represented in the Faubourg Saint-Honoré district"), make possible the reproduction of a semi-individually tailored model.

Could two women wearing the same dress meet in a Paris restaurant? Next question, please. (It once happened at Henri Soulé's Le Pavillon in New York, though the two women were not wearing Dior. Soulé reacted with customary poise and seated the two women in different rooms.) Exclusivity is always expensive, and why not? The idea, gentlemen, is that if Madame wants a Dior dress that only she will have, she has to see the Master. Maybe he'll design one of the eighty models for her. Maybe. In that case, she will be well advised to listen to him. Marc Bohan has been known to tell a customer, "You can't wear that," or "That's not for you."

"Usually they listen to me," M. Bohan said, rather wryly.

Today the big money at Dior is earned not by the *couture*, more or less *haute*, but by the accessory and licensing departments. The accessory department alone accounts for one third of the French turnover and includes "already traditional activities" (ties, scarves, luggage) as well as men's and women's sweaters and bathing suits.

The licensing department negotiates licensing contracts around the world. It is so powerful that it can propose "important new themes" to the styling department. The firm has granted more than 130 licenses for about thirty articles in over eighty countries. The most widely licensed articles are women's stockings (in eighteen countries), men's ties (in ten countries), scarves, lingerie, women's shoes, men's shirts and socks, luggage and handbags, men's shoes, gloves, and sweaters. All licensed items have the status-symbolic Christian Dior label. This is the least expensive (and most widespread) way of wearing something with Christian Dior on it.

All this may seem coldly commercial to you, far from Marc Bohan's artistic dreams, but it has enabled the firm to survive while many others have disappeared. In 1947 the firm had a staff of eighty and annual sales of 1,300,000 francs. In 1975 Christian Dior (with the English and American subsidiaries and the ready-to-wear ateliers in Orléans and Blois) employed more than a thousand people. International sales reached over 550,000,000 francs. One third of the sales are in France. The Christian Dior fur atelier under Frédéric Castet, who creates the annual *haute couture* fur collection, "enjoys one of the world's best reputations for quality," for its selection, technique, and elegance.

Christian Dior Monsieur—that is, ready-to-wear for men—was developed by Bohan himself and is now manufactured under licensing agreements and sold in the United States, Japan, Italy, Great Britain, and Brazil. Bohan has a staff of expert designers but personally approves each item in the collection. There is big money in ties, shirts, cuff links, bathing suits, and sunglasses; these articles now account for one fifth of the company's annual business. Never underestimate the power of a man. It is to be remembered that the very first licensing agreement in the entire fashion industry was signed in 1949 by Christian Dior in the United States for neckties. The independent Christian Dior perfume company now belongs to Moët-Hennessy.

—

They had shown me the *haute couture* department, both the elegant front and the more modest backstage, before I saw the Master. The backstage was the more interesting part. Each of the girls had an exact sketch of the model on which she was working, complete with measurements, accessories, and a sample of the material stitched to the drawing. All this was strictly top secret. The name of the customer was not marked on the sketch, only her code number. Each steady customer is represented by her own mannequin, a dummy of her body beautiful. When, God forbid, the ladies gain, both in years and pounds, the dummies are brought up to date, if you'll pardon the expression, by material and pieces of paper pinned or pasted to certain danger spots.

My visit took place shortly after November 25, when the midinettes of the Paris fashion houses celebrate the feast of Saint Catherine, their tutelary saint. All *directrices, vendeuses, premières* and *secondes d'atelier, petits mains,* models, and apprentices had joined in the fête. The Queens of the day (and queens for a day) are the *catherinettes,* the unmarried girls who will celebrate their twenty-fifth birthday within the next twelve months. Obviously a girl can be a *catherinette* only once in her lifetime; it's always beautiful and a little sad, like one's first love. In my youthful days in Paris a *catherinette* had the right, though not the duty, to kiss every man she wanted to. . . .

Ignoring the past, I walked around the room where the midinettes worked. I remember specifically an *haute couture* creation hanging there, prepared for a fitting. It was a raincoat made of a silky fabric, fur-trimmed and fur-lined, with a hood; it was beautiful, feminine, exquisite. It was deceivingly "simple," the kind of simplicity that is hard to describe and much harder to achieve, and it showed the hand of the Master.

Back to the Master in his office. He said he was going to his country place to work on the new collections. Could he, well, indicate some of his ideas? He looked at me and probably decided it was not an impertinent question. What could I, what could *anyone* do with his ideas?

"We are now informal even on occasions when we used to be more formal," he said. "I'm giving some of my evening things an almost informal look. I find myself thinking a great deal about colors. I've always been sensitive to colors; I have always liked red and black. I believe the colors of the immediate future will be less somber, much brighter, and there will be stronger contrasts. Fashions will be more vital, more alive."

Bohan loves flowers, simple flowers like lilies of the valley but also roses. His daughter, Marie-Anne, lives in England and is pretty; until a while ago she wore her father's Miss Dior dresses. (The Miss Dior line no longer exists.) In Paris she stays with her father at his nearby apartment where he has combined "antique furniture with modern art"—which is not a bad combination. He likes, among others, Tinguely, Warhol, Rosenquist, and Uriburu. He also likes small parties and good food. Sometimes he plays around in the kitchen, making cold cucumber soup or an omelette with truffles.

When I got up to leave, Bohan was no longer reserved and withdrawn. He seemed almost pleased. Perhaps he's learned not to be afraid of an "interview." And I too had learned something—though I still don't know how much he charges so-and-so for an evening dress. I was later told (not by him, of course) that "several thousand dollars" might be correct. The women who go to Marc Bohan to have a dress made are convinced he's worth it. I'm sure they are right.

July 1976

SOLD!

Joseph Wechsberg

For a long time I've wanted to see the Hôtel Drouot, Paris's famous public auction house, which some people call the Hôtel des Ventes, but like most foreigners I never got there. The Hôtel Drouot is a large, forbidding building, very popular with Parisians, poor and rich, who want to buy or sell something. The other important public auction house comparable to it that I know is Vienna's Dorotheum, a veritable treasure-house, where people who know their way around can find many good things, often at reasonable prices. There are people who have taste and money, both in Vienna and Paris, who get everything for their houses at these institutions. Both auction houses are state-supervised, with strict quality controls and none of the funny business that sometimes occurs at private auctions.

The rue Drouot, off the Grands Boulevards, is hard to find; I suggest going by taxi. The best time to visit is Saturday afternoon, when there are no auctions and innumerable things are displayed for interested viewers. I went there on a Monday afternoon. I didn't want to buy anything; I wanted to see what happens, and I had no idea what I was going to find. The auction rooms, on the ground floor and second floor, were crowded with what the pollsters call a cross section of people—*clochards,* elderly gentlemen in camel hair coats that had seen better days (both the coats and the gentlemen), frantic housewives rushing from one room to the next, righteous-looking citizens with cold cigarette ends in their mouths, and, I'm glad to report, even a few not-unattractive ladies who seemed to give me an encouraging smile. Well, let's not jump to conclusions.

In one room shabby household goods were auctioned off for very little money. People bought cheap pictures without frames and cheap frames without pictures, used mattresses, children's carriages (maybe connected somehow with the mattresses), and some lovely old straw traveling baskets. These last brought back memories of my mother and Fräulein Gertrud packing our things for summer vacation at the North Sea or Baltic Sea—never the Mediterranean.

A commissionaire in a dark-blue jacket who had nothing better to do didn't mind giving me a few pointers. On Saturday afternoons between two and six, experts will take potential bidders around, tell them whether a piece is genuine or fake, and give them an estimate of its value. Those who find something that interests them come back the following week when the item is scheduled for auction. If they can't make it, the commissionaire will do the bidding for them. They tell him their limit and also pay the charges, from 10 to 16 percent. After the sale one can pay in cash or by check. One takes one's purchase home the same day or the following day. There is a transport office at the side entrance on the rue Chauchat, with vans and sturdy men standing about. They'll deliver anyplace, at the purchaser's expense. "Couldn't be easier," said the commissionaire. "Our Parisians love it. Some practically live here. All sales are announced on Friday in the *Gazette de l'Hôtel Drouot*. You American, *hein?* You can have it mailed there, ninety-five francs a year's subscription."

I happened to be lucky that afternoon. Room 14, on the right side of the ground floor, was crowded with an unusual group of people: wealthy-looking men with a gleam in their eye, obviously connoisseurs; tough career girls "acting for somebody else," no doubt; and well-fed characters who were, I was almost sure, restaurateurs or chefs out of uniform. Everybody had a red-bound catalogue in his hand and checked off numbers. Looking over the heads of the people I saw row upon row of wine bottles on long tables and cases of wine on the floor.

The auctioneer sat on a raised platform behind a table. In front of him two men were holding up wine bottles while he carried on his business, occasionally bringing down his hammer.

I bought a catalogue. Mes. Ader, Picard et Tajan, Commissaires-Priseurs Associés in Paris (with fancy addresses in New York City and Lausanne), had arranged a public sale of Grands Vins de Bordeaux, Bourgogne, et Champagne, *"appartenant à divers amateurs"* (belonging to various amateurs). I pushed through the crowd. There were many young people who noted all sales, making meticulous entries in their catalogues like system players in Monte Carlo. I talked to an elderly gentleman next to me who happened to be one of the "various amateurs." He wasn't here to buy, he said; he was selling his cellar and wanted to see what was going to happen.

"Doctor's orders," he said, feeling perhaps that an explanation was needed. "He claims I must stop drinking wine. I'm seventy-seven."

"You don't look it."

"That's because I've been drinking wine all my life. Mostly white ones that are said to be full of acid. Acid! Ha! Don't you ever believe a doctor!"

"I'm trying not to," I said, and I meant it and nodded.

"Don't nod, for goodness sake," he said, and gave me a push in the ribs. "If the auctioneer had seen you, he might have thought you were bidding. Down goes the hammer, and you're stuck." He looked at the rows of chairs that were all occupied. "I see no British," he said. "Where are they? They always used to attend these wine auctions."

"Maybe they don't have as much money now," I said.

"Are you kidding? Maybe they don't have money at home, but here in Paris and in Lausanne they have plenty of money. Now, don't move your head; be careful."

I kept standing like a soldier on guard duty. One of the assistants held up a bottle of Grande Chartreuse Jaune, *"D'avant 1910."*

"Nine hundred francs," somebody behind me said. "I hope he doesn't drop the bottle." One dollar was about five francs then; thus the bottle was $180.

"They never drop things here," said my neighbor. Some truly great wines would come up in small lots for sale: eight bottles of Château Cheval-Blanc '34 (estimated price 1,300 francs for the lot); five bottles of Château Lafite-Rothschild '45 (1,500 francs, $300, which means $60 a bottle, truly a super-bargain); seventeen bottles of Château Mouton-Rothschild '07, just my age, for a mere 1,200 francs. The most expensive item in the catalogue was lot No. 533, nine bottles of Château Mouton-Rothschild '28, a super-year, starting price 3,000 francs. A steal!

While I watched fascinated, trying not to move my head, some spectacular bargains were auctioned off. Twelve bottles of Vosne-Romanée '46 that went for from 300 to 820 francs. Thirteen bottles of Château Latour '39, from 300 to 550. One lucky buyer got a bottle for less than $9. Imagine!

But: There seemed to be a *but*. I noticed that the people sitting in front, on the chairs, hardly moved their heads, spoke in whispers when they made a bid, made mysterious signs. I asked my amateur friend.

"Insiders," he said. "Some of them bidding for hotels and restaurants or rich individuals. Everybody here knows everybody, and they know how high to go. This is real science, *mon cher,* nothing for dilettantes." He gave me a hard stare, leaving no doubt whom he considered a dilettante.

"I still wonder about the British," he said. "They always used to buy things that they could not afford. Certainly they cannot afford these wines. Where are they? See that fellow over there with the bulging neck? A German!" He gave me an unhappy look.

Just then a lady friend appeared in the door and waved to me. She had promised to meet me at the Hôtel Drouot. I waved back and prepared to leave.

"Do you like Champagne?" my neighbor asked abruptly.

"I'm not supposed to drink Champagne. Doctor's orders."

"Then why did you raise your hand? You almost acquired lot No. 53. Look at your catalogue: seventeen magnums of Pommery and Greno Brut '43. 500 francs."

"Mon Dieu!" I said, really terrified. What would I be doing with seventeen magnums of Pommery?

"Quiet, both of you!" said a connoisseur behind us.

I said good-bye to my amateur friend, trying not to move my head, and slipped out. My lady was waiting. I wanted to get away from all magnums of Champagne as fast as possible. I'd had it.

Outside, a taxi drove up. The woman next to the driver got out, paying no fare and not saying thanks, and quickly walked into the auction house. We got in.

"There you are," said the driver, an elderly man, turning on the meter. "My wife's got a job from seven in the morning to one in the afternoon. Then she comes home, makes something to eat quickly, and we rush out and I bring her here. She'll spend the whole afternoon at that damn place, looking for a diamond she's been talking about. Not for herself, for a friend. She knows everybody at the Drouot, and her friends ask her to buy things for them. Ah, you can find bargains if you are smart and lucky. Last year my wife bought a pearl necklace for our daughter for 480 francs plus sixteen percent, with a certificate of authenticity. At the Drouot you are always sure of quality. Later a jeweler told us the necklace was worth at least 2,000 francs." He turned around to see our astonished faces. "Not bad, what?"

I said it was certainly not bad.

"This afternoon," he said, "my wife will meet a group of women who spend every afternoon at the Drouot when they have sales, standing around, just watching, mostly not buying. Sort of Monte Carlo, if you know what I mean."

I said I knew what he meant. Wasn't he afraid, though, that she might once lose her head and his earnings?

"You don't know her. She never loses anything. Only thing I don't like is that we always have to eat in a hurry. Gives me indigestion. She feels she must go back quickly to Drouot. Sometimes I think she feels that Drouot is her home. But she does get good things. We even have an old upright Pleyel piano at home, though no one plays it."

I said I knew other people who have pianos in their houses that are not being played.

The driver nodded sagely. "*Standing*," he said, "that's what the Americans call it, I think. You've got to have it. Well, as long as she knows her limit. That's the important thing. When you get out I'll give you my card. If you ever need anything special, call me, and my wife will try to get it for you at the Drouot. As long as you know your limit."

October 1974

BIBLIOTHÈQUE DU GOURMET

Joseph Wechsberg

Monsieur Edgar Soète, a cheerful man of indefinable age, is the proprietor of the Librairie Salet, at 5, quai Voltaire, on the Left Bank.
In his large, bright store that looks like a living room M. Soète keeps
thousands of books on gastronomy. An early one is the famous volume by Platina de Cremona published in 1474 under the title *De
honesta voluptate*. The author's real name was Bartolommeo de' Sacchi
(1421–1481), but because he was librarian at the Vatican he didn't
want to endanger his job. The French version that M. Soète showed
me is a great rarity, translated by Didier Christal, prior of Saint-
Maurice near Montpellier. "Only two copies have been sold at auction
in London in our century," it says in the catalogue, which quotes a
price of thirty-two thousand francs. M. Soète implied that values and
currencies have changed and he wouldn't sell the book for the quoted
price now.

Occasionally he puts out a catalogue. He is not worried about suppliers and/or customers. "I find the books everywhere," he said, "and
I sell them everywhere." There are similar bookstores in other cities,
certainly in New York City, but being located on the Quai Voltaire,
with a view of the Louvre, where one can admire the *Mona Lisa* and
other, highly select masterpieces, M. Soète is in a somewhat privileged

position with his "Bibliothèque du Gourmet." He owns some treasures that he will show you only if you are a connoisseur and collector, with plenty of money, seriously interested in buying treasures.

And treasures there are. One of the latest catalogues offers Antonio Adami's *Il Novitiato del Maestro di Casa* (1636) along with the cookbook of Apicius, translated from the original Latin, and the second edition of *Banquet des Savants* by Athenaeus, "which belongs in every gastronomic library." A history of Italian wines, *De Naturali de Vinis Italiae Historia* by Andrea Baccius, in a beautiful seventeenth-century binding, is only seventy-five hundred francs. Lorenz Fries's *Von Allerley Speysen,* published in Mulhouse in 1559, is eleven thousand francs. And so on.

M. Soète is not only a theoretical connoisseur and a respected expert who conducts his own auctions at Drouot, he also likes to eat well. Like many experts, he speaks about the subject with obvious reluctance. He confessed that he does not like *la nouvelle cuisine française,* though he sells books by Michel Guérard and the Troisgros brothers. He frequents bistros on the Left Bank, which he didn't bother to name, but he admitted that he likes Allard, which is easy to understand. He doesn't cook himself but knows a lot about cooking. That, too, is easy to understand. His catalogue has the "Bibliothèque d'un Gourmand" on the cover; instead of books there are sausages, hams, cheeses, bottles of wine, and other good things. The back page shows the cover of *Le Cannaméliste Français* by Joseph Gilliers, "or a new instruction for those who wish to learn the office." The second edition is "of one of the most important culinary essays of the eighteenth century. The author was *chef d'office* of King Stanislas and his book contains a great number of recipes. . . ." Only fifty-two hundred francs, but M. Soète said the catalogue had been printed some time ago and the prices were outdated.

M. Soète also publishes cookbooks and gastronomic books "when I have time for it" and tries to keep all cookbooks, new and old, in stock. That must be a formidable task.

"This is not something you learn in a day," he said. "It takes a great deal of time and also a great deal of love. Sometimes a collector comes here with a specific idea and wants a specific book, but one cannot have everything. So I try to sell him something similar that will please him. One must know the literature and one must understand the customer's psychology. No use offering him a first edition of Brillat-Savarin's *Physiologie du Goût* if he hasn't got that far yet. Incidentally, have you ever seen the first edition?"

I shook my head. M. Soète got up and walked toward the rear, opened a locked bookcase, and showed me the precious volume. It had the author's inscription to a lady of whom he must have been fond. I asked M. Soète how much the book was worth. He smiled and said it wasn't for sale. Perhaps he meant it wasn't for sale to me, though if an important collector came, or somebody from an important museum, he might reconsider.

"I could find you an early copy of the Escoffier book," he said. "An excellent book." I acknowledged it was excellent but not in the same league as the first edition of the Brillat-Savarin.

"Certainly not," M. Soète said emphatically.

A customer came in and wanted a book about *la nouvelle cuisine française*. Without blinking M. Soète got up and showed her two books, and she bought both of them. Business is business. If you have something rare and valuable in mind, you just might find it at 5, quai Voltaire.

January 1979

FEEDING A CITY

A Night at Les Halles

Alaire Johnston

Situated a mere stone's throw from the Louvre, spilling out in the center of the city like some giant horn of plenty, are Les Halles centrales, Paris's earthy, noisy central market. Through Les Halles passes the daily food supply of most of France in a phantasmagoria of waste and confusion. They have been called outmoded and burlesque, and have even been charged with looting the French pocketbook, but they still throb with a colorful life all their own.

It was in 1110 that good King Louis the Fat authorized some peasant women to set up fish stalls outside his palace walls. The fishmongers flourished, other vendors bought space from the crown, and from the twelfth-century fish stalls the world's largest marketplace came into being.

Today Les Halles sprawl over more than twenty-one acres of choice Parisian real estate, and concessionaires—some of whose families have been in the market for many generations—handle every comestible known to the food-conscious French. A few of the main avenues have been widened and much of the market has been moved under glass-roofed pavilions, but the carnival air and the web of picturesque little streets still recall medieval times.

You can't buy swans on the rue Cygne—and no stags roam the rue du Grand Cerf—but butter and dairy-product stalls line the rue au Lard and every conceivable variety of *champignon* is sold on Mushroom Alley. And in the narrow, Hugoesque rue de la Grande-Truanderie, there are grimacing and whispering women with arrogantly swinging hips.

The time to see Les Halles is at night, for the market wakes while the rest of Paris sleeps. As late as midnight there is little stirring except black-caped *"flics"* on patrol or revelers restaurant-bound. Then, about one o'clock, great trucks from every corner of France begin inching their way through the narrow streets.

Visitors to Les Halles find no shortage of amusements with which to pass the time while the market is being set up. In fact, there is so much to do in the neighborhood that fun-loving Parisians have been coming there in the early hours of the morning for well over a century. In 1850 the crush was such that the authorities closed down a number of all-night establishments. However, some of the old restaurants survived and are still flourishing today, among them Au Pied de Cochon, Le Grand Comptoir, Pharamond, and Le Père Tranquille.

Which one to try first is largely a matter of taste. If you're a tripe enthusiast, there's Pharamond. The specialty of the house at L'Alsace aux Halles is *choucroute garnie*. For snails, there's the famous L'Escargot-Montorgueil. Just let your appetite be your guide.

One way to begin a night at Les Halles is with dancing at The Smoking Dog (Le Chien qui Fume), the oldest of Les Halles' bistros. In 1740 it was a village tavern where the poor of the quarter gathered to have a bowl of soup and to sing the *chansons* of Paris. The Smoking Dog has been a popular and colorful nightspot ever since.

The bar is crowded with truck drivers and white-coated *"forts des Halles,"* or porters, refreshing themselves with *vin blanc* or *café exprès*. In the rear, a two-piece combo is already in action. About now the haunts of the *haut monde* are closing and the night owls begin drifting in. The place is as crowded as a Brueghel canvas, the long tables that ring the dance floor filled by theatergoers, tourists, actors, and assorted refugees from the clubs of Montmartre.

The *ambiance* is irresistible. "Why do you pass me by," the guitarist sings. "Our time is short, our love is young ..." Then comes a rollicking parody on "Mademoiselle de Paris." The crowd sings familiar *chansons* in chorus or claps hands in unison. Between numbers everyone eats grilled pigs' feet or onion soup.

By three in the morning, The Smoking Dog is jammed. But now the din outside is heard, as if some gigantic carnival had begun. Les Halles are open for business.

The trucks have been emptied and the bounty of all the French provinces is on display. The giant *"forts"* shuttle through the narrow alleys with heavy burdens of meat, vegetables, or dairy products. Produce-laden pushcarts dodge in and out, amidst swelling cacophony.

On the rue Carême—the central avenue of Les Halles named, appropriately enough, for the famous chef—an infinite variety of meats and foodstuffs fills the stalls, congests the walkways, and spills into the streets. There are succulent *volailles de Bresse,* hams from Bayonne, *rillettes* from Tours, *fruits de mer* from Brittany and the Riviera, marbled filets from Norman cattle.

There are stalls upon stalls of *triperies,* specializing in tripe, liver, and oxtails; of *volaillers* selling pheasants and ortolans as well as more common birds, and of *boucheries chevalines* selling the horse meat of which Parisians are so fond. Restaurateurs are doing their daily buying, selecting *entrecôtes,* picking over mounds of cabbages and cauliflowers, eggplants and tomatoes, arguing about price, quality, and measure.

Farther along, in a slightly less crowded section of the market, we find the peaks of gourmandise: cheeses of the Jura, baskets of huge black truffles, pots of *foie gras* from the Périgord, luscious beribboned stalks of asparagus, and *fraises des bois,* tiny wild strawberries. Everywhere the abundance of France, arranged with a sensuous love of symmetry and color, assails the nostrils, dazzles the eyes, and stirs the appetite.

Dawn is on its way now. The bargaining grows more frenetic, the tempers shorter. Refuse accumulates as stocks decline. Soon the greengrocers and housewives will descend upon the market to haggle over what is left. Then the carters and grinders of refuse and bones take over.

If I spend a night at Les Halles, by this time I am getting hungrier every minute. However, on my last visit, awed by the immensity of the spectacle, I deferred the usual *omelette au lard*. The Office Central des Halles was just a couple of stalls away and I had questions to ask, so I sought out the *Commissaire*.

"*Monsieur le Commissaire*," I asked, "how many tons of fruits and vegetables pass through Les Halles on an average day in May, for example?"

The *Commissaire* rustled through some papers before coming up with an answer: 4,374 tons.

"But, of course," he said, "fruits and vegetables account for only about half the total tonnage passing through, and the figures are much higher at peak season."

The tonnage reflects the fact that Les Halles serve some eight million people. About one third of the amount goes back to the provinces, with generous profits to middlemen and handling charges tacked on. This situation causes many French housewives anguish, for a two-cent-a-pound rise in the price of beef is a real blow in the solar plexus. Government efforts to decentralize Les Halles have thus far failed, probably because of the pressure that their 1,620 concessionaires have been able to exert in French politics.

"Another question, *Monsieur le Commissaire*," I said archly. "Isn't this an expensive operation? Isn't the government going to abolish Les Halles?"

This was too much. "*Mon Dieu*," he exclaimed. "Of course it's expensive. But do away with Les Halles? That's ridiculous." Then he added firmly, "The markets, they are *traditionnels*."

I got the picture. Necessity or menace, Les Halles are likely to remain, for they are part of a way of life. Governments rise and governments fall, but Les Halles go on forever.

As I leave the Office Central des Halles, every avenue, every alley, and every impasse is solid with vehicles. The forty gendarmes assigned to Les Halles are having their problems. The rue de la Ferronnerie is blocked as it was on the hot humid day in 1610 when Henry IV was assassinated there, his carriage stalled between two vendors' carts that had been overturned in the narrow lane. The rue Saint-Denis, the royal road to Paris, is a mass of outraged vehicular traffic.

"Well, that's life at Les Halles," I thought. And now for that *omelette au lard* . . .

———

For those who are not attracted to The Smoking Dog, there remain the regional restaurants of Les Halles. The Pharamond, at 24, rue de la Grande-Truanderie, has opened at daybreak since 1832 to sell small containers of its specialty, *tripes à la mode de Caen,* to local marketers. But during the dinner hour the soft banquettes of this brightly tiled Norman restaurant are crowded with a discriminating clientele, drawn to the Pharamond by this same *spécialité.* Here is the recipe for tripe after the fashion of Caen as transcribed by chef Henri Guilhem.

TRIPES À LA MODE DE CAEN

Simmer 1 veal shank in water to cover until it is tender and drain it, reserving the stock. Put the shank in a large earthenware casserole. Sauté 4 large carrots, 4 stalks of celery, and 3 large onions, all sliced, in ¼ cup butter until the vegetables are translucent and arrange them on and around the meat. Cover the vegetables with 4 pounds tripe, previously rinsed in cold water 3 times and cut into 2-inch squares. Sprinkle each layer of tripe with salt and coarsely ground black pepper. Add a bouquet garni composed of 6 sprigs of parsley, 3 bay leaves, 2 sprigs of marjoram, and a sprig of thyme. Pour 1½ cups white wine, 1 cup Calvados, and the reserved veal stock over all. There should be enough liquid to cover the tripe. Seal the lid with a roll of dough made of flour and water. Bake the casserole in a very slow oven (260°F) for 6 hours or longer. Serve in the casserole accompanied by a green salad and French bread. Serves 8.

Of course, if hearty Alsatian fare is more to your taste, you may prefer L'Alsace aux Halles. Jutting out into the rue Coquillière at the angle of the rue Jean-Jacques Rousseau, this chalet-styled brasserie, with its scenic murals of Alsace, provides a grandstand seat overlooking Mushroom Alley. You can sit and watch the vendors peddling every variety of mushroom, from the tiny button *champignons de Paris* to the giant cèpes of gourmet cookery. And Maître Robert, formerly of the S.S. *Normandie,* will enlighten you on the characteristics of mushrooms, on Alsatian cookery, and on the lore of Les Halles.

Here is the recipe for that great Alsatian specialty, *choucroute garnie*, just as it is prepared in great porcelain-lined casseroles atop the range at L'Alsace.

CHOUCROUTE GARNIE
(*Sauerkraut L'Alsace aux Halles*)

Line the bottom of a casserole with 1 pound salt pork. Add 3 onions, each stuck with 1 clove, a few juniper berries and caraway seeds, and 1½ pounds sauerkraut. Sprinkle with black pepper and finely chopped garlic. On the sauerkraut arrange 3 pounds smoked pork and sprinkle once more with pepper and garlic. Arrange another 1½ pounds sauerkraut on the pork and cover with 1 pound thinly sliced bacon. Pour 3 cups thin consommé and 1 bottle Champagne over all, cover the casserole tightly, and simmer for 1 hour. Remove the smoked pork, recover the casserole, and simmer for 4 hours. Return the smoked pork to the casserole along with 1 pound thinly sliced ham, 6 *Knackwürste,* 6 *cervelat* sausages, and a few truffle slices. Cover the casserole and cook the *choucroute garnie* for 30 minutes longer. Serves 8.

Perhaps it's the Champagne touch, but this hearty fare of the burghers of Strasbourg is one of the most succulent dishes in all France. Don't miss the province of Alsace if you can help it, but if you can't, there's always L'Alsace aux Halles.

The third and last restaurant of this little tour of the markets isn't regional, but on its elegant little menu you'll find many great regional specialties: *suprême de barbue bordelaise, grenouilles provençale,* and *côte de veau jurassienne,* to name but a few. The great golden snail perched over the door of 38, rue Montorgueil identifies this restaurant as L'Escargot-Montorgueil.

The emphasis at L'Escargot is, naturally, on snails, and a snail restaurant has existed on this spot since the reign of Henry II. As its fame spread through the years, other "snails" opened all over Paris: The Snail of Gold, The Snail of the Butte, The Snail Grégoire, The Gilded Snail.

The original Escargot was slow to fight back, but a few years ago, in self-defense, it became L'Escargot-Montorgueil. Resplendent in its rococo fin de siècle décor, it is probably the best-known snail and seafood restaurant in Paris. The great and famous of many eras have made their way up squeaking spiral staircases to the private rooms upstairs. Today, Rolls-Royces and vendors' carts compete for parking space at L'Escargot.

The average patron, plucking a juicy Burgundian snail from its shell, probably hasn't the slightest idea of the toil that has gone into making it so eminently edible. One night at L'Escargot, Maître Gabriel Pacaud gave us the inside story of the trimmings, washings, scaldings, and simmerings through which the snails pass before they are ready to be returned to their shells. Our recipe, for Americans, assumes that the snails have been so processed before they reach the kitchen.

LES ESCARGOTS BOURGUIGNONNE
(*Burgundy Snails*)

Allow 12 snails for each serving. Cream 1¼ cups butter with 1 teaspoon olive oil and blend in 1 tablespoon parsley, 2 teaspoons shallot, and 1 teaspoon tarragon, all finely chopped, and salt and pepper to taste. Place a small amount of the seasoned butter in each snail shell, replace the snail, and seal the opening with a thick coat of the butter. Put the snails on snail dishes or on a flat baking pan and set them in a moderate oven (350°F) for 6 or 7 minutes, or until they are heated through and the butter is melted. Serve very hot.

The snails, accompanied by a bottle of Pouilly-Fuissé, and followed up with *chateaubriand béarnaise, pommes soufflées,* and a fine Bordeaux—perhaps a Haut-Brion—make an auspicious beginning for a night in Les Halles, especially for those with a fondness for the atmosphere of bygone days.

Spend a night at Les Halles, savoring the riches of French cuisine, French gaiety, and French history. Then you may agree with *Monsieur le Commissaire:* "Of course they're expensive, but *vive Les Halles!*"

December 1961

LES HALLES: A LAST LOOK

Naomi Barry

The string beans were packed in an ordinary wooden crate, the type of light wooden box you see in any grocery store. They were very special beans, however. Having been picked so young, they were almost as fine as blades of marsh grass, and their selection had been so careful that they were uniformly slender. Someone had tenderly laid them in the crate in an even basketry pattern. Then, with a burst of good humor, this unknown genius had looked at the carefully braided beans and decided a little touch was lacking. So he, or more probably she, punc-tuated the top layer at regular intervals with the smiling head of a yellow-and-white daisy.

What a court presentation to tempt a grocer gathering his supplies in the dark hours of the predawn! We are accustomed to ribbons for bonbons, but furbelows for a bean?

However, all this took place in Les Halles of Paris, the city where food and dressmaking were raised to the twin pinnacles of *haute cuisine* and *haute couture,* both as respected as any of the fine arts.

These particular *halles* (the word simply means markets) were the most gigantic, historic, robust, amusing, and artistic in the world. The constructions of fruits and vegetables were a fantasia. At eleven P.M. you saw nothing but bare pavements. By one A.M. you walked between embankments of onions, past turrets of tomatoes, through alleys of lettuce. Cabbages were massed in bulwarks, but the more fragile peaches were cosseted in cotton batting.

My particular love has always been the watercress. Tiny bunches were delicately arranged until they formed wreaths as large as life preservers. The leafy rings were placed with infinite care, one above the other, in baskets high as your waist. No packing down. The heat of crowding would have killed the fragile cress. But who was the anonymous peasant with the soul of an artist who devised the rapturous solution of a wreath?

With a pang of nostalgia, I am already using the past tense. In the beginning of 1969, this gorgeous, paradoxical, centuries-old ephemeral garden, which vanished each morning only to reappear again each night, will fade away for good. Les Halles are being forced out of Paris. The city has become too big. Its streets are a distemper of traffic, without even counting the additional four thousand food trucks choking the heart of town, where the roads are so narrow they must have been jammed even in the days of carts. Les Halles, iron-corseted in a colorful Casbah of fish, fruit, and fowl, have become an anachronism. They make as much twentieth-century sense as pushcarts and stands in the middle of Times Square during rush hour. (At that, there are many who might cheer it as an improvement.) After more than ten years of arguments, negotiations, stalling, and lobbying, the gavel has come down. Paris can no longer support the oasis that bloomed on stone. Les Halles must move to a no-place called Rungis, ten kilometers outside of town, near Orly Airport.

Recently, I made a farewell sentimental journey through Les Halles. It was all color and smell: square fortresses of pale-green and pearl-white leeks; feathery ferns topping carrots, suggestive of the headdress plumes at the nearby Folies-Bergère; small, innocent-looking ivory melons with mint stripes, and only an incredible aroma to tell you of the refreshing juicy flesh within; eggplants, purple, sleek-skinned, a shape to fondle, the most sensual of vegetables.

Every turning was a delight: impudent scarlet radishes with white bunny-tail bottoms, gathered small for extra sweetness; the intoxicating fragrance of thousands of raspberries, picked only after they had tasted the full passion of the sun; neat little bundles of chives; mangoes flown in from Mali; avocados flown in from Israel; pineapples from the Azores; and hot red peppers from Spain. Produce from near and produce from far, coming by ship, by plane, by truck for the Belly of Paris.

All products were sized with precision. A basket of button mushrooms meant button mushrooms right down to the hidden bottom row, and a bushel of peas was as uniform as if each one had been sprung out of the same pod. A restaurateur in Grenoble could order four hundred ducklings for a banquet and know that he would receive four hundred ducklings, each weighing five hundred grams.

The huge trucks crawled through the maze of ancient streets arriving from Brittany, from Belgium, from Holland, from the Mediterranean. Moving like remote-control toys, they pulled up to their appointed stations, nothing but coded chalk marks on the sidewalk. With incredible and silent speed, the contents were discharged into waiting brawny arms. In a twinkling began the erection of the mounds, the pyramids, the still-life displays. The whole ballet was beautiful. Woe unto you, if in your openmouthed admiration you were impeding the structure of a scallion skyscraper. Your French would have to be very good to understand the words, but the tone was unmistakable.

While I enjoyed a regiment of enormous artichokes scandalously tipped with purple, I was reminded in a far-fetched way of a four-masted schooner, a training ship for naval cadets, I once saw sail proudly into the harbor of Hamilton, Bermuda. Suddenly the shore seethed with people. There was a single collective lump in the throat before those romantic billowing sails. It was a world of grace and drama few of us had ever expected to see; most likely we would never see its equal. The roistering, jolly, earthy loveliness of Les Halles belongs to such not-to-be-forgotten and sadly lamented lost worlds.

I have a kaleidoscope of memories. One joyous morning about three A.M., ten years ago, a wholesaler let me "sell" his apples. Mixed in with the buyers came a rollicking band of fashionables. Among them was Mary Jane Poole, of *Vogue*, who also had a suppressed desire to sell apples.

Our boss was as enchanted with his two *américaines* as a producer who had unexpectedly discovered two hit stars. Les Halles may have been serious business, but it was always a lot of fun. When we finished our stint, we accompanied the market people for dinner at dawn.

There always was an exceptional camaraderie. So much handshaking went on, you'd think you were at a reunion of bankers. Hello, goodbye, handshake. Two hundred kilos of oranges. Handshake. Thirty turbot. Handshake. "My little chickadee, your cheeks are roses tonight." Pinch at the cheek of the smiling lady fishmonger, crimson with cold. Handshake. Buyers and sellers had known each other for years, in fair weather and foul.

Transactions were made in a whisper, a habit that goes back to a consideration when the buildings surrounding Les Halles were residential. During the trading hours of the night, families were sleeping. (The buildings are still there but in recent years the apartments have become offices.) When a deal was made, a piece of paper was given. Payment was to a group of cash desks at the end of a buying tour.

Fortunate restaurant owners with wives devoted enough to join them on a tour of duty were able to divide the work and shorten the time spent. The men would select the supplies they required for the day while the wives would trot off to the cashiers.

One night I accompanied the fruit and vegetable buyer of Fauchon, the most luxurious fancy grocer of Paris, on the Place de la Madeleine. No wonder their merchandise is so exceptional. The vendors in Les Halles never even put their finest commodities on the market until he had passed by. If he shook his head, the item was put on sale for others, but not until he had made his choice.

The timetable was rigorous in order to avoid a pileup of customers all arriving in little cars and pickup trucks. First to go on sale about midnight were the fruits and vegetables. At regular intervals during the night came the poultry, the meat, the fish, and the dairy products. At nine A.M., a bell was rung to terminate the wholesale trading. This was also the signal for anything left over to be sold to retail customers during the cleanup hour.

Like Sooners rushing into the opening of the Oklahoma Territory came nuns with orphanages and other institutions to feed, thrifty housewives, the respectable poor, and the *clochards*. Some etymologists say that the slang word *clochard*, meaning bum, is derived from the ringing of Les Halles' bell or *cloche*.

Although the Revolution of 1789 and the Rights of Man never completely eradicated a sense of class in France, Les Halles were remarkably free. Apparently nobody, not even the wealthiest dealer in citrus fruits, felt particularly privileged if he had to get up every morning at four.

Furthermore, everyone who had any work connected with Les Halles wore a coverall or *blouse*. It had the same leveling influence as the obligatory smock worn by French schoolchildren. Employers and employees alike were dressed in these button-down-the-front work coats. A light gray *blouse* indicated some aspect of the food trade. Dark gray signified that one was in fish. White was for the butchers. I knew a merchant in Les Halles who kept a Thoroughbred saddle horse at Rambouillet and a yacht on the Riviera. But during the week, in his light gray *blouse*, he was just plain Jacques to everybody.

"We are a little republic, a *commune libre*," he once said to me. "Nowhere can you find a better human contact between employer and employee than here."

Most visitors were familiar with the white uniforms of the butchers. Generally the butchers were young and strapping, and had ferocious appetites. As soon as their work let up a little (about three A.M.), they would troop to the nearest bars and bistros to restore themselves.

During the twenties and the thirties, an evening at the nightclubs, bars, opera, or theater in the smart quarters of Paris was not considered properly climaxed unless it ended with onion soup, steaks, or seafood in Les Halles. Evening clothes sat next to blood-smeared white aprons, and there was much bantering and laughter between the stalwarts and the swells.

When in the restaurants of the *quartier*, even the outsiders found themselves talking to each other like old buddies. Joyous informality among strangers has never been a trait of the French bourgeoisie. But in this atmosphere so redolent of all the products of earth and sea, stiff behavior just disappeared.

The beating heart of the district, of course, was the markets themselves. The ones known to us were erected during the 1850s under Napoleon III. The delicate ironwork construction of the twelve pavilions was of an architectural daring that thrilled and delighted all Europe. The use of such light iron skeletons was positively revolutionary at the time. Remember that Les Halles predated the Eiffel Tower by more than thirty-five years.

Underneath the pavilions were vast warehouses and storage vaults, never seen by the public. The grillwork gates were locked until four in the afternoon, when they were opened for the Flower Market. The brilliant masses of color, the heaps of blooms beyond the imagination, and the forest of green plants made the few hours of the Flower Market one of the ravishing enchantments of this world.

The police kept careful watch to make sure that no private customers intruded. But at six-thirty P.M., for a half hour, the public could buy bunches at deliriously cheap wholesale prices. What an intoxication to walk away with two dozen long-stemmed roses for a fraction of the cost at a florist on the avenue George-V. Parisians planning a party would try to come during that precious half hour and buy enough to flower their apartments extravagantly.

Whenever I felt stifled by the city, I would stroll over to Les Halles in the daytime. Even though the markets were closed during these hours, the area was a fascinating hive of specialized shops, bistros, restaurants, and throbbing local color. Surrounding the actual marketplace is a teeming quarter filled with accessory trades: jobbers, demiwholesalers, makers of sausage casings, restaurant suppliers, cheese refiners, preparers of foie gras, and sellers of toques and aprons.

People who love their kitchens come to the neighborhood for all sorts of special items, most of which are used by professionals. French *charcuteries* traditionally have stunning receptacles in which to display their wares; crocks and pickle jars and distinctive white rectangular dishes. You can find these at the Verrerie des Halles in the courtyard of 15, rue du Louvre and at A. Simon, 32, rue Étienne-Marcel. At Nortier, at 10, rue Coquillière, the cheeses are so perfectly aged you need never poke an exploratory index finger. Next door is Battendier, celebrated for their whole fresh foie gras, which they send all over Paris, particularly at Christmas.

At 18, rue Coquillière is Dehillerin, since 1820 a headquarters for chefs seeking pots, pans, knives, molds, terrines, and a thousand other utensils absolutely necessary for classic French cuisine. The firm's great specialty is copper of a quality hard to find today: heavy copper casseroles, cocottes, and sautéing pans lined with tin, which Dehillerin will reline during the slow months of January and February. Their weight could break a wrist.

The ancient streets of this area have delicious names like rue de la Lingerie (Street of Underwear), rue de la Poterie (Street of Pottery), rue des Déchargeurs (Street of the Moving Men), rue Mondétour (Street of My Detour), and rue du Plat-d'Étain (Street of the Pewter Plate). The neighborhood is a treasure of exquisite but dilapidated mansions of the seventeenth and eighteenth centuries. You might not notice them because of the warehouses and jobbers installed on many of the ground floors. However, if you raise your eyes, you will discover some of the finest old buildings in Paris. Looming over the whole jumbled ensemble is the glorious Gothic Renaissance church of Saint-Eustache, famous for its organ music.

What is going to happen now? There is no clear-cut answer. Everything under the roofs of the pavilions—fruits, vegetables, fish, dairy, and poultry—will go to the new, spacious, efficient, hygienic buildings and hangars at Rungis. Meats will be transferred to the already existing meat market at the Porte de la Villette. The flowers, too, are going to Rungis, to the dismay of thousands who had hoped and agitated to keep them in the city as an explosion of beauty in the middle of stone urbanism. Unable to make the trip will be the local color and the special Rabelaisian atmosphere of Les Halles. Like good little wines, it is doubtful that they can travel.

Exactly what is to be done with the soon-to-be-cleared space, no one yet knows. Will it be transformed into a park, a parking lot, a sports center, a university complex, a cluster of administration buildings, or a real estate development of offices and apartment houses? All the enterprises in the surrounding area of the pavilions can stay on. Nobody intends to move unless evicted because his building has been condemned. For health and safety, some buildings are to be demolished. There is an uneasy malaise throughout the *quartier*. No one

knows if the neighborhood can survive when the heart has been removed.

Dehillerin is expecting a drop in business. However, they have prepared a simple catalogue to mail out to friends and customers around
the world.

That the Halles district was home to a number of good restaurants
is not news. But they are in a particular bind, according to one merchant in Les Halles. They have falsified their tax returns for so many
years that the indemnity, if they leave, would be next to nothing. The
future is uncertain. Will the bourgeois fun-lovers still come after the
robust workers have gone?

Certain restaurants will not be too much affected because their
clientele does not depend upon Les Halles. L'Escargot has been at
38, rue Montorgueil since 1830, when it used to feed the passengers
arriving by diligence. The décor is so *Merry Widow,* you expect someone to break into song at any minute.

The six macramé curtains are a marvel, and it is estimated that it
would cost two thousand dollars to replace one of them. However,
they can't be replaced, because no one is left to crochet linen thread
into complicated lace patterns of château life. Every August during
the annual closing the curtains are sent to the Jura where they are
laundered by careful old ladies and laid to dry on the mountain
prairies.

At L'Escargot, I ate a delicious fillet of sea bass that had been
poached in a *fumet* with white wine. It was served in a ring of cooked
chopped mushrooms and tomatoes. The décor and the food will attract the clientele, no matter what happens in the neighborhood.

I left the restaurant with an upward look toward the vestibule ceiling, painted to represent a group of cherubs in chefs' toques cooking
up a sauce in heaven. This confection had been bought from the Brittany summer house of Sarah Bernhardt. Sarah, who liked to paint, was
supposed to have applied a few of the brushstrokes herself. After her
death, L'Escargot acquired the fresco in tender memory of a very
spectacular client.

In contrast to the plushy grandeur of L'Escargot, there is a very
ordinary little zinc bar at 13 bis, rue Montmartre. On its walls is a

smashing series of ceramic murals, showing Les Halles in its nineteenth-century bloom. One depicts the scramble to buy food after the bell. Another portrays the arrival of the little merchandise train that used to puff-puff directly into the market.

The little train chugged into oblivion years ago. Now the mammoth trucks soon will be going down another highway. When they get to Rungis, I wonder if they will find a few winking daisies lovingly placed among the string beans for no reason beyond the poetic pleasure.

December 1968

La Vie Moderne

Joseph Wechsberg

Many Parisians were unhappy when their City Council decided to tear down the beautiful old Halles and move the operation to a suburban no-man's-land at Rungis near Orly Airport. The Halles, built between 1854 and 1866 (actually the market had been there since the twelfth century), was a landmark of Paris, like the Eiffel Tower or the Arc de Triomphe. Petitions were signed, and the decision went all the way up to President Pompidou, a connoisseur of beautiful things, but Les Halles was moved to Rungis. They say that the last pavilion, still standing, will be dismantled and rebuilt in Vincennes as part of a permanent exposition.

During the general excitement no one bothered to take a fair look at the Marché d'Intérêt National (MIN) in Rungis. I went there one morning with M. Jean Vialetto, the technical director of the Hôtel Lancaster, who drives out three times a week to buy flowers. The Lancaster spends more money on flowers than it does on electricity. On the way out M. Vialetto told me that the elderly habitués of the Halles had been unhappy about the move and were still trying to get used to Rungis. "The Halles was crowded and uncomfortable but also cozy and convenient. One knew everybody there. One could walk around and make all his purchases within a couple of hours. Rungis is six hundred hectares (almost fifteen hundred acres), and the buyer has to drive around to purchase different things. The operation is more efficient, but somehow it got dehumanized. The spirit has changed. One no longer knows many people there; one feels lost." He gave a shrug. "I suppose it was inevitable. Rungis reflects the patterns and modes of *la vie moderne.*"

We got off the *autoroute du sud* and stopped at a tollgate. M. Vialetto showed his permanent buyer's card. (Other people pay five francs. There was no entrance fee in the old Halles.) It was seven in the morning, just the time to see the windup operation at Le Pavillon de la Marée (the fish market). The men begin their work at five in the morning and end about three hours later. To avoid traffic congestion the various departments at Rungis operate at different hours. After the fish market closes the dairy pavilion is open; the fruit and vegetable markets are next, and then the flower market. The whole system has changed. In the old Halles the small producers sold their goods in small stalls; it was the era of the individualist. Now many small producers form cooperatives to share the overhead. Some sold out to the big companies. The new market is almost anonymous. "The technocrats and the police have taken over," M. Vialetto said.

The fish market, located in a very large hall, was clean and air-conditioned, spacious and well organized. There were stacks of white plastic containers with fine fish and shellfish resting on crushed ice—turbot, sole, *crevettes, langoustes.* The containers were lifted and moved by small vehicles. There was the strong, pleasant scent of the incoming tide. The "fishmongers," mostly large firms, were installed in heated offices behind glass panels. Men in blue or white overalls stood around writing orders. In the not-so-old days the chefs of many good restaurants did their shopping at the Halles, selecting fine fish, *primeurs,* anything that looked especially good. Rungis is too far away for them to come out. Instead they have *commissionaire-négociants* who do the buying for them. Gone are the pretty girls who worked as shopgirls or cashiers, adding the feminine touch. Only a few women are left, and they wear white skirts and white boots.

I asked M. Vialetto what had happened to the lovely old restaurants where one went for *soupe à l'oignon* at five in the morning before going to bed. He took me to a large kiosk across from the main entrance to the Marée hall. It was called Le Grand Pavillon and looked like a California roadside restaurant surrounded by parked cars, but inside the atmosphere was still Parisian. On one side was the café and brasserie. Sturdy men wearing blue aprons were having *un petit verre de vin blanc* at the bar. Others sat at small tables eating. We talked with Mme. Jeanne Baldit, the *patronne* who has run the place with the help of thirty-five employees since the untimely death of her husband, who was well known around the Halles. She showed us photographs of her former restaurant, Aux Deux Pavillons. "We were surrounded by flower women," she said wistfully. *"Ah, comme c'était joli!"* One Saturday night in March 1969 the restaurant closed, and the following Tuesday morning it reopened in Rungis. There are twenty-two such restaurants all over the terrain, compared with one hundred and fifty in the former Halles district. Some have remained, and others have closed up.

"It was difficult in the beginning, but now we do more business than before. We are open day and night except on Sundays. I have three chefs. One works from six in the morning until four in the afternoon; the next, until two in the morning; and the third, during the early morning hours when the Marée people come in. We already have a steady clientele from the outside: Industrialists and executives arrive from nearby enterprises, and some of our old friends come out for dinner. They say it's easier to drive out on the superhighway than it was to travel through the congested streets of the old Halles district; the new market is only twenty minutes from the Concorde. They know they'll get the freshest and best fish from the Marée."

There were a dozen fish dishes on the menu. Mme. Baldit said that Champagne was being sold by the glass at the bar. The restaurant side of the building was cheerful with yellow tablecloths, amusing lighting fixtures, and prints and historical pictures of the old Halles. It was eight-fifteen in the morning, and the bosses of the large fish firms sat down for dinner. The waiters brought bottles of Beaujolais and large steaks. Having seen nothing but fish since three in the morning, they preferred to eat meat. Mme. Baldit had awakened at four, and it would be five in the afternoon by the time she got home. She was getting used to the new pattern of life.

"It's more civilized," she said. "The merchants no longer think they own the place. There was a lot of shouting, you know. This crowd is more businesslike, almost polite. I think even the onion-soup clientele will show up sooner or later."

We left and drove around. M. Vialetto showed me the fruit and vegetable pavilions and took me to the flower pavilion, large and air-conditioned and very clean. Blue signs said Allée des Tulipes, Allée des Roses, and so on. A surveillant member of the Préfecture de Police (who preferred to remain anonymous) told us that the laws are more strictly enforced nowadays. It is impossible to buy without an invoice. Only wholesale buyers are admitted. Housewives can no longer come out on Saturdays to buy what is left at lower prices. The officer admitted that the place has no *ambiance familiale.* "But we have a drive-in cinema, a hotel, even a *centre de loisir.* One cannot do one's shopping as one did around the old Halles. But everything considered, Rungis isn't bad. It was necessary. Maybe someday people will even admit it."

January 1973

PURVEYORS

COLD COMFORT

Joseph Wechsberg

Ice cream and sherbet enthusiasts, who account for a large percentage of the Parisian populace, have long thought Monsieur Berthillon *un peu difficile*. Few know his first name (Raymond); fewer still have seen him. Friends told me I wouldn't be able to talk to him: He had no time for reporters and such. *"Il s'en fiche royalement,"* they said; he couldn't care less. And why should he? M. Berthillon is without doubt the Stradivari of Paris *glaciers* (ice-cream makers).

Ice creams and sherbets (water ices) are part of French gastronomy. "When they are well prepared and daintily dished, they are the consummation of all that is delicate and good," wrote Escoffier, who started out as a *pâtissier* and often made his own sherbets. Flavored ices were introduced in Paris in the 1660s by Francesco Procopio dei Coltelli, "a gentleman from Palermo," who later served sherbets in his Café Procope, said to be the oldest coffeehouse in the world. But the glory of having invented flavored ices goes to the Chinese, who later taught the art to the Persians and the Arabs.

Back to M. Berthillon. His ice-cream parlor is a modest café in the Hôtel de Bourgogne, a charmingly run-down building on the rue Saint-Louis-en-l'Île, in one of the ancient *quartiers* of Paris where time seems to stand still. A historical marker on the façade informs the visitor that the house was built in 1642 for Maître Tailleur Jacques Pichon, perhaps an early Cardin.

Berthillon's café displays two nondescript flowerpots in the window and a sign informing passersby that it is possible to *emporter* (take home) ices Wednesday through Sunday and that there is table service after one o'clock. The price is eight francs for a half liter, sixteen francs for a liter. Some guidebooks mention that the place is closed on Mondays, but when we arrived there on a Tuesday morning, a sign said, CLOSED MONDAYS AND TUESDAYS. The building's entrance, next to the café, has an old-fashioned black-and-gold sign reading, CHAUFFAGE CENTRAL, EAU ET GAZ, which reminded me of my student days when *eau* did not mean *hot* water. The door seemed locked. I pushed a button. Nothing happened. I wanted to leave, but fortunately my companion, a lady of charm and persistence, boldly turned the doorknob. The door opened into a dim corridor. Always trust a woman. The paint was peeling off the ceiling. Along one wall were boxes of strawberries, rhubarb, and asparagus and bottles of cream and milk. The scent of the fruit was fresh and fine. A large cardboard box was marked "380 *oeufs.*"

We proceeded cautiously down the hall. At the end was a spiral staircase and a glass door leading into a pantry and kitchen. A man wearing a white shirt and cook's trousers stood with his back to us, ordering more milk and cream on the telephone. When he finished, I opened the door and asked him where I might find M. Berthillon.

"I am Berthillon," he said. "How did you get in? What do you want?" He glared at me and at my charming companion, who had wisely remained in the shadows. I explained the purpose of my visit. M. Berthillon, a heavyset, ruddy-faced man with a mustache and bright eyes, said gruffly that he was *très occupé* and had no time for idle conversation. Fruits had to be peeled and pressed, and he was already behind schedule. The girl who was supposed to help wash up had gone home and hadn't returned yet. *"C'est un désastre,"* he said darkly and was about to close the door when I quickly slipped my foot in the entrance in my best door-to-door-salesman style and asked Berthillon about himself. No, he had never been a *cuisinier*, never a *pâtissier*, always a *glacier*. He'd been right here for nineteen years. First, he'd been all alone in his kitchen, but now his son-in-law was helping.

At that point, a slim young man, Berthillon's son-in-law, Monsieur Bernard Chauvin, came down the stairs. He shook hands with us, and then M. Berthillon had to shake hands with us too. He was still holding the door, but the ice (unflavored) was slowly melting between us. Thirty minutes and much information later, we were permitted brief access to the small kitchen, with its large, modern ice-cream freezer, refrigerators, and tables. The floor was sticky with syrup, and the girl wasn't back yet. *"Une catastrophe,"* said the son-in-law.

M. Berthillon turned out to be that refreshing, rare specimen, an uninhibited individualist disdainful of any compromise. He said he didn't know what flavors he would make tomorrow; that depended on supplies. Twice a week the two men drive out to the new Halles at Rungis and buy what is good—and, alas, often expensive. In late spring he had found some fine *fraises des bois* and had had to charge twenty-five francs for a liter of strawberry ice, which he hated to do, but at the regular price he would have lost money. The summer's melons were expensive, too, "but good."

On Bastille Day, when it can get humid and hot in Paris and everybody wants ice cream or sherbet, M. Berthillon closes his shop and goes away with his wife, daughter, and son-in-law for two months. The *maison* reopens on September 14, when the warm weather is almost over. Within a few hours word mysteriously reaches customers, from the nearby concierge to the Baronne de Rothschild in her *hôtel particulier,* and everybody arrives and lines up.

"Je m'en fiche," M. Berthillon said with feeling. "I am not interested in people who come here during a heat wave. I like them to come when it's snowing and zero outside. Then they come to enjoy my fine ices and not just to cool themselves."

One can't expect a Stradivari to tell his secrets, and M. Berthillon is no exception. "Anybody can make ice creams and *sorbets,*" he said. "Ice cream is, in principle, fruit or chocolate or something else with egg yolks, sugar, and cream. Sherbet is fruit juice or liqueur with sugar dissolved in water. We have good water on the Île. It comes all the way from Fontainebleau, but we boil it just to be sure there is no taste of chlorine. No coloring, no powders, nothing artificial, either. Two thirds of our sales are water ices, which are refreshing and good for the digestion and haven't many calories. Personally, I don't mind calories. We like to eat well during our vacation. I am from Burgundy and forty-nine." He nodded and smiled as though that explained everything—and it did. We talked about good restaurants for a while, and then M. Berthillon said, almost regretfully, that he really had to go back to work, otherwise he wouldn't be able to serve twenty-five different flavors on Wednesday. "Come back tomorrow at ten when the shop opens," he said. We shook hands and left. No one can convince us that M. Berthillon is difficult.

We returned the next morning. By ten-thirty, a line had already formed in front of the small café. The proprietor of the bookstore next door said that sometimes there is a real *bagarre*, a scuffle, among the impatient customers. Inside, Madame Berthillon and her daughter, Madame Chauvin, were trying to run the madhouse, answering the phone, checking lists, taking ices out of the freezers, and scribbling orders, which they entered in an old-fashioned ledger. The whole operation was amateurish but curiously efficient. In the afternoon a young girl would come in to help serve the tables, but the *maison* was strictly a family enterprise: no waitresses in starched uniforms, no computers, just wonderful ices.

A sign on the wall says that *cornets* (cones) must not be consumed on the premises; little and big boys, take notice! Another sign informs customers of the morning's ice-cream flavors: *vanille, café, chocolat, caramel, noix de coco, Agenaise* (prune with Armagnac), *Créole* (with rum and raisins), Grand Marnier, *plombières* (with glacéed fruits), *noisette,* and *banane.* There is also a list of the available sherbets: *fraise, framboise, cerise, mûre* (blackberry), *myrtille* (huckleberry), *cassis, pêche, reine-claude* (greengage), *mirabelle* (yellow plum), *poire, abricot, citron, mandarine, orange, pamplemousse* (grapefruit), *pruneau* (with Armagnac), *thé, ananas,* and two superspecials, *fraise des bois* and *melon.* A coupe of sherbet is only three francs. They also serve coffee, tea, *café viennoise,* mineral waters, fruit juices, quinine water, and beer, according to a sign, though I wouldn't advise anyone to go to Berthillon for a bottle of beer. Goodness knows what might happen.

The line of customers is a demonstration of the blessings of democracy. Elderly ladies and very chic young women, all wait their turn to ask meekly for a liter of ice. Strawberry and vanilla are the best sellers. Most women know what they want, but some men do not. The day of our visit three bachelors said they had a party for ten that night and asked what they should take. Mme. Berthillon counseled them, and they thanked her. The ices are packed in square white boxes lined with foam rubber, and they keep for at least two hours outside the freezer. The boxes are two francs extra, which is refunded when the customers return them. But they will probably be needed when the customers come for more sherbet; once people have tasted M. Berthillon's ices, they always come back.

When Madame had a free moment, I asked her why her husband and she hadn't expanded the business. She smiled. "You talked to my husband yesterday, didn't you? Well, you noticed that he is a perfectionist. He wants to do everything himself. He admitted Bernard into his sanctum only a few years ago. But we plan to open up the second floor and enlarge the kitchen—just a little. We don't want a factory. We just want to make the best ices in Paris." More power to the House of Berthillon! "Everybody has to come collect his ices here. We do not deliver."

"Even to Madame Pompidou or the Rothschilds?" I asked.

"I don't care about the names of our customers. Everybody gets the same product." She shouted toward the kitchen in the rear, "Will there be rhubarb in the afternoon?" and a man's voice shouted back, "Yes!"

October 1973

THE PRESIDENT OF PASTRY

Joseph Wechsberg

The tale of Monsieur Gaston Albert Celestin Lenôtre, born in 1920 on a small farm in Normandy, is a fine rags-to-riches story. He began as a *petit pâtissier normand* in Pont-Audemer, near Deauville. Word soon got around that Lenôtre made wonderful *tartes,* brioches, *mille-feuilles,* petits fours, and *génoises.* Thus encouraged, Gaston and his wife, Colette, moved to Paris in 1959 and opened *une petite pâtisserie* at 44, rue d'Auteuil.

M. Lenôtre is no longer a *petit pâtissier.* Among his colleagues he is known as *"le Président des Pâtissiers-Traiteurs de Paris."* Among those Parisians who can afford Lenôtre, he is much admired as one of the finest *traiteurs* (caterers) in a city with a distinguished catering tradition. Today the firm Lenôtre calls itself *"Pâtissier, Glacier, Chocolatier, Traiteur."* Pâtisserie, M. Lenôtre's first love, still accounts for 40 percent of the firm's activities. The small pâtisserie has become a large enterprise with three hundred employees, several factories (called *laboratoires*) where the various delicacies are developed, tested, and prepared, and its own training school, the École Lenôtre. So great is the fame of Lenôtre that its founder has been accepted by a group of the younger great French chefs as the only *pâtissier-traiteur* member. Among the other eleven members of the group are the Haeberlins

(Illhaeusern), the Troisgros (Roanne), René Lasserre (Paris), Louis Outhier (La Napoule), and Paul Bocuse (Collonges-au-Mont-d'Or), the head of the group. All of them are aware that *la grande cuisine* must not stand still if it isn't to become stale. They revere their elders, but they agree that the chefs of today must go along with the new times. The once-small pastry shop on the rue d'Auteuil remains the germ cell, focus, and showplace of the firm. The cold pâtés, terrines, meats, and salads are exhibited in the middle of the vitrine. On the left is the pâtisserie, on the right are the chocolates, and in between are the ice creams and sherbets. The catering department offers such rare items as *gratin dauphinois* (scalloped potatoes) and *crêpes aux épinards* (spinach-filled crêpes), which can be bought and taken home and must only be warmed up. The *gratin dauphinois* is a tricky thing, but, if heated carefully, it may taste as though it were freshly prepared. All items, from the two hundred different *plats cuisinés* to the special ice-cream creations, are so prepared that they will withstand the journey from the factory to the six Lenôtre shops (five in the Paris region and one in Deauville) or to the customer's place—a house, an embassy, the private dining room of a large corporation.

The various departments produce 165 different kinds of pâtisserie, including 36 petits fours both *secs* and *glacés*; 31 different sherbets, parfaits, and ice creams, as well as 24 *entremets glacés*; 110 kinds of chocolate candies, *pâtes de fruits*, and caramels; and hundreds of *plats cuisinés*, pâtés, terrines, hams, and sausages, not to mention 42 condiments and sauces.

"In fact," says Alain Lenôtre, a son of the founder, "you can order almost anything, and it will be delivered to your house and will taste as though you'd made it yourself. It may even taste a little better because our first-rate chefs use only first-rate ingredients. We cannot afford anything that's second-class. Our stores offer a different plat du jour every day of the year. We are very strict; we must be. Practically everything not sold tonight will either be eaten by our employees— we have to feed three hundred people day after day—or be given to charitable institutions. But it will not be sold tomorrow. We have to make certain compromises because a few of our articles, ice creams and sherbets, for instance, are not eaten the same day. I was at Paul Bocuse yesterday. Had a wonderful lunch, finished with a wonderful ice cream. He uses only 125 grams of sugar per liter because his ice cream is eaten the same day. Ours must be kept a few days; we use 300 grams of sugar. Otherwise there is no difference between something made at home by a very good cook and something we make and deliver to you."

Alain Lenôtre is young, dynamic, and tough, not the sort of Frenchman some people would expect from novels and the Sunday papers. Lenôtre is no longer a firm of artisans making good pastry; it is a computerized, highly organized business—getting the best ingredients at the right moment, turning them into fine goods, and selling them in the best possible condition. Lenôtre *père* no longer takes part in the commercial affairs, leaving them to Alain.

"My father spends all his time at the laboratory, designing and testing new recipes," says Alain, "but his heart still belongs to pâtisserie." Which is clear to customers when they see the wonderful pastry made by Lenôtre's pâtissiers. Along with the pâtisserie, his ice creams and chocolates are imaginative, elegant, well prepared, and beautifully presented. By the time this is read, Lenôtre will have opened a store in Manhattan, selling pastry, ice creams, and chocolates. The catering will come later; no pâtés, no refined terrines yet.

"We're going to have problems," says Alain. "Butter, for instance. My father thinks that the best Normandy butter is the finest on earth. But we'll manage. Lenôtre is a family affair; there are ten of us in the firm. My wife is in charge of our store at Parly 2. Annie will be in New York. And there are Marcel and Patrick and Colette and Josette and . . ." Even Papa's grandmother is involved, in a manner of speaking. On the labels of Lenôtre's excellent confiture it says, *"Préparée selon l'ancienne recette de ma grand-mère Éléonore Lenôtre."*

January 1974

Paris's Haute Chocolaterie

Naomi Barry

In extremis, when nothing else is at hand, there is always the baking chocolate. Such is my credo, but I didn't expect to find fellow weaklings among the All Gauls: slim, sleek, deceptive types who look as if they were nourished on a string bean. Micheline Haardt, the neat-as-a-pin stylist, whispered that designer Sonia Rykiel is also an unbridled fanatic of chocolate.

Generally speaking, chocolate in the French capital is seductive, refined, recherché, noble, and expensive. And, as I came to discover, the best part of this town is at the rarefied top. *Haute couture. Haute chocolaterie.*

The Paris passion for *haute chocolaterie* is shameless in contrast to my wholesome background of divinity fudge and frosted cupcakes, where those who binged did so in private and were advised to keep it that way. Parisians, on the other hand, extol a bash of indulgence as a *péché mignon* (an adorable little sin). Just one more proof of Gallic greatness.

For the past few hundred years the population of Paris has been treating chocolate as a suave, voluptuous, and amusing commodity. Back in the eighteenth century a witty confectioner upped his business by numbering, literally, his chocolate truffles from one to ninety.

The rich bought big bagfuls for conducting family lotteries in their gilded salons. Win or lose, everybody received a consolation prize.

One of the most publicized meals of the 1970s was a lunch at the Élysée Palace prepared by three-star chef Paul Bocuse and a few of his "pan pals" for the then President Valéry Giscard d'Estaing. The opening bang was an extravagant black truffle soup, all its heady perfume held captive under a dome of puff pastry. Chosen as the climax for the sophisticated menu was a chocolate cake dubbed "Le Président." It too was a domed masterpiece, smothered under a froufrou of chocolate rufflettes. The cake—created by Maurice Bernachon, the famed Lyons *chocolatier,* and still a favorite in his repertory—resembles a saucy dancer dressed as a cancan incarnation of the Black Swan.

Bernachon, a specialist in the finesse that lifts frivolity to an art, occasionally decorates a cake with chocolate leaves. To obtain them he paints melted chocolate over a fresh leaf to capture the veined imprint. Once the chocolate hardens, the leaf is thrown away.

In Paris the contemporary taste is for a chocolate that is dark, unsweetened, and intense. Lovers of the Chocolate Kiss won't like it. They are not yet ready for the True Bite.

———

Christian Constant's small shop and tearoom, at 26, rue du Bac in the stylish Seventh Arrondissement, specializes in his own artisanal production. Constant is revered as the Chocolate Prince. He is affable and attractive, qualities that help quiet the tantrums of exigent clients on a day when supplies fall short of demand.

When professional cooks in Paris make pastries and candies, most of them buy blocks of chocolate from Valrhona, an exacting little factory in Tain-l'Hermitage in the Drôme *département* in southeastern France. Constant is such a fanatic that he has Valrhona send him the cocoa beans themselves. In the laboratory behind his shop he blends cocoas from Venezuela, Indonesia, and Trinidad to fabricate his own bars. Part of the result is sold to the public in hundred-gram weights.

Constant's goal is a chocolate stripped of sugar yet still palatable. He crashed through the sugar barrier with Bitter Plus, with only 20 percent sugar. A cult of devotees sprang up immediately. Constant ventured even further to achieve a "Pure Pâte Sans Sucre." For straight-out eating, this is beyond me, but I may come to it yet.

Recently, a doctor at the Hôpital Bichat, engaged in some research on chocolate, discovered that in its unadulterated state chocolate is capable of producing a gentle high. She announced her felicitous findings on a television program with Constant. The immediate reaction was a rash of customers at the rue du Bac shop, asking furtively from behind the back of one hand for some "Pâte Pure."

"To get the high," says Constant, laughing, "would require more chocolate than anybody could stomach."

Constant serves a *sorbet au chocolat amer* that is a marvel. He wanted no sugar but found that the "Pâte Pure" didn't work. In the end pure cocoa did. Into it he incorporates raisins that have been soaked in Scotch, the whiskey cutting any possible cloyingness from the chocolate's intensity. It is a darkly delicious sherbet with a texture as smooth and rich as ice cream.

Constant is full of praise for America's food and wine but feels the country has not yet grown up to chocolate: "America looks upon it as a bonbon. France has always regarded it as a jewel."

"Vive la différence," I sighed as I set off to further my investigations.

———

La Maison du Chocolat, 225, rue du Faubourg-Saint-Honoré, hit Paris in 1981, and it didn't take long to become an institution. Something like three weeks. Faces staring into the windows are studies in anticipation. The chocolates are made below the shop in what used to be a wine cellar. Owner Robert Linxe is less interested in chew than in flavor and melt. Marriages made in heaven are his forte: chocolate and coffee, chocolate and rum, chocolate and orange. An occasional flirtation with kirsch is permissible. For the more indissoluble union of chocolate with the well-defined personality of coffee, Linxe frequently has his coffee and cocoa beans ground together.

"Good chocolate won't make you sick," he said as he urged us to taste a Romeo, a Bohème, and a Rigoletto. "It won't even make you fat. Look at me, and I eat it all day long." True, he was as svelte and active as a live wire and as persuasive as a faith healer.

"Bitter chocolate is full of potassium and magnesium."

Convinced that it was so good for me, I could hardly refuse a Bacchus.

"Extraordinary subtlety, this," said Linxe. "It contains Smyrna raisins that have been macerated in rum and flambéed before going into the chocolate."

La Maison du Chocolat is located near the Salle Pleyel. An enormous amount of energy is expended in the making of good music, which makes it quite right that upper notes of the range, with names like Daniel Barenboim, Itzhak Perlman, and Barbara Hendricks, should get together as serious clients of La Maison's *chocolat amer.*

"I always know when Zubin Mehta is expected, because I get so many orders to be sent to his hotel. Mehta goes through a kilo of my chocolate in a day and a half," said Linxe proudly.

"Opéra," a flat cake, square or rectangular in shape, with alternate fillings of chocolate and coffee and a satin-smooth chocolate icing, seemed to be a popular number in quite a few restaurants and pastry shops. Some *pâtissiers* aver that it was a favorite at the court of Louis XV. Others assume it was invented to coincide with the opening of the present Paris Opéra in 1874.

Such confusion over the confection's origin is an indication of its settled position in society; it is a modern classic. In January 1986, Dalloyau—the celebrated *pâtisserie* at 99, rue du Faubourg-Saint-Honoré—held a huge fête for the thirtieth birthday of its version of this famous creation. A neat twist: a party given for a cake instead of a cake produced for a party. The Dalloyau rendition of "Opéra" is flecked with twenty-four-karat gold supplied by one of the last two artisans in France still working the precious gold leaf. It can be bought in almost any size, from petits fours to a reception piece good for forty generous portions.

"We do not give out the recipe. We are often imitated, but the copies are never quite the same," says Madame Andrée Galavin, Présidente Directrice Générale of this temple to gastronomic temptations that has been flourishing at the same address for eighty-five years and even offers table service for those in chocolate crisis with time to linger. "This is *pâtisserie* as I respect it. Rich and with butter. I am antimousse," she adds, dismissing the current vogue for cakes that pretend to be lighter than air because of mousse fillings.

———

The original Dalloyau opened his catering establishment in 1802, about the time Paris began to recover its brilliance after the Revolution. Foreign visitors and émigrés were returning. Parties were given again. Monsieur and Madame Bonaparte, the First Consul and his wife, were holding court at the Palais des Tuileries. The year saw new lighting in the Place Vendôme; the Temple of Mars was transformed into Saint-Louis des Invalides; and the lycée system of secondary education was established.

And Monsieur Grimod de la Reynière, the first gastronomic chronicler, with his *Almanach des Gourmands,* praised the confectioner Berthellemot for using as mottoes on his bonbons citations from the works of the most celebrated poets of the "New France."

Questing chocolate in Paris can become a fun foray into social history. The Spanish princess Anne d'Autriche, who married Louis XIII, made chocolate fashionable in France. The Spanish in turn had first encountered the cocoa bean when the conquistadores brought it back from the New World in their curio bags. According to Alexandre Dumas, who recounted the hegira with his usual gusto, Spain—particularly the women and the monks—went mad for the new cocoa drink. The señoras even carried it to church with them, mollifying their reproachful confessors with a proffered cup from time to time. Both sides were absolved from sin by the Reverend Father Escobar, who with metaphysical subtlety formally declared that drinking chocolate prepared with water was not to be considered as breaking a fast.

The monks of Spain and France were a sharing community. During the fifteenth century they busily exchanged the sage theories that helped Columbus make his first trip west. Later the Spanish monks sent samples of chocolate as presents to their brethren north of the border.

If the Spanish made chocolate known, the French made it luxurious, packaging it in gift containers of hand-painted silk and delicate porcelain. La Maison du Chocolat's cardboard boxes are as chic as those of Hermès. With good reason, as both come from the same supplier.

One of the first references to chocolate in French literature was made by Madame de Sévigné, whose name now graces fine chocolate shops at 21, place de la Madeleine and 1, place Victor Hugo. In February 1671 she recommended it to her daughter, Françoise, as a cure for insomnia. The ever-anxious-to-be-modish woman of letters probably overdid the chocolate, however, because she soon complained that the stuff caused dizziness, palpitations, and a burning sensation. Still, she apparently couldn't keep away from it for long, because in October of the same year she wrote Françoise that she'd tried some as a digestive and "it acted as it was supposed to."

Brillat-Savarin (1755–1826), the erudite lawyer-gastronome from Belley, took up the torch from Madame de Sévigné and touted chocolate as a stimulant and restorative for night workers, intellectuals suffering from mental blocks, and any other soul in torment. His personal recipe for combating old-age lassitude was a cup of strong chocolate well dosed with ambergris (a waxy substance from the sperm whale) and prepared according to the precepts of Madame d'Arestrel, Mother Superior of Belley's Convent of the Visitation. A good chocolate drink should, she counseled, be made the day before in an earthenware coffeepot. "The overnight rest provides a velvety concentration that makes it all the better. The Good Lord can't be offended by this little supplement, for He Himself is 'all excellence.'"

No doubt it was in deference to the good gourmand sisters of France, led by the likes of Madame d'Arestrel, that the *pâtissiers* of Paris created an éclair in the form of a brioche and baptized it "Une Religieuse."

———

Early in the nineteenth century a clever Parisian pharmacist, Sulpice Debauve, allied himself with a confectioner named Gallais to produce a line of "agreeable medicaments." Chocolate with an additive of iron salts became the recommended tonic for those whose pallor indicated circulation problems. "Chocolat des Dames," bonbons injected with orange-blossom water, promised relief from migraines and shocks to the morale. Chocolate incorporating almond milk was prescribed for sore throats, gastritis, and indispositions resulting from overheated temperaments.

———

The following recipes use fine-quality unsweetened, bittersweet, and white chocolate, which are available in domestic and imported brands. (Bittersweet chocolate has a more pronounced chocolate flavor than chocolate labeled semisweet because there is less sugar added; unsweetened has no sugar whatsoever.)

Pots Noirs Sonia Rykiel Hôtel de Crillon
(*Chocolate Custards*)

2 cups milk
3½ oz fine-quality bittersweet chocolate, chopped fine
1 oz fine-quality unsweetened chocolate, chopped fine
5 large egg yolks
½ cup plus 2 tablespoons sugar
fine-quality bittersweet and white chocolate at room temperature
     (about 72°F), shaved with a vegetable peeler into curls and
     chilled, covered loosely, for garnish

In a heavy saucepan combine the milk, the chopped bittersweet chocolate, and the unsweetened chocolate and heat the mixture over moderately high heat, whisking occasionally, until the chocolate is melted and the mixture just comes to a boil. In a large bowl whisk together the egg yolks and the sugar until the mixture is combined well, add the chocolate mixture in a slow stream, whisking, and strain the mixture through a very fine sieve into a heatproof bowl or measuring cup. Divide the mixture among six ½-cup ramekins and cover each ramekin with foil. Put the ramekins in a baking pan, add enough hot water to the pan to reach halfway up the sides of the ramekins, and bake the custards in the middle of a preheated 400°F oven for 25 minutes. Transfer the ramekins to a rack, let the custards cool, and chill them, covered, for at least 4 hours or overnight. Top the custards with the chocolate curls. Serves 6.

Le Jour et la Nuit Hôtel de Crillon
(*White and Dark Chocolate Mousse Cake*)

9 large egg yolks
1 cup sugar
6 tablespoons cornstarch
3 cups milk
1 tablespoon vanilla
14 oz fine-quality bittersweet chocolate, chopped
4 cups well-chilled heavy cream

14 oz fine-quality white chocolate, chopped

For garnish
6 oz fine-quality white chocolate at room temperature
   (about 72°F)
4 oz fine-quality bittersweet chocolate at room temperature
   (about 72°F)

In a large bowl whisk together the egg yolks and the sugar until the mixture is combined well, add the cornstarch, sifted, and whisk the mixture until it is just combined. Whisk in the milk, scalded, in a slow stream, transfer the mixture to a heavy saucepan, and bring it to a boil, whisking constantly. Boil the pastry cream, whisking, for 1 to 2 minutes, or until it is very thick and smooth; strain it through a fine sieve into a heatproof bowl and stir in the vanilla. Lay a piece of plastic wrap on the pastry cream and chill the pastry cream for 1 to 2 hours, or until it is cooled completely.

In the top of a double boiler or a metal bowl set over barely simmering water, melt the bittersweet chocolate, stirring occasionally, and let it cool until it is lukewarm. Transfer half the pastry cream to a large bowl, whisk in the chocolate, and whisk the mixture until it is combined well. In a chilled bowl with an electric mixer beat 2 cups of the heavy cream until it holds soft peaks, stir one fourth of it into the chocolate mixture, and fold in the remaining whipped cream gently but thoroughly. Pour the dark chocolate mousse into a lightly oiled 10-inch springform pan, at least 2½ inches deep, spread it evenly, and chill it while making the white chocolate mousse.

In the top of a double boiler or a metal bowl set over barely simmering water, melt the white chocolate, stirring occasionally, let it cool for 2 to 3 minutes, or until it is lukewarm, and whisk it into the remaining pastry cream until the mixture is combined well. In a chilled bowl with an electric mixer beat the remaining 2 cups heavy cream until it holds soft peaks, stir one fourth of it into the white chocolate mixture, and fold in the remaining whipped cream gently but thoroughly. Pour the white chocolate mousse over the chilled dark chocolate mousse, spread it evenly, and chill the cake, covered loosely with parchment or wax paper, overnight.

Prepare the garnish: Grate fine 2 ounces of the white chocolate and reserve it. Working over a foil-lined baking sheet or tray, shave curls from the remaining 4 ounces white chocolate and from the bittersweet chocolate with a vegetable peeler, keeping the white and dark curls separate, and chill them, covered loosely, for at least 1 hour or overnight.

Run a thin knife around the edge of the cake, remove the side of the pan, and smooth the side of the cake with a spatula. Put the cake on a rack set in a shallow baking pan, press the grated white chocolate onto the side, gathering the excess in the pan and reapplying it until the side is coated evenly, and transfer the cake to a platter. Mound the white chocolate curls carefully on half the cake and the dark chocolate curls on the other half and chill the cake, if desired, for up to 4 hours. Serves 14 to 16.

BOIS MORTS AU CHOCOLAT THE RITZ

(*Chocolate Cake Layered with Chocolate Mousse*)

For the cake
 3 tablespoons unsalted butter, softened
 ⅔ cup sugar
 4 large eggs at room temperature
 1 cup all-purpose flour
 1 teaspoon double-acting baking powder

For the syrup
 ⅓ cup sugar
 ¼ cup *crème de cacao*

For the mousse
 ¾ lb fine-quality bittersweet chocolate, chopped
 2 cups well-chilled heavy cream
 3 large egg yolks
 3 oz fine-quality bittersweet chocolate at room temperature
    (about 72°F), shaved with a vegetable peeler into curls and
    chilled, covered loosely, for garnish
 1 tablespoon unsweetened cocoa powder for dusting the cake

Make the cake: In the bowl of an electric mixer cream the butter with the sugar until the mixture is light and fluffy and add the eggs, 1 at a time, beating well after each addition. Into the bowl sift the flour with the baking powder and stir the mixture until it is just combined. Pour the batter into a buttered and floured 8½-inch springform pan and bake the cake in the middle of a preheated 350°F oven for 30 to 35 minutes, or until the top is golden and a tester comes out clean. Let the cake cool in the pan on a rack for 10 minutes and remove the side of the pan. Invert the cake onto the rack, remove the bottom of the pan, and let the cake cool completely.

Make the syrup: In a small saucepan combine ½ cup water and the sugar, bring the mixture to a boil, stirring, and simmer the syrup for 5 minutes. Let the syrup cool and stir in the *crème de cacao.* Halve the cake horizontally with a serrated knife, arrange the 2 layers cut side up on racks set in a jelly-roll pan, and brush them with the syrup.

Make the mousse: In the top of a double boiler set over simmering water melt the chocolate, stirring occasionally. In a chilled large bowl with an electric mixer beat the cream until it just holds stiff peaks. Whisk the egg yolks all at once into the warm chocolate, whisk in half the whipped cream, and fold the mixture into the remaining whipped cream gently but thoroughly.

Put 1 of the cake layers cut side up on a plate, spread it with half the mousse, and top it with the other cake layer. Spread the side of the cake with the remaining mousse and top the cake with the chocolate curls. Chill the cake for 4 hours and sift the cocoa powder over it. Serves 8 to 10.

ENTREMET VENDÔME HÔTEL MEURICE
(*Frozen Chocolate Mousse Cake*)

1 lb 10 oz fine-quality bittersweet chocolate, chopped
4 cups well-chilled heavy cream
14 large egg whites at room temperature
¾ cup sugar
⅓ cup Grand Marnier

For the ganache
¼ cup heavy cream
3 oz fine-quality bittersweet chocolate, chopped
1 tablespoon unsweetened cocoa powder for dusting the cake

In the top of a double boiler or a metal bowl set over barely simmering water melt the chocolate, stirring occasionally, and let it cool. In a chilled large bowl beat the cream until it holds soft peaks. In the large bowl of an electric mixer beat the egg whites until they are frothy, add the sugar, a little at a time, beating constantly, and beat the whites until they just hold stiff peaks. Beat in the chocolate, beating until the mixture is combined well, stir in the Grand Marnier, and fold in the whipped cream. Spoon the mixture into an 11-inch springform pan, at least 2½ inches deep, smoothing the top, and freeze it, covered with plastic wrap, for 4 hours.

Make the ganache: In a small saucepan bring the cream to a boil and remove the pan from the heat. Stir in the chocolate and stir the mixture until the chocolate is melted and the mixture is smooth.

Remove the side of the pan from the cake and set the cake on a platter. Spread the ganache quickly over the cake and freeze it, covered, for at least 1 hour and up to 24. Sift the cocoa powder over the cake just before serving. Serves about 20.

MOUSSE AU CHOCOLAT EN TASSE DE THÉ LE PETIT BEDON
(*Chocolate Mousse in a Teacup*)

½ lb fine-quality bittersweet chocolate, chopped
1 cup milk
2 tablespoons unsalted butter, cut into bits
⅔ cup confectioners' sugar
2⅓ cups well-chilled heavy cream

For garnish
2 cups well-chilled heavy cream
   fine-quality bittersweet chocolate, grated coarse and chilled,
      covered loosely
   sliced almonds, pistachios, and lightly toasted hazelnuts
   julienne strips of candied orange rind*
   candied violets*

*available at specialty foods shops

In a saucepan combine the chocolate and the milk and heat the mixture over moderately low heat, stirring occasionally, until the chocolate is melted and the mixture is smooth. Whisk in the butter until it is melted and whisk in the confectioners' sugar, sifted, and ⅓ cup of the cream. Let the mixture cool and chill it, covered, for 1 hour. In a chilled large bowl beat the remaining 2 cups cream until it just holds stiff peaks; whisk half the whipped cream into the chocolate mixture and fold the mixture into the remaining whipped cream. Divide the mousse among ten 1-cup teacups and chill it, covered, for 1 hour.

Prepare the garnish: In a chilled bowl beat the cream until it holds stiff peaks, transfer the whipped cream to a pastry bag fitted with a large star tip, and pipe a tall swirl of it on top of each mousse. Sprinkle the cream with the grated chocolate, the nuts, the candied rind, and the candied violets. Serves 10.

FONDANT AU CHOCOLAT CHIBERTA
(*Chocolate Mousse on Sweet Pastry Rounds with Coffee Custard Sauce*)

For the custard sauce
- 3 cups milk
- ½ cup dark-roast ground coffee beans
- 9 large egg yolks
- ¾ cup sugar

For the pastry rounds
- 1¾ cups all-purpose flour
- ½ cup confectioners' sugar
- 2 tablespoons plus 1 teaspoon chopped blanched almonds, ground fine in an electric spice or coffee grinder
- 8½ tablespoons cold unsalted butter, cut into bits
- 1 large egg
- ½ teaspoon vanilla

For the chocolate mousse
- ⅓ cup dried currants
- ¼ cup dark rum
- 6 oz fine-quality bittersweet chocolate, chopped
- 1 cup strong brewed coffee
- 7 tablespoons unsalted butter, kneaded with the heel of the hand until softened slightly
- 3 large egg yolks
- 3 tablespoons slivered blanched almonds
- ⅓ cup plus ½ teaspoon sugar
- 2 large egg whites at room temperature
- ⅔ cup well-chilled heavy cream
  chocolate coffee beans for garnish (available at specialty foods shops)

Make the custard sauce: In a heavy saucepan scald the milk, remove the pan from the heat, and stir in the coffee. Let the mixture stand, covered, for 5 minutes, then strain it through a paper coffee filter into a large measuring cup. In a bowl whisk together the egg yolks and the sugar until the mixture is combined well, add the coffee-flavored milk in a slow stream, stirring, and transfer the mixture to the cleaned pan. Cook the mixture over moderately low heat, stirring constantly with a wooden spoon, until it is thick enough to coat the back of the spoon and a candy thermometer registers 175°F (do not let the mixture boil). Strain the custard through a fine sieve into a bowl set in a larger bowl of ice and cold water and let it cool, stirring. Lay a piece of plastic wrap on the custard and chill the sauce. *The custard sauce may be made 1 day in advance and kept covered and chilled.*

Make the pastry rounds: In a bowl whisk together the flour, the confectioners' sugar, and the almonds until the mixture is combined well, blend in the butter until the mixture resembles coarse meal, and make a well in the center of the mixture. In a small bowl whisk together the egg and the vanilla, add the egg mixture to the flour mixture, and toss the mixture until it is combined well. Knead the dough lightly with the heel of the hand against a smooth surface for a few seconds to distribute the butter evenly; form it into a ball and flatten it slightly. Chill the dough, wrapped in plastic wrap, for 1 hour. Roll out the dough ¼ inch thick on a lightly floured surface, cut out 10 rounds with a floured 3-inch cutter, and transfer the rounds to a baking sheet. Prick the rounds lightly and bake them in the middle of a preheated 375°F oven for 10 to 12 minutes, or until the edges are golden. Transfer the pastry rounds to a rack and let them cool. *The pastry rounds may be made 2 days in advance and kept in an airtight container.*

Make the chocolate mousse: In a small saucepan combine the currants and the rum and bring the rum to a boil. Remove the pan from the heat and let the mixture stand for 1 hour. In a heavy saucepan melt the chocolate in the coffee over moderately low heat, stirring, until the mixture is smooth; remove the pan from the heat. Add the butter in pieces, stirring the mixture until the butter is incorporated and the mixture is smooth. In a bowl whisk the egg yolks, add the chocolate mixture in a slow stream, whisking, and stir in the almonds and the currants, drained. Transfer the chocolate mixture to a bowl, on it lay a piece of plastic wrap, and let the mixture cool to room temperature. In a small heavy saucepan combine 1½ tablespoons water and ⅓ cup of the sugar, bring the mixture to a boil over moderately high heat, stirring and washing down any sugar crystals clinging to the sides with a brush dipped in cold water until the sugar is dissolved, and boil the syrup until a candy thermometer registers 248°F (tilt the pan so that the thermometer can register). While the syrup is cooking, in a bowl with an electric mixer beat the egg whites until they are frothy, add the remaining ½ teaspoon sugar, and beat the whites until they just hold stiff peaks. Add the hot syrup in a slow steady stream, beating constantly, and beat the meringue until it is cooled to room temperature. In a bowl with the electric mixer beat the cream until it holds soft peaks. Into the whipped cream fold the meringue gently, stir one fourth of the meringue mixture into the cooled chocolate mixture, and fold in the remaining meringue mixture gently but thoroughly.

Put the pastry rounds, trimmed if necessary, into ten ½-cup ramekins, measuring 3 inches across the bottom. Divide the chocolate mousse among the ramekins, smoothing it, lay pieces of plastic wrap on the mousse, and chill the desserts for at least 3 hours and up to 8 hours. Run a thin knife around the edge of 1 of the desserts and unmold the dessert onto a metal spatula. Transfer the dessert pastry side down to a plate and discard the plastic wrap. Unmold the remaining desserts in the same manner, top them with the chocolate coffee beans, and around them pour the custard sauce. Serves 10.

ENTREMET CHOCOLAT CARAMEL AVEC SAUCE VANILLE GÉRARD BESSON
(*Chocolate and Caramel Mousse Cake with Vanilla Custard Sauce*)

For the chocolate cake
   1 large whole egg at room temperature
   4 large egg yolks at room temperature
   4 oz almond paste, crumbled (about ⅓ cup, available at specialty foods shops and some supermarkets)
   ⅓ cup plus 1 tablespoon confectioners' sugar
   2 tablespoons plus 2 teaspoons all-purpose flour
   ⅓ cup unsweetened cocoa powder
   1 teaspoon granulated sugar
   2 tablespoons plus 2 teaspoons unsalted butter, melted and cooled

For the chocolate mousse
   3 oz fine-quality bittersweet chocolate, chopped
   2 oz fine-quality unsweetened chocolate, chopped
   ½ cup sugar
   2 large eggs at room temperature
   1 cup well-chilled heavy cream

For the caramel mousse
> 4 large egg yolks
> ½ cup plus 2 tablespoons sugar
> 1 cup milk
> 1 envelope of unflavored gelatin
> 1 cup well-chilled heavy cream

For the custard sauce
> 12 large egg yolks
> 1 cup plus 2 tablespoons sugar
> 4 cups milk
> 5 vanilla beans, halved lengthwise
>   confectioners' sugar for dusting the cake

Make the chocolate cake: In a bowl with an electric mixer beat the whole egg, the egg yolks, the almond paste, and the confectioners' sugar, sifted, until the mixture is thick and pale, sift together the flour, the cocoa powder, and the granulated sugar into the egg mixture, and stir the mixture until it is just combined. Stir in the butter until the mixture is just combined and turn the batter into a buttered 8-inch springform pan, 2¾ inches deep and the bottom lined with a buttered round of wax paper, and bake the cake in the middle of a preheated 400°F oven for 20 to 25 minutes, or until a tester comes out clean. Let the cake cool in the pan on a rack. Run a thin knife around the edge of the cake, remove the side of the pan, and invert the cake onto a flat surface. Remove the bottom of the pan, peeling away the wax paper carefully. *The cake may be made 2 days in advance and kept covered tightly with plastic wrap.* Cut the cake into 2 layers with a serrated knife, making the bottom layer twice as thick as the top, and reserve the layers, wrapped tightly in plastic wrap.

Make the chocolate mousse: In the top of a double boiler or a metal bowl set over barely simmering water melt the bittersweet chocolate and the unsweetened chocolate, stirring, and let the mixture cool completely. In a small heavy saucepan combine 2 tablespoons water and the sugar, bring the mixture to a boil over moderately high heat, stirring and washing down any sugar crystals clinging to the sides with a brush dipped in cold water until the sugar is dissolved, and boil the syrup until a candy thermometer registers 238°F (tilt the pan so that the thermometer can register). While the syrup is cooking, in a bowl with the electric mixer beat the eggs until they are very thick and pale. Add the hot syrup in a slow steady stream, beating constantly, and beat the mixture until it is cooled to room temperature. Beat in the melted chocolate. In another bowl with the electric mixer beat the cream until it holds soft peaks, stir one fourth of the whipped cream into the chocolate mixture, and fold in the remaining cream gently but thoroughly.

Into the bottom of the cleaned 8-inch springform pan fit the thicker layer of reserved chocolate cake, add the chocolate mousse, smoothing it with a spatula, and top it with the remaining layer of reserved cake. Chill the chocolate mousse cake, covered, while making the caramel mousse.

Make the caramel mousse: In a bowl whisk the egg yolks with 2 tablespoons of the sugar, add the milk, scalded, in a slow stream, stirring, and transfer the mixture to a heavy saucepan. In a small bowl sprinkle the gelatin over 3 tablespoons cold water and let it soften for 10 minutes. While the gelatin is softening cook the milk mixture over moderately low heat, stirring with a wooden spoon, until it is thick enough to coat the back of the spoon and a candy thermometer registers 175°F (do not let the mixture boil). Add the softened gelatin, stir the mixture until the gelatin is dissolved, and reserve the custard in the pan, covered. In a small heavy skillet cook the remaining ½ cup sugar over moderately high heat, stirring constantly with a fork, until it is melted completely and a golden caramel and add the caramel carefully in a stream to the reserved custard (the caramel will bubble up and seize). Heat the mixture over moderately low heat, stirring constantly, until the caramel is dissolved, strain the caramel custard through a fine sieve into a bowl, and on it lay a piece of plastic wrap. In a bowl with the electric mixer beat the cream until it holds soft peaks. Set the caramel custard into a larger bowl of ice and cold water and stir it until it is the consistency of raw egg whites. Stir one fourth of the whipped cream into the caramel custard and fold in the remaining whipped cream gently but thoroughly.

Spread the caramel mousse over the chilled chocolate mousse cake, smoothing it with the spatula, and chill the cake, covered with plastic wrap, for 24 hours.

Make the custard sauce: In a large bowl whisk together the egg yolks and the sugar until the mixture is combined well, add the milk, scalded with the vanilla beans, in a slow stream, stirring, and transfer the mixture to a large heavy saucepan. Cook the mixture over moderately low heat, stirring constantly with the wooden spoon, until it is thick enough to coat the back of the spoon and a candy thermometer registers 175°F (do not let the mixture boil). Strain the custard through a fine sieve into a bowl set in a larger bowl of ice and cold water, let it cool, stirring, and chill it, covered, for at least 1 hour, or until it is cold. *The custard sauce may be made 1 day in advance and kept covered and chilled.*

Remove the side of the springform pan, transfer the cake (still set on the bottom of the pan) to a platter, and over it sift the confectioners' sugar. Serve the cake with the custard sauce. Serves 12.

SOUFFLÉS ÉTONNANTS À LA MENTHE ET AU
CHOCOLAT AMER LE DIVELLEC
(*Mint Soufflés with Bitter Chocolate Mousse*)

For the pastry cream
    1   cup milk
    ½   cup firmly packed fresh mint leaves, chopped coarse
    2   large egg yolks
    ½   cup sugar
    2½ tablespoons all-purpose flour

For the chocolate mousse
    ½   cup heavy cream
    3   oz fine-quality bittersweet chocolate, chopped fine
    ¼   cup sugar
    3   large egg whites at room temperature
    unsweetened cocoa powder for dusting the soufflés
    2   mint sprigs for garnish

Make the pastry cream: In a small heavy saucepan scald the milk, remove the pan from the heat, and stir in the mint. Let the mixture stand, covered, for 5 minutes and strain it through a fine sieve into a measuring cup, pressing hard on the mint. In a bowl whisk the egg yolks with the sugar until the mixture is combined well, sift the flour over the yolk mixture, and whisk the mixture until it is combined well. Add the milk in a slow stream, whisking; in a heavy saucepan bring the mixture to a boil over moderate heat, whisking, and boil it, whisking, for 1 minute. Transfer the pastry cream to a bowl, on it lay a piece of plastic wrap, and let the pastry cream cool. *The pastry cream may be made 1 day in advance and kept covered and chilled.*

Make the chocolate mousse: In a small heavy saucepan bring ¼ cup of the cream to a boil and remove the pan from the heat. Stir in the chocolate until it is melted and the mixture is smooth, lay a piece of plastic wrap on the mixture, and let the mixture cool to room temperature. In a bowl with an electric mixer beat the remaining ¼ cup cream until it holds soft peaks, stir one fourth of the whipped cream into the cooled chocolate mixture, and fold in the remaining whipped cream gently but thoroughly. *The mousse may be made 8 hours in advance and kept covered and chilled.*

If the pastry cream has been chilled, bring it to room temperature. Sprinkle 1 teaspoon of the sugar into each of 2 lightly buttered 6-inch ovenproof bowls, 1½ inches deep, and divide the chocolate mousse between the bowls, spreading it evenly. In a bowl with an electric mixer beat the egg whites until they are frothy, add the remaining 3 tablespoons plus 1 teaspoon sugar gradually, and beat the whites until they just hold stiff peaks. Stir one fourth of the whites into the pastry cream and fold in the remaining whites gently but thoroughly. Working quickly, divide the mixture between the bowls, spreading it to cover and seal the chocolate mousse completely, forming a dome shape, and bake the soufflés in the middle of a preheated 400°F oven for 13 to 15 minutes, or until they are golden. Sift the cocoa powder over the soufflés, top the soufflés with the mint sprigs, and serve them immediately. Serves 2.

March 1987

LA VIE EN ROSE

Frank J. Prial

A quarter of a century ago, when I was living on the Île Saint-Louis, I would stop by a wine shop just over the Pont Marie on the rue Saint-Paul. It was a wine shop from the past. It had no name other than a sign over the door that read VINS DU SUD-OUEST. Inside, a counter reached from one wall to the other. Behind it were four metered pumps, much like the ones at an old country gas station. Three of the pumps, for the reds, had a number: 11 on the first, 11.5 on the second, and 12 on the third, representing the alcohol content. Nowhere was there any mention of vintage, provenance, or grape variety.

The customers, mostly women, didn't seem to mind. They arrived with their own bottles or plastic jugs and ordered, say, three liters of 11, or perhaps two of 11.5. It was Zola's Paris, intact. The wines, wherever they came from, were not much, not even the most expensive, the *douze*, with its extra kick and high price of fifty cents a liter. I'd buy a little of the white wine, which had a pump of its own, and lug it home in my plastic jug to make *moules marinière*. It was exciting to discover this backstreet gem because, even in the 1970s, so much of the old wine scene in Paris had disappeared. Gone, for example, were Nicolas's little three-wheeled motorcycle trucks that, until the 1960s, scurried around the city delivering wine the way we used to deliver milk in this country. Housewives or cooks would leave a wire bottleholder full of empties at the back door or in the courtyard, and the Nicolas man would replace them with twelve full bottles. Just about every week, usually.

Gone, too, were the old wine sheds at Bercy and Jussieu, at the eastern end of the city, where, long before the railroads arrived in the nineteenth century, wine came up the river by barge to be blended and bottled. By the time I got to Paris, most of the wine sheds at Jussieu had been replaced by a grim-looking extension of the University of Paris. Bercy also stood empty, its wine sheds and cellars crumbling, until the early 1990s, when the city turned the place into a park. There's a small vineyard there now, probably to remind Parisians where their wine comes from. At Moissonnier, a bistro across the street from Jussieu, they still serve wine in a forty-centiliter *pot,* just as they did a hundred years ago, when the wine merchants dined there with their customers. Nicolas stores were everywhere in Paris in the 1970s, as they are today, but a lot of people—and restaurants—preferred to buy directly from the producers.

So did we. One day, in my office, someone produced a catalogue from a well-known Beaujolais shipper. Half a dozen of us chipped in and sent off for thirty or so cases. Two days later, I came home from work to find the wine sitting on a pallet in my courtyard, in the rain. Others would send off for a barrel of Beaujolais and then bottle it themselves to save money.

Champagne producers were just as eager to ship to us as the Beaujolais makers. But we preferred the ninety-mile Champagne run. It required a car, a convivial group of three or four, some orders from a few friends, and a day off. We would avoid the big houses like Mumm and Mercier. Small producers like Bonnaire, in Cramant, and Ricciuti-Révolte, in Avenay, were always happy to offer a "tasting" to visitors intent on loading up a car. A bottle or two would appear on the kitchen table and be quickly finished off and, of course, pronounced superb.

Parisians, like most of the French twenty-five years ago, took wine for granted. It commanded little more attention than the baguettes they ate at every meal. Expensive wines—Bordeaux or Burgundy—

were for special occasions and rare dinners out. No one read wine books; no one took wine courses. Instead, they depended on wine merchants. There were good ones around, people who knew their wine, unlike the current breed, who meekly run critics' ratings in their advertising. Two favorites were Lucien Legrande, near the Place des Victoires, and Jean-Baptiste Besse, in the Latin Quarter. Both were *épiciers* who sold coffee, tea, exotic foodstuffs, and beer and liquor as well as wine. But both had an encyclopedic knowledge of wine.

———

Lucien Legrande was proud to be the third generation in his family to sell wine. Even as a youth he often spent his weekly day off visiting growers in the Loire, sometimes driving all night to get there. His cellars in the rue de la Banque actually belonged to an old abbey. He not only stored his wine there but bottled much of it himself. Legrande would sell you a famous Bordeaux if you insisted, but he often suggested something at a third the price, saying, "Try this. It's just as good."

Jean-Baptiste Besse was an ancient but rugged little peasant from the hardscrabble Corrèze region of France. Like Legrande, he had a passion for wine. He bought his wines in barrels, bottling half and selling the rest directly from the spigot. His seventeenth-century cellars on the rue de la Montagne Sainte-Geneviève were chaotic—chock-full of bottles, many piled precariously on the floor, ready to fall upon and crush anyone foolish enough to venture among them. Besse shrugged off complaints. "I have a photographic memory," he'd say. "I know where every bottle is."

Restaurateurs, too, had a different relationship with wine. How vividly I remember the Sancerre at Allard. The bistro's list of Burgundies was impressive, but the signature wine was the Sancerre, cold, sharp, and green-gold in color. Who supplied it, I never knew; there were no labels, no promotional materials, just an endless succession of icy green bottles.

Allard was a friendly place. Once I watched a young American couple order half a bottle of Sancerre and then protest when the waiter brought a full bottle. "We only serve full bottles," the waiter said. "Just drink half." At the end of the meal, the couple admitted sheepishly that they'd finished the entire bottle. "Good for you," said the waiter. "A full bottle for half price." Allard is still there on the rue Saint-André-des-Arts, but after Madame Allard sold the place, all the old waiters, who knew everybody in Paris by name or face, quit.

Those were thrilling times for wine lovers in Paris. On the rue du Marché-Saint-Honoré, old Léon Gouin was serving such good Beaujolais at Le Rubis that the lunchtime throngs—bankers, firemen, saleswomen—clustered around upturned barrels on the sidewalk outside the café to enjoy a plate of charcuterie and a *ballon* of Juliénas. Gouin would survey the crowd. An imperceptible nod to the bartender meant that a regular was up for a refill on the house.

I remember in 1976 when a young Englishman named Steven Spurrier startled the wine world with his famous Académie du Vin tasting, at which a group of prominent French wine figures judged several California wines to be superior to some of the most famous Bordeaux names. The Académie du Vin, along with Spurrier's wine shop, Les Caves de la Madeleine, and his delightful restaurant, Le Moulin du Village, was in a little street called the Cité Berryer, just off the Place de la Madeleine. With its outdoor market and absence of motor traffic, the Cité Berryer was an astonishing bit of old Paris that managed to survive almost into the twenty-first century. Almost, but not quite. Developers found it, stole its soul, and rendered it banal at great expense.

To savor each day and still revel in the past is a rare talent. Except in Paris. Sitting at one of my favorite cafés, like Le Viaduc, on the avenue Daumesnil, or even back at Le Rubis—still there, even if it's not the same without Gouin—I can pull it off with ease. Every time.

December 2002

THE BISTRO SCENE

HOME AWAY FROM HOME

Joseph Wechsberg

Having settled on a hotel, travelers must turn their attention to food—especially in Paris. One solution is the bistro, but what exactly *is* a bistro? The trouble begins with the definition. Even the spelling is controversial. Is the word written with or without a final *t*? It depends on how one feels about the word's history. According to legend, its origin goes back to the Cossacks who came to Paris with their then-allies, the British and the Prussians, in 1815. They camped in the Place de la Concorde and under the trees of the Tuileries and the Champs-Élysées. They were hungry and thirsty and ran into the nearby cafés and restaurants asking for something to eat and drink, mainly to drink, and shouting *"Bistro, bistro!"* (quick, quick). No one knows whether the story is true, and some eminent French-language experts don't like the foreign sound of a cherished French institution. They have come up with several alternative etymologies. One holds that the name goes back to the French word *bistre*, the brown shade reflected by the bottles behind the bar on the traditional zinc counter. Personally, I prefer the French spelling to the Russian one, though many dictionaries do not bear me out.

Actually, the Frenchman who speaks of his bistro doesn't think of a restaurant but of the small, often shabby café that is his home-away-from-home. Foreigners rarely understand the importance of the bistro-café in the life of the average French citizen. At the bistro, the small place at the corner or down the street, he spends much of his leisure. There he sees his *copains*—they are pals, not friends—whereas he sees his relatives at home. He invites you, the foreigner, to his bistro but rarely to his house. When he is late for dinner—the average Frenchman eats at home—*Maman* sends her son to the bistro to fetch *Papa*.

To Frenchmen the bistro is more than a little café. It is the hub of democracy, the last remnant of what older people nostalgically call *la vieille France*, the final refuge of *le vrai individualiste*. The bistro resembles another civilized institution, the English pub. In such places a man may speak his mind and be listened to. After he has made his point and drinks up, the other fellow speaks. In pubs and bistros there is still genuine conversation. It can't be interrupted, as happens all the time in New York bars.

Certain topics are always discussed at bistros: sports, especially the preceding week's soccer games and, in summertime, the Tour de France, long before it starts and long after it is finished; politics, either on the national or local level; and the cost of living, which goes up all the time. The bistro remains the ideal place to gripe. There are experts who remember vintage years for gripes, just as others remember vintages of wines.

The neighborhood bistro is petit bourgeois, unsophisticated, and very French. Often it consists of two rooms, the front room with the bar, where the counter is still called *le zinc* even when it is made of plastic. There may be a few marble tables and simple chairs and there may be a sidewalk extension, but it isn't as important as in the big Champs-Élysées cafés with their large sidewalk installations, where people sit to watch the world go by. In a genuine bistro no one watches; everybody talks. There may be a small back room, with banquettes and brass rails on top of wooden partitions, but it is rarely used. The bistro is not a place where one sits alone in the back. People stand together at the bar. The smell of the bistro is as dearly familiar as that of the Paris *métro*. At the bistro the smell is a mixture of beer, white wine, Pernod, and the smoke of Gauloises. The clients like it better than their wives' perfumes.

I explain all this at great length because we foreigners have little hope of being admitted to the inner circle of a genuine bistro. For some time I believed I'd almost made it—that wasn't in Paris where the bistro exists mainly in the workingmen's districts—but then I noticed that the *patron* never dried his hands to shake hands with me, as he always did when a client, a Frenchman, came in. The *patron* is not just the proprietor; he is the soul of the bistro. He looks around with a permanently suspicious expression on his face, he knows everything about everybody in *le quartier,* and he enjoys death and disaster as much as the concierge in the buildings where the *copains* live. I have often wondered how a Frenchman stopped being a customer and became a client, an insider. It's hard to say; there seem to be unwritten laws. Apparently he must conform to the standards of the establishment. He must come regularly, and in the beginning he should be seen but not heard, like a freshman senator. He should be conservative in his drinking habits. The real *apéro* is out of fashion. When a client comes in for *petit déjeuner* because no one at home will make it for him, he has *un petit vin blanc.* People who sit down in the rear and want coffee and croissants are considered *voyageurs,* here today, gone tomorrow. They don't belong.

Once a man belongs and is accepted, he need never be alone. He may break into the Banque de France—how nice that would be—and his *copains* will rally to his aid. The bistro remains the citadel of camaraderie.

About 1900 some foreigners discovered informal neighborhood restaurants where the food was more important than the décor; they called them bistros or *bistrots.* No one was quite sure what a bistro was, and people began talking about a bistro-type restaurant, which left matters pleasantly ambiguous. After World War I, people in Paris began collecting bistros. As in the case of Impressionist paintings, most collectors were foreigners. They started the bistro (or *bistrot*) trend, and Frenchmen followed. The French won't admit it today. They still collect bistros, and if they find one that is really good they keep the address to themselves. In that respect nothing has changed.

Still, what exactly *is* a bistro? The definition has expanded to include quite a range of small places. Price is not the criterion; there are bistros now that are very expensive. Even the décor is not the measure.

Most experts agree that the food matters more than the ambience. The *Guide Michelin,* which listed bistros in former years, said: *la table prime le cadre* (food takes precedence over the setting). That is true but not the whole truth. Bistro purists agree that what matters most is who runs the place. A bistro is a family affair: the husband in the kitchen, the wife in the dining room, or the other way around. The young man or the girls who work in the kitchen are relatives, and so are the waiters and waitresses, even though they may be cousins twice removed. As a rule the service is fast—*bistro*—and the tables are sometimes occupied three times during a meal.

Bistros became fashionable after World War II because of the idea that they were less expensive than more formal restaurants. That too is doubtful now. Some highly rated bistros have been invaded by refugees from Lasserre and La Tour d'Argent. Some even take telephone reservations, which was unthinkable in the old days. If you wanted to be sure of a seat, you came early, before twelve o'clock, or late, around two. In between the place was crowded with *gens du quartier* (neighborhood people). Even today the clientele is quite different at noon and in the evening. Strangers rarely come for lunch; they wouldn't feel at home then. At lunch everybody seems to know everybody else, and often the waiters don't even ask for an order, because they know what their clients like best. The atmosphere is friendly; people sit close together. At noontime most guests are men who like to eat and drink well—that is important—and at night there are often women as well, couples who don't live in the neighborhood but have heard about the bistro and want to try it. At night the pace is more leisurely. People don't mind sitting around and enjoying their meal.

I have to warn you: The real bistro is on its way out. I've been told by several *patrons,* "When my wife and I can't do it anymore, we'll close. Young people don't want to carry on. *Pensez-vous!* They can make more money and have fewer problems working in a large place, with regular hours. We get up early to do the buying, and we close very late, and what with all the taxes and costs we discover at the end of the year that we've just managed to break even."

There you are. A few celebrated restaurants will go on, subsidized by the super-rich and by people with expense accounts. But the *quartier*-type of bistro, the small, often quaint eating place, will not be with us much longer. In such a place the menu is still handwritten, not typed, with ordinary dishes in violet ink and special dishes in red ink and very special things written upside down, so you cannot possibly miss them. Such a bistro is not necessarily a workingman's hangout.

There is one in the rue de Berri in the Eighth Arrondissement, not exactly a workingman's district, called Aux Amis du Beaujolais, which is precisely what the customers are: friends of Beaujolais. Martin, the *patron,* is said to have one of the best Beaujolais *caves* in the neighborhood. He comes from the lovely village of Fleurie, in the hills of Beaujolais, and he goes there every year after the harvest, buys a few barrels of the wine he likes best, has them shipped to his restaurant, and bottles them himself. These are *vins de provenance directe,* wines that neither bottler nor merchant has played around with. When I was there, the *vin du patron* was a Chénas, another community in Beaujolais, and it was served in a plain bottle with neither label nor cork. I was charged only for the portion of the bottle I drank.

The front room with the bar was crowded with executives from nearby firms having a drink and masons from a building site around the corner having a beer. There was a disturbing detail, however. A few people, apparently in a hurry, didn't sit down but had their plat du jour standing at the bar. That would have been unheard-of in the old days. No one in a bistro would eat standing up. Obviously, at a time when the bistro has to compete with pizza parlors and snack bars, Wimpys and McDonald's, it has to compete with the standing-up school of eating.

Otherwise little has changed. I saw two bookish-looking executives, perhaps publishers, and a garageman sitting at the same table. At the bistro one doesn't have one's own table; one is glad to have a seat. The executives approved of the wine, offered the garageman a glass, and asked what he thought about it. He approved; it was a decent Beaujolais, quite fresh and fruity. You will admit that this nice little scene could take place only in a bistro in France.

The menu too had the structure of an old-fashioned bistro menu. The hors d'oeuvres were almost the same as I'd had in the old days:

carottes râpées (grated carrots), *pâté de campagne* (country pâté), *rillettes* (spiced pork spread), *thon à l'huile* (tuna in oil), hard-boiled eggs with mayonnaise, *jambon blanc* (ham), *terrine de foie de canard* (duck liver pâté). Among the entrées were all-time favorites: *pot-au-feu* (boiled beef), *paupiette de veau, purée de pommes* (veal roll, mashed potatoes), *andouillette de Chénas, purée* (chitterlings, mashed potatoes), *tripes à la mode de Caen* (tripe with onions and carrots), *jambon lentilles* (ham with lentils), *entrecôte grillée* (grilled shell steak), *escalope aux pms. frites* (veal scallop with french-fried potatoes). There was an astonishing collection of cheeses—Brie, Cantal, Camembert, Boursin *aux herbes*, Crottin de Chavignol, and a few others—though not many, perhaps, if you think of the 480-odd ones made in France; but they were all very good.

In the upper left corner of the *carte* was the *menu conseillé* (recommended menu) for 25,80 francs. There were a few special wines listed, among them a Moulin-à-Vent at forty-four francs, the most expensive bottle, and there was a choice of desserts, from the familiar *crème caramel* (caramel custard) and *gâteau chocolat* (chocolate cake) to such innovations as *tranche vanille cassis* (vanilla ice cream with black currant syrup). I was pleased that most people waited patiently for a table. When they sat down, they studied the menu carefully. When the food came, they tasted it and nodded their approval. They knew what they were eating and they liked it.

Most of them were habitués. The waiter shook hands with them and greeted them as old friends. In a bistro you will be liked only if you come regularly and indicate that you want to belong. In some bistros there is a pigeonhole rack for the regular clients' napkins. The waiter hardly greeted me, but he brought me bread and an open bottle of red wine. I ordered the *terrine de foie de canard*. He didn't write it down; rather he went over to a small table near the bar, cut a thick slice of the terrine, and brought it to me. He nodded his approval when I kept my knife and fork after the hors d'oeuvre, and for the first time he gave me a glance. He saw that I knew the rules. In the old days, bistros rarely changed knives and forks.

There were other people that day who did not belong, but they were treated like everybody else. They got their food in the same manner, large portions served on the plate. I had the *paupiette de veau* with the *purée de pommes*. The dish was well prepared, with a homey touch. The guests did their own seasoning. On each table were salt, pepper, and mustard. Many people peppered their food though few used salt. The bill was written by the waiter on a piece of paper. In old bistros it had been added up on the paper tablecloth. When a guest got up, the tablecloth was removed, a new one was put down, and the place was ready for another guest. No chichi, but good value.

Chez Pauline, at 5, rue Villedo in the First Arrondissement, is an entirely different sort of place, though it can be considered a bistro. There is the *comptoir* downstairs, which is necessary, and behind it two severe, elderly ladies keep the reservation book. The place is famous, and one needs a reservation. But there is a cheerful lack of formality; the bread is placed on the table and the *pâté maison* is put before you in a large container, serve yourself. Unless you order a special wine— and why should you—an open bottle of very good Beaujolais is put on the table with two glasses. No one bothers to fill the glasses, and the sommelier won't sniff the cork. There is no cork and there is no sommelier, but the wine isn't *bouchonné* (tasting of cork); it couldn't happen here.

I also recommend Chez René, a good and genuine bistro at 14, boulevard Saint-Germain in the Fifth Arrondissement, just around the corner from La Tour d'Argent, which is more elegant and also more expensive. Monsieur and Madame René Cinquin run the place from behind the bar. Already the younger generation, M. Cinquin *fils* and his wife, is working. Everybody employed at Chez René is related to M. Cinquin, as they should be in a bistro. The Cinquins come from the Beaujolais country and always have good wines. For years Mme. Cinquin did the cooking, genuine *cuisine ménagère* (home cooking). The waiters wear dark aprons and throw utensils and plates at you, but they never spill anything.

There is no heat in wintertime on the theory that the clients, sitting close to each other, will do the heating. After the third glass of the Juliénas no one cares. There are flowers on the tables and paintings on the walls. The tables are small but the portions are large. René is famous for *andouillette du pays,* a fine sausage filled with chitterlings. Please do not ask him whether the *andouillette* is good. Yes it is; he had it himself for lunch.

If you don't like *andouillette,* there is *poulet rôti* (roast chicken), *coq au vin* (chicken in red wine), *haricot de mouton* (mutton stew), and a fine *boeuf bourguignon* (beef stew in red wine). There are good hors d'oeuvres, many fish dishes (an excellent *lotte à l'américaine*—anglerfish with tomato sauce), and wonderful *mousse au chocolat* (chocolate mousse). At Chez René you will not be received and served like a prince— if you insist on that, you must go around the corner to the Tour d'Argent—but you will eat as some princes wish they could eat.

There are a few rules you should follow if you want to be happy at bistros. *First, be humble.* In a bistro one doesn't complain. At Lasserre the guest is always right (even when he is wrong). At a real bistro, only the *patron* is always right. *Second, don't ask for anything.* In some bistros, they don't bother to write a menu. They may bring you something, and you eat it, or else. *Third, no praise.* The *patron* knows his is the best place on earth; he doesn't need you to confirm it. At a famous restaurant they are always glad when you compliment them. Not at a true bistro. They *know* they are good.

July 1979

BISTROS

Naomi Barry

One way of identifying a real Parisian is by the quality of his bistro list. A good list is considered part of his cultural baggage along with a knowledge of period furniture, modern art, and the fashion positions of Courrèges and Chanel.

Word of a new bistro with potential flashes around the city by means of some undefined underground. Since location means nothing, the place may be in any outlying arrondissement and down any unprepossessing street. Yet, if the cooking is right, within a few months that mysterious group known as "everybody" or *"le Tout-Paris"* has the address marked in its little bistro book.

Doctors and young Paris journalists have high gourmet ratings and are among the first to discover a new place. The presence of both groups is easy to spot since they tend to go out with very pretty young women.

Don't be misled into thinking that an absence of décor is accompanied by low prices. In some top-rated Paris bistros you pay royally for the privilege of having no red roses on the table, no thick carpet on the floor, and no bowing headwaiter. Contemporary chic says that if you have money, spend the maximum to heighten the effect of the minimum; so when you want to sup on fresh foie gras and pheasant you may choose a little restaurant with sawdust on the linoleum.

The list of treasure bistros is part of the craze for "playing it down." The acme of local fashion is a $750 *haute couture* dress stripped of everything but line. To ensure that rich-poor look, one design dictator forbids his clients to wear any jewelry with his dresses—not even a wristwatch. In prestige, a chauffeur-driven Austin Cooper is miles ahead of a space-consuming American car. The coveted apartment is a top-floor studio walk-up. It probably cost the owner a fortune to convert it from a series of six miserable maids' rooms into a spacious two-room suite.

In this current atmosphere of less is more, there is a staggering choice of recommendable bistros. The following are among my favorites, because I am fond of the people who run them. They are not in the ultra-fashionable category like Chez Allard, where a week's advance reservation is a necessity. Nor are they particularly expensive.

In each case the bistro is a family affair with the husband doing the cooking and the wife running the dining room. All of these couples are relatively young. They are warm, friendly, and charming. In their simple but pleasant establishments even a first-day tourist feels himself a part of the city.

AU PETIT COQ

This endearing bistro exists under the sign of the colorful Gallic cock. The rooster is everywhere: on the walls, the shelves, the counters. He appears in paintings, in drawings, and on faience plates. Customers bring figurines of roosters made of wood, straw, and painted terracotta from Portugal, Sweden, Finland, Russia, and Mexico as presents for Monsieur and Madame Pommier. The client-*patron* relationship here is one of real affection. I have never brought any resident of Paris to the Petit Coq who did not become a regular customer.

The specialties of slender, modest Francis Pommier include *fond d'artichaut langouste, turbot à l'oseille, gratin de langouste, noisette d'agneau à l'estragon, steak au poivre, coq au vin, caneton aux pêches,* and *andouillette au Beaujolais.*

I can never resist the turbot with sorrel. The turbot is one of the finest fish found in European waters. The great gastronomic writer Ali-Bab declared that "if the sole has been justly called queen of the seas, the turbot deserves to be their king."

Monsieur Pommier exalts his turbot with a sauce fashioned from fresh cream, Sancerre wine, and generous amounts of chopped sorrel. (The addicts of sorrel can never get enough of this pleasantly tart herb; it appears only on a few Paris menus.) Monsieur Pommier is so exacting about his turbot that he claims he will accept only those which have been caught at the end of a fishing line. He has a complicated theory to the effect that the delicacy of the flesh is impaired when the turbot is caught in nets.

I also like his baby lamb chops, presented on a giant pancake of shredded potatoes, and, for dessert, the pear tart in a pillow of puff paste, served warm.

Another dessert specialty, the *pavé du Petit Coq,* is made of the simplest ingredients—two thirds of a pound of semisweet chocolate, four eggs, and a third of a pound each of sugar and butter—but the result is delicious. Monsieur Pommier says that after the chocolate is melted it is removed from the heat and the butter is added in small bits and mixed in well with a wooden spoon. The yolks are whisked into the sugar in a bowl, and the beating is continued in the upper part of a double boiler until the mixture forms a ribbon, at which point it is thoroughly mixed into the chocolate. The egg whites, beaten *en neige,* are folded into the mixture before it is poured into a mold to be refrigerated overnight. At serving time, the *pavé* is unmolded and covered with *crème anglaise.*

LA CHOPE D'ORSAY

This is the neighborhood restaurant par excellence. It benefits from being in a fine Left Bank neighborhood full of antiques shops, art galleries, and publishing houses. It is only a five-minute walk from my house, and I come here often. So does Virgil Thomson, the composer, whose Paris apartment is around the corner. A number of the residents of the quarter eat here regularly.

You get an occasional glance at Roger Pical via the pass-through to his inadequate kitchen. He is a good-looking young man with black hair, black mustache, and warm, smiling brown eyes. In addition to eleven main dishes always on his fixed menu, Roger prepares four or five different specialties for each day. Out of the tiny kitchen come sumptuous dishes such as a *blanquette de veau à l'ancienne,* a fillet of beef in a brioche crust with a *sauce périgourdine,* and a monumental *sole meunière.* In season he presents pheasant, partridge, quail, and other game birds.

If you are fortunate, you may chance upon a day when Roger has decided upon his superb *tarte aux tomates,* a sort of tomato quiche. For each tart he lines a pie plate with classic puff paste, punctures it with a few holes, covers it with wax paper weighted with beans, and bakes it for fifteen minutes. He dips four large tomatoes in boiling water to loosen their skins, peels them, halves them crosswise, and gently squeezes out the seeds. Then he sprinkles them with salt and pepper and lays them, cut sides down, in the shell. He mixes well three eggs, a pint of crème fraîche, and a scant four ounces of grated Gruyère, pours the mixture over the tomatoes, and bakes the tart in a gentle oven for fifteen or twenty minutes.

Don't wait for Roger to make his outstanding soufflé of chicken livers—he prepares it only upon special order. It is one of the neatest attractions of any bistro in town. Half of its glory lies in the accompanying brown sauce enriched with green olives, mushrooms, and quenelles of veal.

CHEZ MICHELLE ET BRUNO

Even if Bruno did not cook so well, I probably would be attached to this little place just to hear Michelle coo in her Toulouse accent. Michelle, who has the round prettiness that Renoir loved, addresses all her customers with affectionate little pet names: *ma fille, mes gosses, mon petit.*

Michelle and her husband, Bruno, worked around Paris for several years as waitress and cook, respectively, until they had saved enough *sous* to open their own bistro. Michelle decorated it with the gaiety of a harvest booth at a French country fair. Clusters of garlic and red pimiento hang from the rafters. The room divider is a lattice of dried ears of corn.

The accent of Toulouse appears again in such regional dishes as the cassoulet (a well-cooked ragout of goose, shoulder of lamb, sausages of Toulouse, white beans, and cubes of bacon), the confit of goose, and the confit of duck. (The confit is a traditional method of conserving fowl by marinating it in salt and then cooking it, well spiced, in its own fat. It is eaten later, either warm or cold.)

A startling contrast to this heavy fare is a light opening dish such as the *salade de Gruyère*. It is a lovely toss of thin sticks of Gruyère, pitted green olives, white heart of escarole, minced shallots, freshly ground black pepper, and a vinaigrette. The salad is a Michelle contribution.

The *cocktail de fruits de mer* is a platter of assorted seafood—scallops, stuffed mussels, clams, and crayfish tails—and frogs' legs. Despite the name, all the elements are cooked. Bruno presented it one night to win an Englishman over to seafood.

Another Bruno specialty is a tournedos served in a *tartelette* of puff paste lined with slices of cooked apple. His *délice du Gascon* is made by covering a four-ounce veal scallop, beaten flat, with a slice of Gruyère, a slice of ham, and a second slice of Gruyère. The *délice* is dipped in beaten egg, rolled in bread crumbs, and sautéed lightly on each side before being cooked in a covered pan over a slow fire.

Michelle's joy is to prepare crêpes suzette, which she does with a theatrical flourish. "I find it very agreeable to watch the customers in ecstasy before the blue flame," she told me one day.

The featured wines of the house are a rosé de Perpignan and a Cahors.

AUBERGE DE L'ARGOAT

Marcel Goarguer has a remarkable wine cellar, albeit a little like a patchwork quilt. There are three bottles of this, four bottles of that. A *rarissime* is hidden at the back of the cupboard. On Sundays Marcel forages the countryside, calling on little cafés in the provinces, hoping to find some buried treasure. It is not an orthodox manner of building up a *cave*, but Marcel has had his own bistro for less than a year and he is short on money. Through his initiative, however, he can offer the connoisseurs among his clients some real experiences.

He has a Pichon-Lalande '26 (three bottles), a Château Latour '33 (also three bottles), a Château Margaux '37 (six bottles), a Château Margaux '47 (ten bottles), and a Chambolle-Musigny '34 (three bottles). When these are gone, he trusts he will have found some more.

Marcel believes in long cooking in a copper casserole on a slow fire.

"My *coq au vin* does not drown in wine," he says proudly, "but it does require five hours of gentle cooking."

Another example of his art is the *lapin à la bretonne*. A three-pound rabbit is cut into six pieces. In a copper *sauteuse* it is sautéed in two thirds of a pound of sizzling rendered pork fat (Marcel uses fat cut from their hams) until it is golden; then the rabbit is flambéed in six ounces of Calvados or Cognac and removed to a large copper casserole. Into the *sauteuse* go a dozen small onions, four shallots, and a pound of mushrooms cut into small pieces; when they begin to color, three quartered tomatoes are added, along with salt and pepper and a bouquet garni including thyme, bay leaf, parsley, and a heavy dose of tarragon. After a gentle cooking, the vegetables are poured over the rabbit and covered with a bottle and a half of Muscadet. The cracklings of the rendered pork and six *chipolata* sausages are added to the rabbit, which is cooked over a slow fire for an hour and a half. After it has rested overnight, the dish is reheated. The rabbit is served on fried croutons with the sauce, to which six teaspoons of crème fraîche have been added, and with *pommes vapeur.*

Since Marcel and his wife, Jeanine, are from Brittany, the menu is strong on fish and seafood, all of which are ordered directly from coastal ports.

The restaurant has a big stone chimney with a wood-burning fire. The dining room is furnished with Breton antiques: cupboards, copper, pewter, pottery, and old guns. As with his wines, Marcel collects lovingly and buys carefully. He often buys antiques for his customers as well.

For dessert, try one of Jeanine's *crêpes Plougastel.* The rolled pancake is filled with beaten egg white flavored with crushed strawberries and a drop of Élixir d'Armorique—a liqueur so scarce that few Frenchmen have ever heard of it.

June 1965

ALLARD

Naomi Barry

Technically, Allard is a bistro. That is, it looks like a bistro. In the front room is the bar, which is indispensable to every bistro. However, here it is covered in gleaming pewter rather than in zinc, which should give you the tip-off. Actually, this is the number-one small chic restaurant in Paris and has been for thirty-five years.

The windows are grilled, with iron bars. Inside, the coats hang on shining brass hooks, and the sausages of Fleurie hang like stalactites. The waiters match the décor in the traditional uniform of long black aprons, black trousers, and white shirts. The menu is written in purple ink and is characteristically undecipherable.

The atmosphere breathes authenticity, for the building—number 41, rue Saint-André-des-Arts, at the corner of the rue de l'Éperon— is very old, dating back at least to the beginning of the eighteenth century. The premises have known earlier bistros, which left no recorded history but a bit of their personality and an undeniable note of veracity. The food is mother's home-cooking style—provided your mother happens to be a very gifted cook from Burgundy.

To this mock-simple place in the heart of the Latin Quarter comes an enviable parade of chauffeured cars choking up the narrow, twisted street. Parking is impossible in this neighborhood. The cars return after the meal. So many of the diners wear the red rosette of the *Lé-*

gion d'honneur in their buttonholes that the two plain little dining rooms sometimes take on the air of a ministerial conference.

Paris is a fickle town. Allard was established in 1931, among the first of the deluxe bistros. That it has never wavered from lead position in this period is almost a phenomenon. During the winter it is wise to reserve a table a day in advance. During the spring and the fall, when Paris entertains visitors, an advance reservation of four or five days is almost a necessity. What is the secret?

The answer, according to André Allard, is an insistence on sameness. Familiarity is solid and comforting, especially in a rapidly changing world.

The business was started by Marcel Allard. His wife, Marthe, handled the kitchen. Now their son André runs the show. But André first stepped in as a young boy in 1939, working behind the counter, and then as a waiter. When he married Fernande, who also hails from Burgundy, she came into the kitchen and cooked at the side of her mother-in-law. By the time André and Fernande took over, the clients were well habituated to them.

So the tradition goes on. Fernande continues to make the dishes that were introduced by Marthe. André continues to shop in Les Halles each dawn and to buy his wines in the same vineyards patronized by his father. Whenever the restaurant is freshened and painted, it is always as before. In 1964, Allard was able to absorb the boutique next door, which meant a slightly expanded kitchen and space for fifteen additional guests. The changes were so imperceptible that no one noticed.

Allard's popularity in large part, of course, is due to the steadfast quality of the cooking and to its gloriously vaulted cellars. "If you have a good dish and a bad wine, all is lost," says André.

He buys his wine by the barrel, concentrating on Beaujolais, Côte de Nuits, Côte de Beaune, and other regional wines from Burgundy, and Chavignol from the Cher. His model cellars—centuries old—have all the advantages. The subway lines and the trucking routes are far enough away to cause no tremors. The building has no central heating plant. The corridors of the *caves* are covered with gravel rather than cement, so that the ground may give a natural freshness.

Allard keeps a specialized cellarman all through the year to bottle wines, label them, and seal them with wax. So subtle is the job that no bottling is ever done on a rainy day.

If you were planning on a whiskey before dinner, forget it. André does not stock whiskey, in keeping with the tradition of Marcel, who died several months ago. As an apéritif, he suggests a Kir, which is particularly appropriate for a Burgundy house.

A Kir is white wine (at Allard, it is Chavignol) and *crème de cassis*. The drink was invented by the Canon Kir, mayor of Dijon, capital of the old province of Burgundy.

"It is a perfect opening for a meal," says André.

After dinner, there are all the brandies and *alcools* you could desire. Cognac, *eau-de-vie de framboise*, and *marc de Beaugency* are suitable products for this sort of restaurant, and so they serve them.

Allard has its plats du jour that have become classics over the years.

Monday: cassoulet.

Tuesday: veal *à la berrichonne*.

Wednesday: *coq au vin* and leg of lamb.

Thursday: *petit salé* with red beans.

Friday: *boeuf à la mode* and *navarin*.

Saturday: *coq au vin* and leg of lamb.

These specialties represent French country cooking at its most traditional. It takes courage for a present-day restaurant to make them because of the long hours of preparation, but Allard is a family affair, which makes it possible.

Various fish *au beurre blanc* are served according to the seasons. The tricky foaming white-butter sauce accompanies turbot, sea bass, and pike. From January until May, it appears with fresh salmon of the Loire.

The delectable scallops *coquilles Saint-Jacques*, sautéed in butter, are served during all the oyster months.

Fernande Allard supervises the making of the pâtés and the terrines of hare, duck, and chicken livers. The *matelote d'anguilles*, a savory stew of eel, sounds more Norman than Burgundian, but this version is done with red Burgundy wine.

Game is always a seasonal affair, but at Allard there are seasons within seasons. For example, the *bécasse* (woodcock) is preferred in November when it migrates south, rather than in March when it moves north again.

"In November, the *bécasse* is larger and fatter," says André, opting for the nourishment of birds in cooler climes.

Now, my favorite dish *chez* Allard is duck with turnips, a dish that once almost caused a permanent break between us.

One day in May, André suggested a *canard aux navets*. "Out of the question," I replied. "I've never eaten a turnip in my life and furthermore I never intend to."

"Lots of people say that," he replied. "But for six weeks a year, turnips are not only edible, they can even be very good."

"Not possible," I retorted.

"Just try them," he insisted. "If you really don't like them, I'll have a side dish of olives for you." (Duck with olives is the usual manner at Allard.)

Loathing myself for being such a pushover, I agreed to order the duck with the hated turnips. My companion and I were desolate, looking longingly at the next table where two rich businessmen were undisguisedly enjoying *entrecôte marchand de vin* and veal *à la berrichonne*. We, too, might have been so happy, and now we were stuck with turnips.

To console ourselves, we opened the meal with a delicate turbot in the suave white-butter sauce, which we shared. Most servings at Allard are so copious that it is not niggardly, but simply sensible, to divide them.

The duck arrived, neatly disjointed and reassembled—and completely smothered with tiny, golden-brown turnips. How glad we were, my friend and I, that we had supple characters, that we had been receptive to the voice of knowledgeable authority. For the despised vegetable, in the tender succulence of its youth, is sweet and gently flavored. In addition, the Allard kitchen obviously knew how to bring out the best of its ephemeral charms.

That happened four and a half years ago, and it has become a standard house story. As for me, I can hardly wait until turnip time next spring.

Fernande makes a cake with fresh raspberries that is celebrated throughout Paris. When there is no more fresh fruit available for the cake and for other fruit tarts, she substitutes a buttery mocha cake.

Marthe Allard has retired to the country home in Burgundy but regularly sends her children in Paris home-preserved string beans, pickled mushrooms, and other delights that she puts up in old-fashioned glass jars.

In the evenings, the women who come to Allard dress with particular care. For some reason the plain background seems to be an ideal foil for fine clothes.

Those who like a taste of history along with their partridge should know that the great playwright Racine lived in a house on the present site of Allard from 1680 until 1684. Furthermore, the rue Saint-André-des-Arts has an added literary charm. *Trilby,* George du Maurier's romantic nineteenth-century novel of English students at the Beaux-Arts, the servant girl, and Svengali, was set in this narrow, winding street.

February 1966

LE BISTROT DE PARIS

Naomi Barry

"Parisians like noise. Parisians like a room where they will be noticed. Especially the women. They are crazy about a restaurant where they can show off a new dress to advantage."

My knowing adviser on such matters is my excellent coiffeur, Serge Simon, an ultra-Parisian among Parisians. "You can divide our restaurants into two categories," he continued. "Those for people who have something to say to each other, and those for people who do not. The restaurants where the people have nothing to say to each other must be full of personalities, droll men, elegant women."

He rattled off a list of spots in this category: "There's Jarrasse, a fish restaurant in Neuilly; Moustache, where you can be sure of seeing people; Le Florence, always a few movie stars and very chic; Le Grand Comptoir in Les Halles—very much on top, I don't know why; Au Vieux Paris—the Duke of Edinburgh recently took over half of it. The restaurant was very correct and did not inform the journalists, but of course there has been enormous publicity from mouth to ear."

These restaurants, known as *très parisien,* are smart, snobbish, humming with activity, and sharp with surface brilliance. And of all this group, the current phenomenon is Le Bistrot de Paris. All over town, which is rather unusual, the fashionable set are discussing it, arguing with acerbity, pro and con. "It's great; it's terrible." The newspaper columnists and the television commentators have been adding their grain of salt. It is hot copy.

The décor and the atmosphere are pure theater. The restaurant opened at 33, rue de Lille last November 11, Victory Day in France. Like a hit show, it has been playing to a capacity house ever since, at both luncheon and supper. It is always jammed, and it turns down an average of twenty-five to seventy-five would-be reservations a day. Everybody in Paris who thinks he counts feels he must be among those present. The noise could bring on a migraine in even a cool head. The women are exquisite, the clothes are from the top of the *haute couture,* and the jewels are real.

At the same time, Le Bistrot de Paris is a marvelous hodgepodge. Next to a carefully groomed blonde in a St. Laurent dress one will see a girl in a jacket with matching trousers. (The coordinated pants suit is the latest style rage of youthful Paris.) Beside a distinguished-looking middle-aged man in a formal dark business suit, enlivened with a red rosette of the Legion of Honor in his buttonhole, will sit a youngster in a black turtleneck sweater. This is the bistro—the bubbling of the pot.

The tables are so close together that separation is only theoretical. It is almost impossible to keep your chitchat out of your neighbor's plate, and as a result everyone with a bon mot is sure of an audience.

To hear the comments later, one wonders if they are talking about the same place.

"The food is superb and the prices are reasonable enough."

"The food is frightful and too much for what it is." And in the next breath, "Oh, your cousin's lawyer knows Michel. Could he get us a table? Certainly, we'll take a week from Tuesday."

Good, bad, indifferent—it is important to get in.

My experience with the food, on three occasions, was mainly on the fortunate side. The veal with olives, a variation of veal Marengo with olives instead of the classic garniture, was so good that I asked for the leftovers of the copious portion to carry home. The brochette of seafood (mussels, scallops, and bits of *langoustine* interspersed with branches of thyme) was consistently excellent all three times. On the other hand, the chicken with cheese stuffing—a house innovation—was passable but pallid. And a purist was furious to learn that the management had shortchanged the traditional preparation of *blanquette de veau* by omitting the egg yolks which add suavity to the sauce. Swinging back the pendulum, I liked an old-fashioned and very French hors d'oeuvre of hot Lyons sausage with cold potatoes in oil. And I love the lemon pie, which is so lemony it bites.

Enormously popular is the *pot-au-feu en vessie,* a stew of *plats de côtes,* bone marrow, veal shins, turnips, leeks, and carrots, done up in a beef bladder and presented to the customer like a tucker-bag on a plate. The diner is given a pair of scissors to cut open the bag, thus making him a participant in the act. Although dozens of these *pot-au-feu* are served each day, I cannot judge their merits, for the mere thought of them reacts on me as did my mother's fricassee when I was a child.

The décor of Le Bistrot de Paris is artfully simple. Its atmosphere, evoking the bustling boulevard restaurants of the turn of the century, is pure showbiz. The lights are old brass-and-globe gaslight fixtures. (Actually, they were piped for gas the first weeks but had to be transformed to electricity because the heat from the gas was infernal.) The walls and ceiling are painted authentic bistro ocher beige, sickly but chic. There is a profusion of green potted plants. At the rear is a winter garden with a long marble bar presided over by a girl at a cash register. The scene could have been painted by Renoir. There are old cabinets with numerous drawers from the era when each regular customer was given a drawer in which to keep his napkin for the week. These days only calling cards and oddments are kept in them. Upstairs is a room with a billiard table, a further touch of grandpa's day. Much may be phony, but the total effect is *parisien,* that acme of compliments.

Behind Le Bistrot de Paris is a dynamic trio—Roland Pozzo di Borgo, Maurice Casanova, and Michel Oliver—who are young, know everybody, and have the kind of energy that lets them enjoy working sixteen hours a day.

Pozzo di Borgo, of the well-known Corsican family, is regarded as one of the most desirable bachelors in town. He is one of the top public relations men in France (a brand-new group), with clients as varied as a chemical company, which wants to sell a loving image of itself to conservative villagers, and a giant new housing concern that he is encouraging to model itself after California with swimming pools, tennis courts, and other recreational facilities.

Maurice Casanova arrived in Paris from Algiers in 1954—stone broke. Starting from zero minus ten, he imposed himself on Saint-Germain-des-Prés, that most difficult of Paris neighborhoods for an outsider, and established two stunning successes—the Bilboquet, a semiprivate supper club with dancing, and Le Bistingo, which for years was a bistro à la mode. "The French in North Africa had a capacity for hard work that the French in Europe have never known," he says in unassuming explanation. Le Bistingo was similar in genre to Le Bistrot, so Casanova and his two partners have ripped it apart and transformed it into a fish grill with the fresh fish trucked in directly from Brittany ports, bypassing Les Halles in Paris.

To open Le Bistrot de Paris, Pozzo and Casanova joined forces with Michel Oliver, son of Raymond Oliver, proprietor of the three-star Paris restaurant Le Grand Véfour. Michel is descended from a family of seven generations of cooks, chefs, and restaurateurs from the Bordeaux region. His two charming illustrated cookbooks, *La Cuisine Est un Jeu d'Enfants* (Cooking Is Child's Play) and *La Pâtisserie Est un Jeu d'Enfants* (Pastry Is Child's Play), have been recent international successes.

The Oliver presence has meant a lot, for the curious Paris public was immediately eager to discover if he had learned anything from his father. He has the Oliver respect for a good cellar. Le Bistrot de Paris buys wine in kegs direct from the vineyards and bottles it in its own *cave*. Already the stock is up to twenty-five thousand bottles, and the three young restaurateurs hope to reach forty thousand within a few months.

June 1966

CLASSIC TABLES

LA TOUR D'ARGENT

Joseph Wechsberg

Parisians rarely agree on their restaurants, but there is nearly unanimous consent that La Tour d'Argent, founded in 1582 and reputedly the oldest restaurant in the city, is one of the most beautiful on earth and a genuine temple of *la grande cuisine*. At the time of Henri III "The Tower of Silver" on the Quai de la Tournelle stood next to the monastery of the Bernardins near the gates of Paris. To get a table a cavalier might pull up his horse, walk in, challenge a diner to a duel, and kill him to take his place. The restaurant has always been popular with writers, artists, emperors, and queens. Balzac and Alexandre Dumas were habitués, as were George Sand and Alfred de Musset. Napoleon III came with Marguerite Bellanger, and in the museum on the ground floor is the table where on June 7, 1867, Czar Alexander II, the Czarevitch, Wilhelm I of Prussia, and *Fürst* Bismarck had a sixteen-course luncheon that must have left them unable to govern for the rest of the day.

La Tour d'Argent is the beloved mistress of Claude Terrail, who was born in the building. Tall, elegant, and dynamic, Claude studied to be an actor, a diplomat, and a lawyer, and now he is a combination of all three as a restaurateur. When his father, André Terrail, who owned the famous Café Anglais, bought the Tower, the dining room was on the ground floor. That space is now the small museum, filled with Gobelins, paintings, brass, old silver, and incredible eighteenth- and nineteenth-century bottles. The wine cellar, with over 150,000 bottles, is a famous attraction. The last time I was there, they showed me some truly old Cognac—1800 and 1805.

The dining room, now on the sixth floor, is a magnificent glass-enclosed penthouse with a superb view of the Seine and Notre-Dame. At night the cathedral is magically lighted. Claude Terrail arranged for the lighting years ago to please some friends. Today he runs La Tour mainly "for my friends and their friends. I wish I were rich enough to invite them all." One rides up in an elevator with engraved metal walls and steps out into the warmth and elegance of a beautiful civilized home: large rounded windows, handsome wood, tapestries, deep rugs, a black-glass ceiling. Last year Claude turned an apartment on the fifth floor just below into a magnificent suite. The entrance walls are covered with velvet and silk, a cocktail room is paneled with wood, and an intimate dining room has silver walls engraved in the manner of old tapestries: very chic, very Parisian, and very much the personal creation of the proprietor, who is dedicated to beauty and aesthetics and who believes that a restaurant must always rejuvenate itself, especially when it is almost four hundred years old.

La Tour d'Argent has had its ups and downs, but it has survived the whims of peoples' tastes, especially of those who can afford to go there. Claude never compromised with quality. The service matches the décor: elegant and unobtrusive. The staff is interested in pleasing the diner. Even a young waiter is able to explain the intricacies of a gastronomic creation. La Tour d'Argent is more than a restaurant: It is an experience.

A little guidance helps the diner appreciate the finesse of the cuisine. I've seen people at La Tour d'Argent who ordered steak and french fries; I don't know why they bothered to go to the restaurant. On the other hand, the *croustade de barbue Lagrené* is a masterpiece—the *barbue* (brill) surrounded by a fluffy soufflé frame and served with a delicate *sauce mousseline*. One could say that the *noisettes des Tournelles* are tournedos made of lamb, sautéed in clarified butter, glazed, and served on artichoke bottoms with a magnificent sauce, but that doesn't explain the dish at all. Or that the *caneton* Marco Polo (wild duck is, of course, La Tour's great specialty) is roasted and served with a sauce made with four peppers, including a very rare one from Madagascar. It still doesn't explain the elegance of the dish; one has to taste it. There are other variations—the duck served with olives, with a *julienne de citron*, with oranges, with pineapple, with peaches, with oysters *à la façon de M. Carême, en terrine*. But there is also a modest salad, *salade Roger*, that shows what these artists in the kitchen do with a few fine lettuce leaves, a very light vinaigrette dressing, thinly sliced mushrooms, and cut boiled potatoes, which take the vinegar out of the vinaigrette and make it mild and soft and wonderful. Years ago I had a similar experience with *purée de pommes de terre*—mashed potatoes, if one will pardon the expression. But *how* they were done—with love.

That is the secret of La Tour d'Argent. Its staff does everything with love, style, and refinement, although they are under pressure and against strong competition, as is everybody else in the big city. Never mind the number your wild duck comes with. The Prince of Wales, later Edward VII, got No. 328; much later Queen Elizabeth and Prince Philip got No. 185,397. The numbers change, but the spirit is still there. Take your lady to the lovely penthouse and make her feel like a queen for a couple of hours.

January 1973

PRUNIER

Naomi Barry

September in Paris is *la Rentrée*. The city fills up as families return to town so that the children can start their classes. The theaters reopen. There is the delicious excitement of the new fashions; the men are eager to see how the women will be dressed for the coming season. The flowers in the gardens of the Tuileries and the Luxembourg are more wildly brilliant than those of the spring. Oysters are back with the *r* in *septembre*, and Prunier reopens after its annual two-month vacation.

Prunier is an important landmark in the Paris restaurant world. For ninety years it has occupied the same location, albeit with more space now, on the short, narrow rue Duphot at number 9—a few hundred yards from the Place de la Concorde and the Place de la Madeleine. The first Prunier had its modest beginnings three years earlier on the rue d'Antin. It has been in the capable hands of the same family since 1872, a restaurant of exacting standards and flawless service.

For oysters, as for all kinds of fish and shellfish, no restaurant in Paris is more superlative than this noble institution. It is amusing to realize that the Prunier *kanak* predates the Eiffel Tower.

The word *kanak*, or *canaque*, originally referred to the Melanesians. Why the name was given to the Prunier boys who made home deliveries with baskets of oysters on their heads, nobody any longer seems to know. Prunier still makes home deliveries of oysters. A *kanak* comes to your house twenty minutes before dinner is to be served. He opens the oysters in your kitchen and arranges them on platters of crushed ice and seaweed. Although he no longer goes around town with the basket on his head, the traditional costume is still worn by the men who open the oyster shells in the stalls in front of the restaurant itself.

On the ground floor of Prunier are a series of small dining rooms and an oyster bar. The *grands salons* and the private dining rooms are upstairs. Upstairs is decorated in a kind of avant-garde 1925 style that I used to think was just terrible. Now that 1925 is far enough back in time to represent a period, the décor has suddenly taken on a certain charm like a stage set for a play of Colette. Furthermore, 1925 was supposed to have been rich, wild, and gay. This nostalgic aura does more than a little for the interior decoration.

The service is peerless. It is very grave and very serious. Each man, from the busboy to the headwaiter, performs his duties with the dignity and pride of people who regard themselves as representatives of a great house.

Simone Prunier, third generation of the dynasty, once said, "The good headwaiter must have the tact of an ambassador, the discretion of a father confessor, the sunny humor of a fashionable doctor, and the memory for faces of royalty. His post is one of those in which the enjoyment of the work is part of its rewards. In addition, he must possess an encyclopedic knowledge of food and drink." With standards like these, no wonder the grand dukes used to head for Prunier's, straight from the steppes.

A meal at Prunier should start with oysters. The house has its own beds and parks on the Atlantic coast. At the beginning of the century, Émile Prunier was largely responsible for the development of an association for the promotion of the oyster cultivation industry in France.

There are three principal varieties of French oysters: the *belon*, the *marenne*, and the *portugaise*. The greenish *marenne* and the grayish *belon* are both flat. The greenish *portugaise* nestles in a deep baroque shell. The first two are considered as being of equal rank. "The *portugaise*," said the headwaiter, "is not of the same class. A mink coat and a muskrat coat are both fur coats but they are not quite the same."

Still, the *portugaise* is not bad. It is pretty good, in fact, but it suffers from a very old prejudice. A Portuguese ship in the 1860s was forced by a storm to jettison its cargo of Portuguese oysters in the Gironde estuary. The French culture of the variety started with this accidental beginning. The *portugaise* became so plentiful that until the First World War well-to-do French families ordered those oysters only for their servants.

During the 1922–23 oyster famine, the one French oyster to resist the mysterious plague was the despised *portugaise*. During that hard year, Prunier put *portugaises* into fattening beds to refine them. They became acceptable to the restaurant's fashionable clientele, who did not wish to be completely deprived of oysters, but the old prejudice never quite died away.

The *belon* and the *marenne* are minkier in price. Preference usually depends quite simply on whether you like your mink dark or light. However, since the former hails from Brittany and the *marenne* comes from the Charente-Maritime, there may be taste fluctuations depending upon weather conditions in the two regions.

Prunier serves four each of the three varieties on the plate it likes to call *le plateau vivant*. The large oval platter also includes a selection of sea urchins, raw mussels, and giant shrimps, and two varieties of clams—all fresh with the taste of the sea. The sea urchins, *oursins,* are presented in their spiky cups to be scooped out with a spoon. These are always from Atlantic waters and far sweeter than their counterparts dredged up from the Mediterranean.

The platter is accompanied by thin slices of buttered brown bread and wedges of lemon. I do not believe a plump *belon* should have its flavor masked with anything more than a few drops of lemon juice. For those who believe differently, the house has developed an oyster sauce concocted of its own wine vinegar and sharpened with minced gray shallots. The gray shallot is rare and refined, and Prunier is rightly proud of the sauce.

When Alfred Prunier first founded his bistro in 1872, the house offered nothing but oysters, snails, grills, and *pieds de mouton poulette* (sheep's trotters with *sauce poulette*). As late as the 1880s, the rule still held that no customer would be served unless he ordered oysters.

The rigid rules were given a body blow in the 1890s by a wealthy Bostonian who shocked Alfred Prunier by telling him he ought to cook oysters. The Bostonian, in turn, was even more shocked when he learned that Prunier didn't know oysters could be cooked.

The American was a rugged individualist of his time. He insisted that Prunier take him to the kitchen, where he prepared an oyster pan stew. The Frenchman was converted and immediately added the new-fangled dish from abroad to his menu. The now famous *tournedos Boston*, a tournedos with a sauce of cooked oysters, is another Prunier memorial to the Massachusetts gourmet.

During the first decade of this century, Alfred's son, the dynamic Émile, developed Prunier into a restaurant celebrated for its fish and other seafood, as well as for its oysters.

Sea perch *à l'angevine* is one of the hundreds of fish recipes that enhance the international reputation of Prunier. The fish is opened, the backbone removed, and the interior seasoned with salt, pepper, and minced savory. The stuffing includes equal quantities of spinach and sorrel, cooked, ground, and combined with melted butter, salt, pepper, chives, and fresh bread crumbs. Once stuffed with this mixture, the perch is baked for thirty to forty minutes, basted occasionally with butter. The sauce is made by cooking chopped shallots in dry white wine over high heat. When the liquid has been reduced by one fourth, the heat is lowered, a spoonful of heavy cream added, and a goodly amount of butter introduced bit by bit. Pepper and salt are added; the sauce is brought to the first suggestion of a boil and served in a sauce-boat.

Homard au Champagne is lobster at its most luxurious. A live lobster weighing a scant pound and a half is cut into slices an inch thick. After the slices have been browned in butter and seasoned with salt and pepper, half a bottle of very dry Champagne and a little fish stock are poured in, and a whole truffle is added. The pan is covered and the lobster cooked gently for twenty minutes. Then it is removed and shelled, and the meat and truffle are sliced thin and placed in a warmed, covered dish.

The sauce is made by straining the cooking liquid, reducing it, and adding a cup of heavy cream before heating. It is not allowed to boil, but is thickened and bound with egg yolks. This sauce goes over the lobster and truffle already dressed on the platter, just before being served.

This dish, cautions Prunier, cannot wait. But then, who, when faced with it, would want to tarry?

Six years ago, during the Floralies—the international flower show held in Paris—the committee asked a few leading restaurants to prepare dishes with a floral touch. Prunier accommodatingly dreamed up a mullet into which a note of jasmine had been introduced. The result was so delicate and exotic it might have been born of a couplet in a Chinese poem.

Prunier has one of the most renowned wine cellars of the city, built up lovingly by the family over the years. Many a bottle in the *cave* survived the great Seine flood of 1910, when the river turned the Place de la Concorde into a lake and lapped up the rue Royale almost to the steps of the church of the Madeleine.

The Prunier cellars, being in this area, quite naturally were flooded too. With characteristic aplomb the house took care of the emergency. Every morning and evening, the cellarmen stepped into square French dustbins and paddled through the watery vaults to fish from the racks for the bottles requested by the sommeliers in the dining rooms upstairs.

September 1965

LUCAS-CARTON

Naomi Barry

When a Frenchman wants to visit the last authentic vestige of the Paris of Les Grands Boulevards, he goes to a restaurant at the corner of the rue Royale and the boulevard Malesherbes called Lucas-Carton. Here the old traditions that made France great have never been interrupted. The splendid era is still a breathing reality. Every dish is prepared in the classical manner, without skimping or shortcut. The atmosphere is cushioned with inbred courtesy and solicitude. Even the fresh-cheeked, beardless busboys seem to have been born to the house.

Like a venerable bank, Lucas-Carton isn't really noticed as one goes by. It has been there too long—for more than a century.

The glass revolving doors lead to an interior so purely 1900 that one must have been delivered by fiacre, and surely the horse-drawn omnibus must still be operating between the Madeleine and the Bastille. The walls are paneled in blond sycamore and sculpted in free-flowing motifs of leaves and thistles. Carved female heads smile from the center of light fixtures curved in flower shapes. Between the arches are rust-vermilion porcelain cachepots planted with greens. The pots were specially made to harmonize in color with the plush velvet banquettes by the Vase Étrusque, a shop across the street where upper-bourgeois Paris families for years have bought their important wedding presents.

The Beaux-Arts administration has wanted to class the restaurant as one of the finest remaining examples of the art nouveau style. Monsieur Alex, who is the soul and the dynamo of the enterprise, as well as its proprietor, refused the honor, saying "The place would no longer have belonged to us."

The jet set—the swinging set—rarely comes here. But the serious gourmets are present, the ones who seem to have developed their taste buds in a school of the 1890s. On Sundays the important old families lunch here with their grown children. Various missions of the French government use Lucas-Carton practically as an official dining outpost. Even Winston Churchill and Konrad Adenauer were guests at intimate dinners here arranged by the Protocol.

There are seven private dining rooms upstairs where old-fashioned methods of discretion set the tone. The rooms can be approached by a side staircase leading from the passage de la Madeleine. A foot placed on the first step sets off a warning bell that rings upstairs. Whenever guests include political figures, waiters are changed with each course to eliminate the possibility of following a conversation. It all has the lovely seriousness of a spy story in the days before wiretapping. Any waiter observed to have carelessly forgotten to shut one of the double doors is fired on the spot.

In a country where closing days, closing weeks, closing months are the rule, the luxurious Lucas-Carton is a startling exception. It is open every day of the week for lunch and dinner, every month of the year. The explanation is weighty with dignity. Says Monsieur Alex, "These days, a big businessman or a diplomat finds himself in Berlin today, in Washington tomorrow. He says to his colleague, 'Let us meet in Paris at Carton on the twenty-third.' He has no doubt in his mind when he makes the date. He knows Carton will be there ready to serve him."

This devotional attitude toward service is an integral part of the grand style. It befits a house that was chosen by the French government to prepare and orchestrate the state dinner given in the Galerie des Glaces of the Château of Versailles on July 21, 1938, for their Britannic majesties, George VI and Queen Elizabeth.

Now the younger gastronomes are finding Lucas-Carton, and I couldn't be more delighted. Henri Gault and Christian Millau, the two Paris journalists who have been rediscovering the city for their fellow citizens, gave Lucas-Carton their ultimate rating for classical cuisine, décor, and treatment of the public.

On November 4, 1965, the publishing firm of Julliard decided to hold a dinner that would be the acme of French gastronomy for Gault and Millau's *Guide de Paris*. The locale chosen was Lucas-Carton. Monsieur Alex regards the Julliard evening as the restaurant's most ambitious effort since George and Elizabeth.

Not long ago two successful young French journalists, a Paris decorator, and I decided to make it a foursome at Carton for a special dish of lark stuffed with foie gras. It was an evening of that kind of mood.

On each table, there were roses in sterling silver bowls and vases. I noticed a waiter deftly prepare a finger bowl. He poured hot water from a pitcher into a silver porringer and added a few rose petals. The remembrance of such things past made me happy.

Another waiter slipped a small round stool under my feet. It was a tapestry velvet stool somewhat worn by generations of slippers—silk, satin, and fine kid. It was an infinitesimal attention but it made me feel cosseted and precious. Monsieur Alex commented offhandedly that thoughtfulness had always been a sign of a great house in La Vieille France.

As we mused over the menu, which is printed on a very large, single sheet of cardboard, the maître d'hôtel gave us suggestions by performing a subdued ballet of presentation. He held before us a bowl of rare morels, black and convoluted as brains. Then he whirled out a dish of *girolles*.

"Look at them. Beautiful, *non*? They are the first to appear in Paris. You can still smell on them the fresh good earth of Périgord." He tempted and excited our admiration by wafting before us the darkly golden mushrooms exuding their fragrant damp, and we were encouraged to try a small dish of them in butter as an entr'acte to our order.

It is a principle at Lucas-Carton to treat each guest to a loving display of the food stars of the day as they appear on the market. There is a special sensory delight in living seasonally, and the superb primary materials make of the year a colorful kaleidoscope. Spring offers delicate young string beans, almost as fine as blades of grass; early peaches blushing with pride; strawberries gloating with the promise of the juice locked within. Autumn is hardly less bountiful: September inaugurates the hunt with wild quail; October brings hares, pheasants, woodcocks, partridges. These are the months of the oysters—the plump *belons* and the greenish *marennes*.

"Ah, France is a rich country," sighs Monsieur Alex. "Only the French do not realize what they have."

The dining-room display of the first of the season's products is theater, and meant to be. However, there is a second reason for showing the customer the treasures culled that day in Les Halles. To see beforehand what is to go into the pot will spare one any surprises.

Serious gastronomes are unashamed to come here and dine alone. Not long ago, a gentleman who seemed to be in his late seventies arrived unaccompanied. "He ordered a beautiful meal and an important bottle of wine," recounted Monsieur Alex. "At the end he called me over. 'Perfect. Nothing has changed. I have not been here in fifty years.' He had come on a pilgrimage. He left like a jaunty young man, with a cigar in his mouth."

Sometimes women come here alone too. Frequently a concierge from one of the big hotels will telephone, saying he is sending over an unescorted woman. "She is sure of a welcome," says Monsieur Alex. "In some establishments she will be neglected. Here we treat her with double courtesy because she is alone."

Alex Allégrier is a boss of the old school. "In life you get nothing without effort. I must show the example. My staff are my children. They will do anything for me. But they know I will do anything for them."

Today he is sixty-four years old and a wealthy man. Yet four mornings a week he is at Les Halles at five o'clock making sure his merchandise is the best the market has to offer. His wife comes along to pay the bills, thus saving time.

She is a chic and handsome woman, well-dressed, well-coiffed, wearing a few discreet jewels as she sits behind the imposing cash desk in the main dining room of the restaurant. She is the daughter of Francis Carton. Despite the fact that she was the boss's daughter, she was working at the same cash desk back in 1924 when young Alex Allégrier came as the new maître d'hôtel.

He was fresh back from London, where he had been a butler for the Baron d'Erlanger and had had free run of the house. "You can touch everything but the chambermaid." One day the baroness called him. "It is not right for a young man never to go out. Don't you have enough money?" He assured her he had ample funds, but the baron and his wife continued to display concern. The following Sunday, consequently, he betook himself, impeccably dressed, to the Savoy, where he treated himself to a meal of the finest dishes and wine. After a very long lunch, and still alone, he returned to the Erlanger residence. The next morning the baron called him in. "Alex, you conducted yourself with the dignity and decorum befitting a butler of the Baron d'Erlanger."

He had been watched all the time.

After dinner, Monsieur Alex took us down into his cellar. He loves to invite guests to descend for a little Champagne, a glass of marc.

The rue Royale is a short street leading from the Madeleine to the Place de la Concorde, and no street could be more aptly named. Its underground is a royal way of wine housing the cellars of Maxim's, Fauchon, and Lucas-Carton. It is an awesome collection, representing an incalculable fortune.

In 1938 Monsieur Alex, sensing the impending war, walled up a section of his cellar, hiding behind it the finest bottles in his collection. Now he likes to show the marks of the wall that protected his treasures.

There are four hidden entrances providing access to the restaurant, three of them through the cellars. One is half a dozen doors away. It is beautifully Hitchcock.

On the wall of one of the private dining rooms is the menu, most modestly framed, of the great state dinner for the British sovereigns in 1938. This meal was the apogee of the restaurant's entire career, which dates back well over a century.

A great menu is like a page of history. This one has the added touch of magic that comes from pageantry and pomp, extravagance and audacity, and culinary genius. Just to read it is to tingle the buds of taste.

Monsieur Alex relived it with relish as he described the great day.

"There were three hundred guests and three hundred waiters to serve them. Actually fifty of them were police dressed as waiters. Supers. Extras. No one suspected they were guards. We had ninety cooks working in the kitchen." He made the appropriate comments and footnotes as he read the menu from the wall.

Perles Fraîches de Sterlet
("Fresh gray caviar from Iran")
Melon Frappé
("The chilled melon had been worked into little balls resembling hazelnuts.")
Sherry Mackenzie Amontillado Grande Réserve
Délices du Lac d'Annecy à la Nantua
("That is the *omble-chevalier* from the Lake of Annecy.
It took three thousand crayfish to prepare the sauce.")
Chevalier-Montrachet 1926
Mignonnettes d'Agneau Trianon
("Medallions of lamb fillet garnished with artichoke bottoms and
tiny fresh vegetables.")
Magnum de Château La Mission-Haut-Brion 1920
Timbales de Cailles Farcies à la Talleyrand
("Wild quail stuffed with foie gras and truffles." When I pointed out to
Monsieur Alex that he had already told me that wild quail is available in
France only in September and this dinner was served in July, he replied,
"But this was an affair of state. The British government cooperated with us
and arranged to fly quail in from Egypt.")
Hospices de Beaune cuvée Charlotte Dumay 1915
Aiguillette de Caneton Rouennais à la Montmorency
("Rouen duckling with Montmorency cherries.")
Salade gauloise
("A touch of olive oil. Cockscombs. Gaulois, you know.")
Magnum Château Mouton-Rothschild 1918
("It is not true!" I exclaimed. We were not much more than halfway
down the list. "That is the reason," he said, "for the . . .")
Granité au Lanson 1921
("A sherbet made from Champagne as a palate clearer.")
Suprême de Poularde de Bresse au Beure Noisette avec
Pointes d'Asperges à l'Étuvée
("Chickens from Bresse. Only white meat.")
Château d'Yquem 1921

Truffles à la Mode de Périgord
("The truffles were specially selected. Each had to weigh ninety grams.
One per person, steeped in port and served in an individual casserole
covered with a pie crust.")
Magnum de Château Latour 1924
Mousse Glacée Singapour
("Frozen pineapple mousse.")
Pêches de Montreuil Princesse
("The peaches were stoned and filled with a praline. They were peeled
at the last moment. A little extra refinement.")
Frivolités en Corbeilles en Sucre
("Small petits fours, *mignardises,* presented in baskets spun from sugar.")
Magnum Champagne Pol Roger 1911
Magnum Champagne G. H. Mumm 1901
Champagne Louis Roederer 1904
Champagne Veuve Clicquot 1900
Champagne Pommery 1905

Lest I might think that all this belonged to the glorious past, Monsieur Alex brought out the extraordinary menu for the Julliard dinner, which was given in November 1965 and prepared by Mars Soustelle, the venerable chef of Lucas-Carton for the past forty years.

There were forty guests, who met at seven P.M. in the extraordinary cellars where 180,000 bottles of wine are stored. "And not one of them is defective," asserted Monsieur Alex.

The cellar prelude began with *marennes* oysters, foie gras from the Landes with black bread, and a Château d'Yquem '55. There were canapés of caviar, smoked salmon, and Parma ham. The fourteen-course dinner proceeded as follows: *Crème du roi de la forêt* (a *velouté* of mushroom soup) accompanied by a sherry from the reserves of Francis Carton; *pâté de brochet "Talleyrand"* with a Montrachet Les Caillerets '62; *noisette d'agneau "Trianon"* with a Château Trottevieille '57; *feuilleté "Chanteclair"* (cockscombs in a puff paste) with a Château Chapelle Madeleine '37; *granité "Alaska"; aspic de homard* with a Corton-Charlemagne Domaine Louis Latour '45; *surprise de Mars Soustelle* (*girolles* mushrooms from Périgord) with a Château La Grave Trigant de Boisser '29; *bécasse à la façon de Francis Carton* (woodcock prepared and flambéed by the maître d'hôtel at the table before the guests) with a Richebourg Domaine de la Romanée-Conti '37; *salade "Ninon"* (a salad of mixed greens); *cardons à la moelle* (cardoons served with a sauce of beef marrow); *poires doyenne du comice; Époisses du Château et Brie de Meaux* (two superb cheeses always featured by Lucas-Carton) with a Magnum Château Latour '04; *pêches flambées "Lucas"* (the peaches covered with granulated sugar and branded with a red-hot poker at the table) with a Champagne Bollinger '29; *le chant du cygne et ses frivolités* with a Clicquot '11; *pot d'armagnac '84, fine napoléon sans age,* Vieille Chartreuse '00, and savories.

—

As long as this sort of table is still set, the good old days are far from dead.

August 1966

A Secret Club

Joseph Wechsberg

Back in 1936, when everybody who was anybody wanted to make a crossing on the wonderful S.S. *Normandie*, the flagship of the Compagnie Générale Transatlantique, somebody at the Plaza Athénée in Paris had the brilliant idea of installing a small grillroom for those who had missed the boat. Later the *Normandie* was destroyed by fire in New York harbor, but the grillroom is still at the Plaza Athénée, a *succès fou* since it was opened. Located on avenue Montaigne, Le Relais Plaza has become a secret club (with unwritten statutes) and a definitive "in" place for the veritable insiders of the *haute couture,* the aristocracy, members of government, and also *the* place for professional snobs, who come to see and be seen. Also present are the last of the *boulevardiers,* jaunty and elegant, with flowers in their buttonholes, who come because, as one told me, "the dear old Relais Plaza is exactly as it was in '36. Now how many places can make that claim?"

Everything has been faithfully preserved (which doesn't always please the barmen and waiters). M. Albert, the dignified Turk of indefinable age, still pours the coffee. The blackboard is carried through with the name of a habitué who is wanted at the telephone. Only habitués dare call the Relais to ask for a fellow habitué. Even the dresses worn by the ladies haven't changed much since '36, only the prices. The service is excellent, and the cuisine is reliable, though no one comes here for the cuisine. The ambience is quite different at lunch and dinnertime. At one o'clock, never before, and never later than one-thirty, the lunch club members, the great names of the *haute couture*, drop in. M. Balmain comes five times a week. M. Givenchy, M. Laroche, and M. Saint Laurent appear frequently. And many others: Prince Paul of Yugoslavia, a sprinkling of the old names of France, and Madame Messmer, the wife of the Prime Minister. Tourists, even in the millionaire class, haven't much of a chance at the Relais Plaza. Some come at noon and are tactfully informed that they must be gone by one when the table "belongs" to someone. Or they may come after two-thirty when it's all over.

The social topography at the Relais Plaza is as strict as it was at Le Pavillon in New York under Henri Soulé, when only God and M. Soulé decided exactly where the guests would sit. There was no appeal against the decision of *le grand Henri*, who used to say with disarming frankness, *"Le Pavillon, c'est moi."* At the Relais Plaza the great decisions are made by M. Claude, who performs with dignity and knowledge and knows the unwritten rules. ("The worst mistake is to ask a man, 'Who are you?' If I don't know who he is, he's got little chance.") Some clients are sent to the bar and told to wait for their table. Some get discouraged or maybe have too many drinks and walk out, which was the idea anyway. The most "desirable" tables are near the revolving door and close to the bar where it is very uncomfortable and one is bothered constantly, but people like to suffer. The most desirable seven tables at the *old* Pavillon (today La Côte Basque) were in the sanctuary, the small entrance room between the checkroom, the rest rooms, and the door. Same old story.

Having been recommended by M. Paul Bougenaux, the general manager of the Plaza Athénée, we were given a tiny table near the kitchen door, the equivalent of Lower Siberia or maybe Outer Mongolia. But M. Claude, who has a heart and a sense of humor, told us, smiling, that the gentleman behind us wearing dark glasses was *"le roi du pétrol,"* and he didn't care where he sat. And that nice, simply dressed woman nearby was "la Baronne Guy"—Rothschild, that is— and *she* didn't care either. I was reminded of Henri Soulé's favorite woman customer, who told him, "Don't worry, M. Soulé. Any table will do. Where I sit, it's chic." *Voilà!*

At lunch the Relais Plaza is the rendezvous of *le Tout-Paris*. Other places in town claim this distinction, but I think the Relais truly deserves it. The day we went, there were practically no foreigners, ourselves excepted. Everybody seemed to know everybody else. The women were good-looking: Some were expensively underdressed, wearing leather jeans and strange garments; others looked like they could be (and probably had been) on the cover of *Harper's Bazaar*. And the men were attractive. This doesn't mean that we were surrounded by wealthy socialites and displaced parasites. On the contrary, there were some very hardworking people around us who like the place because it's convenient, one doesn't have to eat much—it's really a sort of glorified snack bar—and one meets one's friends there. M. Claude told us about the Marquis de la Bruyère, a faithful club member and client of long standing, who had been away for two years, arrived in Paris in the morning, came for lunch at one o'clock, got *his* table, naturally, and saw all his friends, immediately feeling *comme chez soi* (at home).

The club members worry continually that the management may decide to modernize things, God forbid. Every year, before the place closes in August, they urge M. Bougenaux and M. Claude not to change anything, neither the décor nor the formula. A number of years ago, when the hotel was sold with the George V and La Trémoille to what was called "British interests" (actually the tycoon Charles Forte), there were dire predictions that the flagship was leaking and might be sinking fast. But Mr. Forte knew better than to interfere. I am not sure he could get M. Balmain's table; that is, unless M. Balmain happened to be away, which is as it should be in this kind of place.

At night the ambience at the Relais Plaza is quite different. Three theaters are in the immediate vicinity, including the Théâtre des Champs-Élysées, where history was made on May 29, 1913, when the premiere of Stravinsky's *The Rite of Spring* caused such a scandal that the composer and Pierre Monteux, the conductor, had to escape through a window. Had the Relais existed then, they might have sought solace there. Today first-nighters gather at the Relais for an early postmortem, many women wearing the creations of the *couture* artists who were there for lunch. When Herbert von Karajan conducted the Orchestre de Paris, he came to the Relais. Georg Solti, sorry, Sir Georg, who now conducts the orchestra, also comes there. I am sure he gets an acceptable table, close to the door.

The Relais Plaza stays open until two A.M. and serves warm dishes until one or one-fifteen, which means they need three crews of cooks and waiters. The cuisine is the same as that at the respected Régence Plaza, where they like fancy dishes such as *soufflé de homard Plaza* (lobster soufflé). But at the Relais the diner is just as welcome if he orders only toast Relais Plaza, smoked eel on scrambled eggs. There is a very large menu, ranging from *soupe à l'oignon gratinée* to *timbale de framboises parisienne.* The wines range from a *Beaujolais en carafe* (twenty-five francs) to a Château Margaux '59 (eight hundred francs). If you, Madame, belong to the three thousand women on earth who can still afford *haute couture*—ten years ago, there were twelve thousand such women—you may want to read the sentence on the last page of the menu, which says, *"Pour vous, Madame, après le charme des présentations de Couture, le Relais Plaza sera votre rendez-vous à l'heure du thé-cocktail."*

January 1974

Maxim's

Naomi Barry

I'm going to Maxim's
Where all the girls are Queens
A sentimental army
To captivate and charm me.
Lo Lo, Do Do, Zou Zou,
Clo Clo, Margot, Frou Frou—

The Champagne I will sip, sip, sip
Could sink a battleship....

It is more than half a century since Franz Lehár wrote *The Merry Widow,* but the aura of romance he created still lingers on undiminished. The world continues to dream of Maxim's as the meeting place of Lo Lo, Do Do, Zou Zou, and Margot.

In the 1900 edition of Baedeker's guide to Paris, the correct and austere German chided Maxim's by describing it as "an elegantly fitted-up restaurant, frequented mainly at night, *for gentlemen only.*" It was his tactful way of indicating that the glittering and gorgeous women who supped with half the nobility of Europe were not exactly "ladies."

At the same period, the dapper Boni de Castellane, husband of Anna Gould and a Maxim's habitué, summed up the situation by quipping, "Virtue is the mediocre attribute of women who have never had a chance to lose it."

Nonetheless, many society women and their daughters during the

Belle Epoque yearned to join the fun. Rumor has it that a few daring ones, heavily veiled, slipped up a secret staircase for a midnight supper in a private dining room for the delicious experience of finding out what it was all about.

So famous, or infamous, was the reputation of the splendid house on the rue Royale, but a few steps from the majestic Place de la Concorde, that at the start of World War I, Kaiser Wilhelm exhorted his generals to hurry up with their western offensive so they could all soon meet again for a Champagne dinner at Maxim's.

History has since transformed the world. Nothing has remained static. What goes on now *chez* Maxim's? Tonight the banana-colored Rolls-Royce of the Maharani of Baroda is at the door. Aristotle Onassis and Maria Callas are at a corner table. The orchid loveliness of a bouquet of South American heiresses blooms under the soft caress of the amber lights. And the Champagne that is sip, sip, sipped could still sink a battleship. *Plus ça change, plus c'est la même chose.*

The clothes may be different, but the décor is rigorously the same. The mahogany walls with arabesque appliqués of gleaming brass, the tall mirrors framed in mahogany whorls, the stained glass, the fleur-de-lis bracket lamps, the potted plants, the murals of rosy-fleshed nymphs are the quintessence of the cosseted hothouse luxury of Paris 1900. The French government has cannily classed the interior as a historical monument, a memorial to one of the gayest and most pleasured periods the world has ever known. Maxim's is what it has always been—an illusion palace within whose walls breathe love, wealth, glamour, high living, power, beauty, magic, and the shadow of that immortal Merry Widow. No alteration can be made in Maxim's without the approval of the Beaux-Arts administration, a permission not likely to be given.

To enter the doors of number 3, rue Royale these days is a formidable security check—of your own ego. The trademark of a Maxim's waiter is deftness of service and a turned-down mouth. Obviously, the regular customers here are solid enough in themselves that they don't need to be bolstered up by smiles from the help.

One day I made a tremendous discovery. It was the middle of the afternoon. The luncheon guests were gone. The waiters had removed their coats. In their shirtsleeves, they were rearranging tables. Even among themselves, their mouths were still turned down.

I breathed like one reborn. The deprecating expressions had nothing to do with me. They were part of the physiognomy. So remember that when you come in shyly from Akron, Dallas, Tulsa, or Duluth and you get a reception like a dash of bitters. Your counterparts from Oslo, Zurich, Madrid, or the *Seizième arrondissement* are not being greeted more sweetly.

One exception to this dour staff is the maître d'hôtel, Edwin Meissner, who grew up in the house over the last twenty years. He is a tall, thin Alsatian with an extraordinary resemblance to Valentin le Désossé (Valentin the Boneless One), the immortal high-hatted dancer in the Moulin Rouge posters of Toulouse-Lautrec. Meissner moves around the crowded dining room like a ribbon of silk, and he carves a *caneton aux pêches* as if he were doing a production number in a ballet. He also does not regard it as beneath him to remember your name.

A few years ago, Serguy Prince Lubomirsky—a Polish émigré— told me he came to Maxim's one evening escorting a wine-sodden and ragged old crone. She was a street vendor of newspapers in his neighborhood. Intrigued by her stylish and rather wicked repartee, he fell into conversation with her. She revealed she was the daughter of Émilienne d'Alençon, a music-hall artist who had been one of the most famous in the galaxy of the ladies of *chez* Maxim's.

Lubomirsky felt it was only fair that the unfortunate daughter should also have a chance to revel for a night at Maxim's. Up on a table nimbly leaped the disreputable-looking old bawd. For hours, in a croaking voice, she sang the nostalgic songs of her mother's repertoire. The dining room was enchanted. Here and there a tear rolled down the withered cheeks of an elderly gentleman who remembered the delectable Émilienne. A note of unrespectability has always been cherished by Maxim's.

Emily Post, that wise and not sufficiently honored arbiter of the social scene, once observed that often the only difference between a smart party and the other kind was the way the women dressed. Maxim's is exigent. On Friday evenings, all guests must come in full formal attire.

However, since it is even more fun to impose your own rules, the unwritten law made up by the guests now demands evening clothes on Tuesdays as well. These gala Tuesday nights belong to the pretty little debutantes of Paris, who, with traditional French thrift, have provided themselves with extra opportunities to wear their ball gowns and thereby amortize for their papas their murderously expensive coming-out dresses. And when, after dinner, the center of the floor is cleared for dancing, the room becomes a whirling parade of Paris *haute couture*.

It is time now to talk of *médaillons de veau Orloff* and matters culinary. The cuisine in this tureen of snobbishness gambols from passable to great. I first realized its potential excellence when I was wandering through the antiquated cellar kitchens and found an unused portion of simplicity in the form of a baked custard. Chef Alex Humbert, who dresses like a banker when off duty, handed me a spoon. The custard was exquisite beyond belief, lifted from its customary blandness by the subtle flavor of raisins previously soaked in rum.

On the other hand, I am not an advocate of sole Albert, which is one of the starred dishes on the menu. I think many people order it because it is named after the late and legendary Albert, who for twenty-five years was the autocrat of Maxim's. During his reign, his icy glare for those whom he did not deem worthy of the gilded life was responsible for sending hundreds of crumpled souls to dine miserably in other restaurants where they were greeted with more welcome.

The great Escoffier catalogued 185 recipes for preparing sole, that incomparable fish from the icy waters of the English Channel. I don't think he would have added sole Albert as his 186th, despite its present popularity. In this dish, the sole is given a topside coating of fresh bread crumbs and baked in a pond of dry vermouth. The level of the vermouth is carefully controlled so that no liquid touches the bread crumbs, which are moistened only with melted butter. The heavy slathering of bread crumbs counteracts the delicacy of the sole and produces a dish far too dry for my taste. Utterly disappointing.

However, I do love *potage Billy By,* closely associated with Maxim's and one of the most festive of party soups. According to the Countess de Toulouse-Lautrec, in her book *Chez Maxim's* (McGraw-Hill), Louis Barthe, a former chef at Maxim's, in 1925 "was working in the kitchen at Ciro's, a restaurant in Deauville known for a special mussels dish with a particularly succulent sauce. One day a very good customer, Mr. William Brand, decided to invite some American friends to Ciro's. Mussels are generally eaten with the fingers in France, using one double shell as tongs to scoop the meat out of the others.

"As Mr. Brand wanted to spare his friends this delicate operation, he requested that the juice be served without the mussels. It was such a success that during the days that followed each of his guests returned separately to Ciro's and ordered the potage Billy Brand." For the sake of discretion, it was placed on the menu as *potage Billy B,* and thus was born the *potage Billy By* which has since become a classic of the French culinary tradition.

At Maxim's, the soup is prepared by steaming the mussels open in a mixture of minced onion, celery, dry white wine, and pepper. The mussels are removed to be reserved for another use, and the soup is made from the liquid, which is first reduced and then reheated after the addition of *fumet de poisson* and heavy cream.

The *médaillon de veau Orloff* is a dish often suggested for private dinner parties at Maxim's. A sumptuous preparation most suitable to the surroundings, it is made of veal steaks cut from the tenderloin. These are seasoned with salt and pepper, lightly dusted with flour, and seared and cooked in butter. Removed from the fire, the steaks are slit and stuffed with sautéed mushrooms puréed and mixed with heavy cream, and covered with a *purée Soubise* (minced, blanched onions stewed in butter, simmered with a thick béchamel sauce, and passed through a sieve). The sauce poured around the meat is made with the pan juices, to which chopped shallots, dry white wine, and port are added before they are reduced by half and enriched with *fond de cuisson* and more butter.

The *poulet aux concombres* is one of M. Meissner's favorite recommendations and is a specialty of Chef Alex Humbert. A chicken is put on a bed of thinly sliced carrot and onion and chopped giblets in a buttered casserole, and brushed with melted butter before being roasted in a medium oven for forty-five minutes. It is turned and basted four times during this period, and a little thyme, bay leaf, and coarsely chopped tomato pulp are added after the first quarter hour. When the chicken is done, it is put in a serving dish, covered with a sauce made by simmering cream with the pan juices, and surrounded with quartered cucumbers, peeled, seeded, blanched, and stewed in a mixture of butter and cream. The chicken breast is decorated with tomato slices warmed in butter.

However, when I go to Maxim's I rarely eat much, having got myself so dolled up that my appestat goes down to where I am satisfied with a dozen plump *belon* oysters and a glass of chilled *brut* Champagne. From sidelong glances at other tables, I gather most of the other women are in the same state.

Frou Frou, Zou Zou, and Margot indeed!

April 1966

MAXIM'S

Joseph Wechsberg

It's easier to explain what Maxim's is *not* than what it is. Maxim's is *not* a nightclub where undressed women appear on the floor while the salad dressing is being served. The management often receives letters from all over the world asking about the "program" and what time it starts. Here it is. At nine-thirty in the evening a small orchestra on the platform begins playing what was once discreetly called "table music." After eleven, people dance, having finished their dinner. Roger Viard ("Roger"), maître d'hôtel and dictatorial ruler at Maxim's, doesn't care much for the doubtful combination of dining and dancing.

Maxim's is *not* just another three-star restaurant, though it has long had the *Guide Michelin*'s top accolade. Few people go to Maxim's to feed themselves. But the late Alexandre Dumaine, not exactly the Maxim's *type*, once told me, "You can lunch very well there ordering the plat du jour, maybe the *côte de boeuf*, from the wagon." Finally, Maxim's is *not*, as some believe, an exhibition of unrestricted snobbism. If it were just that, Maxim's couldn't have survived for over eighty years as the citadel of Parisian chic, a rendezvous of the world's VIPs.

No, it's more complex. Jean Cocteau called it *"le véritable théâtre de quelques grandes actrices."* Paul Valéry compared Maxim's with a "submarine immersed with its décor Jules Verne." Maxim's is the quintessence of Paris, a mixture-as-never-before of history and legend, elegance and impertinence, showplace and snob appeal. You feel it the moment you walk through the woodwork-and-gilt entrance at 3, rue Royale: It is the reflection of what was called La Belle Epoque in Paris and the Edwardian era in London. The 1900 décor must not be changed; the French government declared Maxim's a national monument. As a heritage of the nation it may not rank with the Louvre or Versailles, but it is as Parisian as the Place de la Concorde just a few steps away. Maxim's (and Paris) have had their ups and downs, but the ups have outshone the downs. It is no accident that Maxim's has often been imitated, but never successfully. Underneath the glamour and the glitter there is something solid and permanent that has attracted people for generations. Maxim's has often been lucky with its public relations. Its most famous (unpaid) press agent was Franz Lehár, who in 1905 placed an entire act of his masterpiece, *The Merry Widow*, in the midst of the restaurant, where he had never been. Ever since, the legend of the forbidden fruit has remained indestructible.

Maxim's also remains a battleground of complex social topography. The only other comparable place was Le Pavillon in New York City in its heyday, under the late, great Henri Soulé. He was totally unimpressed by fame and wealth, as many rich and prominent would-be customers came to learn, grievously. Soulé alone decided who got in and who would sit where, and though he repeatedly proclaimed that all tables were "desirable," the customers knew very well that some tables were more desirable than others. For many years Maxim's was arrogantly run by Albert Blaser, the rotund, tough arbiter of the social Who's Who. Albert's decisions were often shocking and always final. He understood that Maxim's existence depended on its prestige as an exclusive club, with no written statutes, whose "members" liked to be among themselves. A few outsiders might be permitted, but only in "Siberia" and provided they "behaved." This uncompromising policy is continued by Albert's handpicked successor, the formidable Roger, who was eighteen when he began working as a *commis* at Maxim's in 1937, was the youngest *chef de rang* at the age of twenty, became Albert's assistant in 1952, and took over seven years later, not long before the death of Albert, the Master.

Henri Soulé used to say, *"Le Pavillon, c'est moi,"* with an invisible bow to You-Know-Who. Roger could say the same about Maxim's. He is more graceful than Albert—times have changed, after all—but he knows his sacred duty to Maxim's and is just as severe in his decisions. The son of a Parisian physician, he lost his father when he was very young, had to work, and almost accidentally slipped into the restaurant business. He was working at Larue, once a famous restaurant in the nearby Place de la Madeleine, when he was noticed by Albert. Like his mentor, Roger learned to see a lot, to know everything, to say nothing. He will not recognize people who under certain circumstances prefer not to be recognized. He can tell you many things without telling you anything; he would have made a brilliant career at the Quai d'Orsay, where the diplomats do just that. Roger conducts Maxim's as though it were an orchestra; he sets the tone and defines the rhythm. He is *très dur* (very tough) with his "players," the personnel, and even more so with his audience, the customers.

Not many people know that Roger leads a bourgeois life once he leaves Maxim's and gets to his home on the rue Cambon. His oldest son is a mathematics professor who wants to have nothing to do with the restaurant business.

"He is right," says Roger. "It's not easy. I cannot afford to make many mistakes. Maxim's greatest asset is its unique ambience." But the ambience depends on more than the ancient mahogany walls and the cut-glass mirrors surrounded by art nouveau arabesques of colored glass and carved wood. It must be painstakingly created and exactly executed. On Friday nights, when black tie is de rigueur, Maxim's often becomes a social jungle where prominent lionesses fight for "desirable" tables and only the fittest survive. Roger nobly rises to the occasion, relying on his knowledge of human nature in general and of his customers' personal histories in particular, as he makes the seating arrangements, which he calls "orchestrating my dining rooms." On other nights—Maxim's is closed on Sundays—he does it only after the customers come in, not before nine o'clock. If you come earlier you will be subjected to the condescending stares of the help, and you are through as far as they are concerned, no matter how much you may overtip.

"I want to have a beautiful *salle*," Roger says dreamily. "Everybody likes attractive, well-dressed women. Mind you, they don't have to be beautiful, but they should have that indefinable quality that makes men sit up and look at them as they walk by. Such women will be prominently seated; they are my best helpers. I receive the guests in the lobby and sometimes give them a sort of X-ray look when I don't know them. Many don't like it. But I know instantly where they are going to sit." There is no appeal against Roger's instant decision; don't even try.

In his demanding task Roger relies on the peculiar geography of Maxim's: *la grande salle,* which is the main dining room, and the narrow, rectangular grill with the "garden" near the windows facing the rue Royale that was always known as the omnibus. There the people sit on the banquettes along the walls, as in an oversize omnibus, staring at each other. This fortunate arrangement makes Maxim's, as its owner, Louis Vaudable, told me happily the other day, *"deux maisons dans une,"* two restaurants in one. At lunch, *the* place to sit is the omnibus, especially the "garden" (the few elegantly decadent plants arranged in the curtained windows), and *not,* God forbid, the *salle.* Within the omnibus the ambience is that of a very exclusive club. Everybody knows everybody else; people talk freely with others at neighboring tables; it's very relaxed. Outsiders are rarely permitted there during lunch. They may sit in the *salle,* possibly ordering *petit homard court-bouillonné à la nage* (lobster cooked in broth) and *sorbet aux fruits exotiques* (exotic fruit sherbet), but are left there in not-so-splendid isolation.

It's *quite* different at night, when the omnibus becomes the least desirable part of Maxim's. (Why? Don't ask. If you feel you have to ask, don't go there.) With certain subtle exceptions. The tables in the omnibus that you see when you come in are highly desirable, but don't even try. They are for Roger's client-friends. "The Duchess," he says, "likes to sit at Number 16, where she can see *everything.*" British royalty traditionally had Number 16. The Duchess of Windsor, a dear client (and one of the few Roger will mention by name), was also a dear client of Henri Soulé's. And Madame Rochas is always happy "over there," still at the omnibus.

The rest of the omnibus is zero at night. And even worse is the right side of the *salle* (as you come in), which is known as *la Sibérie* among the help. Yes, Siberia. Oil nabobs, the third divorced wives of department store plutocrats, and assorted lesser millionaires are seated there, take it or leave it. But the left side of the *salle* is only for clients or friends that Roger *likes* to have there. The Monday night in March— Monday is usually quiet, and March is even quieter—we were there, only two tables on the left were occupied, but many tables on the right side and even in the middle around the small dance floor were filled. Why didn't Roger relent and let some temporary visitors to Siberia sit on the left side. Ah, I have learned not to ask silly questions. I never asked Soulé, and we were friends. And I didn't ask Roger, and that is perhaps why we were seated at the most desirable left side table. The help was puzzled, and no wonder, no one knew us.

———

Maxim's owes its name to Maxime Gaillard, one of the waiters at the nearby Reynold's bar, who bought the premises at 3, rue Royale in 1893 from an Italian ice-cream vendor named Imoda. Gaillard didn't have the money to pay for it and borrowed from a neighborhood butcher and wine dealer. He dropped the *e* from his name to make it more English-sounding (the English clientele was very important) and opened Maxim's on May 21, 1893. Business was pretty bad—only coachmen of hansom cabs and fiacre drivers seemed to be patronizing his establishment—and Gaillard was almost bankrupt when he had a lucky break in 1894. Irma de Montigny, vaudeville star at the Palais de Glace, had been refused a table at Weber's, an elegant restaurant on the rue Royale, walked out, and went over to Maxim's. Perhaps she knew Gaillard, who had once worked at Weber's.

Irma liked it and came back with a wealthy admirer, Baron Arnold de Contades, profession: "sportsman." (The profession of "playboy" had not yet been invented.) Maxim's was in business, and where is Weber's now? In 1900 the Paris Exposition opened, and Maxim's cele- brated the event by getting a new, sumptuous décor of the Belle Epoque, with frescoes by Martens and Sonnier and other lovely fea- tures that are now much admired. (The management still has some of the receipts from bills paid for the decorations in 1900.) Poor Gaillard was no longer around though. He had died in 1895, leaving the estab- lishment and considerable debts to one Eugène Cornuché, his head- waiter.

Smart fellows. The year 1900 ushered in the golden age of Maxim's and the immortal legend of wine, women, and sin. The legend and its factual background are linked to several kings and to some ladies of charmingly doubtful virtue, known as the *grandes cocottes,* perhaps in order to distinguish them from the many not-so-*grandes cocottes.* The famous protagonists in the sumptuous farce performed at Maxim's were King Edward VII, who liked large French blondes and slim English brunettes; Leopold II, King of the Belgians, who liked them all, blondes, brunettes, even redheads; Alfonso XIII of Spain, who once tossed five hundred (gold) francs over his shoulder to hear his favorite song. Also present were Russian grand dukes, maharajas and sultans, American millionaires, British lords, artists and spies, embezzlers and jockeys. And why? Because of *les dames de chez Maxim,* the ladies from Maxim's.

Nowadays they don't like to talk about the Ladies. Naturally. Some of them were no ladies, sitting near the bar waiting for customers and "doing all right by themselves." They really overdid it sometimes, and Maxim's was almost . . . well, you know—but it must have been great fun while it lasted. Georges Feydeau wrote *La Dame de chez Maxim,* and Yves Mirande wrote *Le Chasseur de chez Maxim's.* There was *The Merry Widow,* and not so very long ago there was *Gigi.* Much of it is fiction, but the *grandes cocottes* were fact. Many were music hall stars and former ballet beauties, and they were the big show at Maxim's as they swept in sometime after midnight, beautifully gowned and hatted, with recently acquired jewels and even more recently acquired lovers. Every night was first night at Maxim's. The Ladies liked jewels, excitement, and a good fight. They provoked duels that took place in the Bois de Boulogne and often ended with a "reconciliation breakfast" at Maxim's. These people had style. I wish I had been there.

Think of Caroline Otéro, yes, *la belle Otéro,* as the Prince of Wales called her, and so did Grand Duke Peter of Russia and another admirer, Kaiser Wilhelm II, who also called her "my little savage." Maybe the Kaiser had better taste than history credits him with. *La belle Otéro* eventually ended up with a Baron Ollstreder, who gave her so many jewels, including the famous necklace of Marie-Antoinette, that he nearly went broke. And that was the end of the liaison, which shouldn't surprise you. No jewels, no Otéro. Her archenemy was the beautiful

Liane de Pougy, who got so angry about Otéro's jewels that she decided to teach her a lesson. One night Liane came in wearing a simple dress. Not a single diamond. She was accompanied by her maid, who took off her coat to reveal all of the jewels belonging to Liane. Everybody gasped, and the confrontation ended with a terrific fight.

The gentlemen were also quite spectacular. James Gordon Bennett, publisher, gambler, and master of high living; Louis Renault, André Gustave Citroën, Émile Levassor, and Ettore Bugatti, of automobile fame; Paul Poiret, who "invented" *la femme moderne;* Prince Murat and Prince Henri d'Orléans; Caruso and Chaliapin, who would share a soufflé for dessert; Roland Garros and Georges Carpentier; Marcel Proust (though it seems hard to fit him in); and Comte Boni de Castellane, who later married Anna Gould.

Edward VII, King of England, would come "anonymously" with Lillie Langtry, the beautiful British actress, whom he couldn't meet in London. He said he liked Maxim's, where he was "known but not noticed." Also present was the celebrated cartoonist Sem (Georges Goursat), chronicler of Maxim's, whose drawings can still be seen there. There were others who wrote about the goings-on upstairs, in the back rooms, and at the bar.

In 1907 Monsieur Cornuché (who had discovered that Maxim's needed beautiful women who would attract rich and powerful men) decided that he had had enough and sold Maxim's to a British company. Under the new management, frivolity was frowned upon and respectability was encouraged. Out went the last of the *grandes cocottes.* In came such public-relations bombs as Madame Sarah Bernhardt and Dame Nellie Melba. The new Prince of Wales (later briefly Edward VIII) made his first appearance and was given his grandfather's table, Number 16.

The shots in Sarajevo caused, among other things, the end of the glorious epoch at Maxim's. The kings disappeared and were succeeded by black marketeers and high-living Allied officers. A mysterious woman, later described by maître d'hôtel Hugo as "grossly mannered," often dined with Allied officers and later delivered war secrets to the Germans. Eventually Margaret Zelle was caught and executed at Vincennes. She remains known as Mata Hari, darling of the Sunday supplements.

Toward the end of World War I Maxim's became the hangout of celebrated aviators: Georges Marie Guynemer, René Fonck, and Charles Nungesser. During the early 1920s, when inflation raged in Europe, spenders of American dollars and British pounds were much appreciated at Maxim's. In London it was said that the directors of Maxim's Limited made frequent "business trips" to Paris "to look after their investment."

Came the Big Depression and in 1932 the British corporation sold out to Octave Vaudable, a well-known Paris restaurateur who decided to give Maxim's a new lease on elegant life. But it was a difficult time, and Vaudable was about to sell Maxim's when he had a brilliant idea and hired Albert Blaser, the famous maître d'hôtel at Ciro's. Maxim's sent out invitations, *"Albert vous recevra chez Maxim's de midi à l'aube* [Albert will receive you at Maxim's from noon until dawn]." Albert's presence pulled Maxim's out of the doldrums within a month, and during the 1930s favored clients included the Prince of Wales, the King of Spain, King Carol of Romania, and the Aga Khan. It was said that "Everybody talks to Albert but Albert talks only to the Aga Khan."

With World War II came the fall of Paris, and the restaurant seemed nearly finished. Octave Vaudable died in 1942, leaving the enterprise and its uncertain future to his son, Louis. The Nazis placed the restaurant under a *Kommissar,* a well-known Berlin restaurateur whose name shall be mercifully forgotten. Possibly owing to its *Merry Widow* fame— *The Merry Widow* and *Die Meistersinger von Nürnberg* were the Führer's favorite musical works—Maxim's became the hangout of Göring, Goebbels, et al. No one likes to remember those years, but Albert later said that "even Göring never got near table Number 16," a modest consolation. It is no longer a secret, however, that the British Secret Service had its operatives at Maxim's. Meetings of the top Nazis in the private dining rooms were at once reported to London. In 1944 Maxim's was closed, but only after Louis Vaudable had managed to remove thirty thousand bottles of wine to a hideout in Burgundy.

———

The reopening of Maxim's in 1946 marks the beginning of the latest chapter in the life of the apparently indestructible institution. The kings were either gone or had become ex-kings, but there were many customers among the old rich (the Rothschilds), the new superrich (Getty, Niarchos, Onassis), the fashion czars (Dior and Givenchy), stars of the stage and screen (Maurice Chevalier, Marlene Dietrich, Noël Coward, Maria Callas, and Charlie Chaplin), also Sacha Guitry, Colette, Arthur Rubinstein, and many, many others. By that time the place had become part and headquarters of the Société Maxim's, under its founder and chairman, Louis Vaudable. Now the corporation's worldwide activities include Les Caves Maxim's (wholesale wine merchants) and Les Cuisines Maxim's (frozen *plats cuisinés* sold in many countries). Maxim's makes guest appearances all over the world: in 1970 at the ninetieth-anniversary ball of the Boston Symphony Orchestra and in 1961 at the Restaurant de l'Exposition Française in Moscow. Ten years later, Maxim's experts arranged the banquets and official dinners given by the Shah of Iran in Persepolis during the 2,500th anniversary celebrations of the Persian Empire.

In short, Maxim's has become Big Business and, incidentally, a third-generation enterprise. In 1970 François Vaudable (who had wanted to become a scientist) decided to join his father in the management of the family empire. Four years later François became a director of Maxim's. He is a modest, relaxed young man who learned the business from scratch; he studied wines seriously with the late Édouard Pommier, the famous sommelier. François is unimpressed by the legend of Maxim's but delighted with it because it pays off handsomely. He is sometimes puzzled by what he calls the secret code of behavior at Maxim's.

"It does exist," he says, "but no one is able to define it. For instance, the same people who are relaxed at lunchtime when they sit at the omnibus and talk to each other across the tables would never do that at night, when Roger takes them into the *salle*. There they are formal, almost stiff. They greet each other correctly but wouldn't talk to people at another table. Strange, isn't it?"

Certain things are just "not done" at Maxim's, but again, it's hard to define them. People are supposed to have a good time, but they shouldn't get *too* drunk, not at Maxim's. Gentlemen will kindly wear a tie or will be lent one by the management. Maxim's is not an open-shirt joint, although elegant turtleneck sweaters are tolerated, especially when worn by world-famous conductors. The busiest seasons are from April to June and from September to December.

Lunch is now more important than it used to be, but it shouldn't be strictly a business affair. Women are welcome at Maxim's for *déjeuner,* particularly the kind of women Roger approves of. Though big deals, sometimes involving millions, are discussed in the omnibus, most men order Bordeaux or Champagne, or both. The Champagne is likely to be Maxim's own, the proprietor's house wine. At night the men bring their ladies (not necessarily their wives) into the *salle* and again order Bordeaux and/or Champagne, but rarely a Burgundy. Maxim's wine cellar is one of the finest in the world, no doubt about that, with over 120,000 bottles of sometimes priceless wines. (As Mr. Morgan might have said, if you ask for prices, don't go to Maxim's.) Originally, the cellars were located on the site where the American Embassy stands today.

———

I now understand (I didn't always) that women and sometimes even men like to see and be seen at Maxim's. Nothing has changed. One comes in and leaves one's coat at the wardrobe, high above. Paulette Payne, the famous hat-check lady and confidante of the high and the mighty, retired in 1974 after more than thirty years of service. On the walls are the playbills, the drawings by Sem, and the framed Peter Arno cartoon from *The New Yorker* showing a highly dissipated gentleman at the bar and the maître d'hôtel saying, "Ah, m'sieu, I have a table for you now." The new-old bar, now called l'Impériale, is on the second floor, created and beautifully decorated by Maurice Carrère. Next to it is the *salle* where the Club des Cent meets for *déjeuner* the first three Thursdays of the month. One member, the *brigadier,* is in charge of the lunch. He composes the menu, selects the wines, and with half a dozen others attends a dress rehearsal, followed by a review. The *déjeuner* is usually attended by one third of the membership. Roger is glad about the difficult guests who help him to keep everybody on their toes.

It's no news that one can eat very well at Maxim's. Alex Humbert, whom they called the *"chef des chefs,"* is no longer there, but his pupil and assistant, Michel Menant, "who possesses all the secrets of his maître," is now in charge of the kitchen *brigade* of twenty-four. The hardest thing is to choose well; there is a very large card with the celebrated *spécialités—sole braisée au vermouth Albert* (sole braised in vermouth), *noisettes d'agneau Édouard VII* (noisettes of lamb), *caneton nantais aux pêches* (duck with peaches), and so on. We wanted something light, so Roger recommended *coquilles Saint-Jacques au safran* (scallops in saffron sauce), also known as *coquilles Saint-Jacques Alex Humbert.* The complicated recipe was beautifully executed and finished, and it was strictly *grande cuisine.*

And the service is as good as it used to be, which means impeccable. Not many people at Maxim's have time to watch the service—there are so many supposedly interesting people to look at—but it is a pleasure to see the help at Maxim's at work under the omnipresent Roger. This is one of the last places on earth where service with a flourish is considered as important as the food and the wines. "The secret of Maxim's," says Roger, "has always been that our habitués are served what they like the way they like it, without having to ask for it." Not many places in the world can claim that.

Lunch may be "important," but the time to go to Maxim's is at night (unless you are a habitué who goes there several times a week, for lunch and dinner). Like an attractive woman of a certain age, Maxim's is most fascinating under soft, artificial lights, when the pink-shaded table lamps, the red-velvet banquettes, the gilt-framed mirrors, and the stained-glass roof bring back the colors and memories of a fin de siècle fairy tale. It is so kitschy that it is beautiful. The night we were there two large tables were occupied by young people. Roger was pleased. Many of them were the children and perhaps grandchildren of former habitués. They had inherited their elders' taste, money, and *snobisme.*

"Some of them are already difficult about where they sit," Roger said, with a fine smile. "They learn fast. Perhaps *papa* or *maman* told them that certain tables are just not possible." Still, he said, the presence of the young people proves that Maxim's remains alive. "They always come in groups, eight or twelve of them. It's rare that we have a young couple. I suppose they are comfortable only when they are together."

The Vaudables, *père* and *fils*, are glad that the young people are beginning to come to Maxim's.

"We don't want to rest on the legends and laurels of the past," says Louis Vaudable. "Maxim's should not be known mainly as a national monument."

"Absolutely," says his son, François. "We'll celebrate our hundredth anniversary in 1993, but, personally, I often find myself thinking of Maxim's at the year 2000."

February 1978

THE CHEFS

WHEN *MICHELIN* COMES KNOCKING

Joseph Wechsberg

How does it feel to be the owner of a distinguished two-star restaurant in Paris and to be told by three anonymous gentlemen who have just finished lunch that the *Guide Michelin* has just awarded you the coveted third star, which in France is akin to canonization? Jean-Claude Vrinat, whose father founded Le Taillevent in 1946, told me how he felt when exactly that happened to him. I was there on March 15, the day the new *Michelin* was put on sale. The Vrinats, *père et fils,* had not the faintest idea what was going to happen. There had been no rumor; no one had "leaked" the good news to them.

"They introduced themselves and told me we'd been promoted. I thought they'd given us another *fourchette*." (In the *Michelin* crossed forks denote the elegance of a restaurant; stars refer to the cuisine.) " 'No,' they said. We'd been given a third star. My first reaction of happiness was immediately tempered by a sense of worry. I knew we were going to have difficult times. I called in Claude Deligne, our chef; the inspectors congratulated him, and we had a *goutte* of Champagne."

Jean-Claude tried to telephone his father, but he was out. At seventy, André Vrinat is semiretired and only comes to the restaurant twice a week to relieve his son. "I finally reached Papa that night. He was pleased but less surprised than I. He said he'd expected it for a long time."

So have many serious eaters in Paris who agree that Taillevent almost never serves a disappointing meal. "It was overdue," one such gentleman with a triple chin told me, and he gave a resigned shrug, probably referring to the unfathomable ways of the Good Lord and the *Guide Michelin*. Taillevent is a wonderful place for people who like to dine in an elegant ambience, don't care to see or be seen, and value a quiet, unhurried atmosphere. The restaurant is located in a *hôtel particulier* built by Napoleon III in 1852 for the duc de Morny. It still has the genuine aristocratic touch: dark colors, deep rugs, wood paneling, old paintings, subdued lights—the sort of place where even captains of industry and members of the government lower their voices instinctively. Bankers and diplomats never raise theirs anyway.

Vrinat *père* comes from the Limousin in central France and was an engineer. Later he worked for Potel & Chabot, the famous catering firm, and finally opened a small place of his own in the rue Saint-Georges near the Opéra. He called it "Taillevent," the sobriquet of the famous chef Guillaume Tirel (1326–95), who wrote one of the oldest cookbooks, *Le Viandier*.

It is a French adage that great chefs and restaurateurs choose their métier under the influence of their mothers and grandmothers. In André Vrinat's case it was his grandmother. (His son didn't want to join the father and studied business administration, but now he loves being a restaurateur and has learned his métier well.)

The restaurant has long been famous for its cellar, considered by some the finest in Paris. In fact, the wines often divert people's attention from the classical cooking. Vrinat *père* had his wine list made up by the late Raymond Baudoin, one of the country's most respected wine connoisseurs, who also designed the wine lists for Fernand Point's Pyramide and Alexandre Dumaine's Hôtel de la Côte d'Or. Baudoin organized a group of fifteen backers, château owners and wine merchants, who sent their best wines to Taillevent and became symbolic shareholders. Among them was Douglas Dillon, the former United States ambassador and proprietor of the celebrated Château Haut-Brion.

In 1950 Vrinat moved the restaurant to its present location. In the cellar he keeps over thirty thousand bottles, and there is a reserve of fifty thousand more in Bougival. The wine list is magnificent in its scope, variety, and rarity. The oldest wine now on the list is an 1846 Château Lafite-Rothschild priced at 2,600 francs. Two years ago one could get an 1806 of that château for eight hundred francs, but we all know what happened to wine prices.

July 1973

La Grande Cuisine Française

Joseph Wechsberg

Michael Guérard is the owner and chef of Le Pot au Feu, an unfashionable-looking small restaurant in the unfashionable working-class suburb of Asnières. The rue des Bas looks like a fine setting for what the French call a *roman policier,* a mystery novel. But M. Guérard is often discussed among serious eaters in Paris, and lately it has sometimes been difficult to get a table at his restaurant, which seats only thirty people. Guérard belongs to the small group (about a dozen members) that calls itself, with frankness and without modesty, *"la grande cuisine française"*—no more, no less, no such old understatement as "Traditions et Qualité." The group includes some of the most interesting artists now performing on the French gastronomic scene. The unofficial spokesman is Paul Bocuse. Two celebrated members admitted to me, "Guérard is probably the most imaginative of all of us." Apparently Michel Guérard has what matters most to an artist— the respect of his fellow artists.

Guérard, a short, boyish-looking man, with thoughtful eyes and his hair combed down over his forehead, is forty and looks twenty-two. By now he may have moved to another location because the building where we went to dine, number 50, may soon be torn down; but he says he is going to stay in Asnières. He feels that if the customers like his place they will come all the way out to eat there; he is right. When we drove up the dark street, a sign at the corner said that the entrance was through *le jardin,* which turned out to be a couple of stunted trees with two small tables and two candles on them. To eat there, one must truly love Guérard's cooking.

The same attitude goes for the people inside. Le Pot au Feu is housed in a barnlike room, which some impressionable guests may call charming and others just so-so, with uncomfortable nylon-covered banquettes along the wall, red tablecloths and napkins, and a bar in the rear. It all sounds terrible but isn't. The night we were there the customers all seemed to know each other, with M. Guérard serving as the invisible link. The diners get two small pots of butter, one filled with sweet, the other with slightly salted. There is a small, exquisite wine list, but no one fusses. We had something I had never had before: a white, repeat *white,* Beaujolais, which was fresh and fruity and light. Though it was served in a pewter pitcher and they couldn't give me the exact source, it was unmistakably Beaujolais.

At the Pot au Feu the excitement is not the people but what is served on the plates. The plates are the largest I've seen for many years—not a bad idea, because the portions are enormous. M. Guérard came to our table, looking absentminded, a poet of the kitchen. I asked him where he had learned his art, and he said, *"Un peu partout,"* which was not particularly helpful. Later I heard that he'd been named "Best Pastry Worker in France" when he was at the Hôtel de Crillon and that he'd spent some time at Reginskaïa, a restaurant specializing in nostalgic Russian dishes.

No one at the Pot au Feu comes to see and be seen. There is a different kind of excitement. A double-chinned Frenchman next to us whistled admiringly as he was served the *merlan à la julienne de légumes selon Fernand Point.* Guérard, one of the few outstanding younger French chefs who is not a member of the School of Point, has long admired the great *maître* and named one of his most original creations in Point's honor. Guérard resembles the *maître* in his philosophy; he loves challenges and likes to make matters difficult for himself, and he has the needed imagination and technical skill. Other famous restaurants serve the expensive varieties of fish—sole, turbot, and *loup de mer.*

Guérard serves the lowly *merlan* (whiting), which, John M. Iversen of the Hôtel Lancaster said, "we serve the staff on Fridays." Guérard is no fool, though, and studied Escoffier, who loved some inexpensive fish, such as cod. ("When it [cod] is really fresh the delicious flavour of its flesh admits of its ranking among the finest of fish.") Guérard's *merlan* was delicious, poached in a consommé with vegetables and served with a farce made of mushrooms and truffles and a sauce containing a little butter but no cream. Characteristically, Guérard asked at the end of our dinner, "Was it light enough?"

The young kitchen artists in France understand that fewer people than before can afford to eat the heavy, creamy sauces made by the older chefs, no matter how excellent they are. Serious eaters are beginning to ask for lighter cooking even in the temples of French gastronomy where the word "calories" was once considered sacrilegious. This complicates matters for the chef. Guérard's light, almost transparent cooking tells the truth and nothing but the truth. One would immediately discover a wrong note. (There was none that night.) On the other hand, a chef who uses plenty of butter and cream may occasionally conceal some shortcomings. Yet Guérard and his friends are on the right track. If Fernand Point were alive, he would approve of the trend.

Taste, for instance, Guérard's *pâté d'anguille à la mousse de cresson*. It sounds easy: a pâté made of eel with a purée of watercress. Actually, the dish is a masterpiece of imagination, design, and execution. A lot of work (perhaps, one should say, of virtuoso technique) is done in the tiny kitchen, smaller than that in many American houses, where Guérard works with three young men and a dishwasher. But the size and appointments of a kitchen have no relation to the quality of the food produced in it. Everything must be carefully thought out and organized. The *salade gourmande* is just that: green beans, foie gras, asparagus, and truffles. The *terrine paysanne Prieuré Saint-Saturnin*, made with chicken and goose livers, was luscious but not very light. Unfortunately, it was not the season to order Guérard's *foie gras frais des Landes préparé à la maison*, which is said to be extraordinary. His latest creation is *poissons cuits sous les algues* (*suivant arrivage*), fish cooked under seaweed, which sounds quite attractive, but there was no *ar-*

rivage (delivery) when we were there. Another specialty is the *ragoût fin Bontoux*, made with *coquillettes*, truffles, foie gras, and sweetbreads. No wonder Guérard's fellow artists admire his imagination. It is matched by his fastidious standards: He makes the best out of the best available ingredients, which is the only way to practice gastronomy. He uses vinegar in some dishes and likes the contrast of sweet and sour—the Chinese influence—and his *canard confit à la maison,* cold or hot, is slightly caramelized and has the color of *canard laqué.*

It is easy to believe that Guérard was once named his country's best pastry worker. The *feuilleté de poire caramélisé* is hot *mille-feuilles* with caramelized pears and is simply exquisite. So is his *salade de pêches et fraises au Bordeaux.* Perhaps more interesting even is the *granité de chocolat amer et brioche rôtie,* a light sherbet made with finely crushed ice and very bitter chocolate. The Italians, who invented *granita,* mostly make it with syrup, flavored with coffee, lemons, or strawberries. Not M. Guérard, who produces a cold, bitter-chocolate sherbet, which contrasts with a hot, sweetish brioche. No doubt this is an artist going places fast. The *Guide Michelin* gives Guérard two stars; perhaps they feel the ambience is not quite up to the third star. He will get it eventually. Guérard understands the basic truth that gastronomy demands new-old ideas or old-new ideas, provokingly developed. He is always experimenting. A great cook never stops doing that.

April 1974

Jacques Manière's Human Factor

Joseph Wechsberg

Among serious Parisian epicures, a modest Left Bank restaurant—Au Pactole, 44, boulevard Saint-Germain—has for the past few years been an oasis of culinary progress and gastronomic imagination. Its owner, Jacques Manière, is a refreshing specimen, a great French chef more interested in creative cooking than in publicity and money. Manière will never get as rich as some of his avant-garde confreres who spend more time appearing on television or giving guest performances in Japan than working in their kitchens. Manière gets up at four in the morning and drives out to the new Halles at Rungis to select the best fish and shellfish and anything else that strikes his fancy, and only then does he go back to his kitchen and design the menu for the day. Once a week a large truck from Normandy pulls up, delivering cream and butter straight from the farm. Manière buys the best available *poulardes* from Bresse, "never less than five pounds," which taste beautiful and melt in the mouth. Manière confounded the pros by admitting that he is an autodidact. He began cooking at an age when other chefs had already opened their restaurants.

At fifty, Manière looks and walks like the young Jean Gabin playing a chef who is also an artist. Manière comes from the Périgord, which explains his love of truffles and truffled dishes, such as his *ragoût de truffes et foie gras.* As a young man he wanted to become a professional soldier. Fortunately for French gastronomy he didn't like the tough *régime* of Saint-Cyr, the French West Point. Instead, he went home and started a truffle-canning factory. Knowing a great deal about truffles but little about business, Manière canned first-rate truffles and went broke. He had always been an enthusiastic eater, and at that point he decided to become an enthusiastic cook.

Enthusiast, amateur, autodidact, artist—no wonder Manière is considered an eccentric in some conservative circles. A famous guide-book refused to list his restaurant because he was unwilling to play by the rules of the culinary game. His fierce sense of independence is demonstrated in some of his dishes done *à ma façon,* "the way I do it," which isn't always the way it's done in the books. But there have been other gifted dilettantes among the great French chefs. Raymond Thuilier of the Oustau de Baumanière was a painter before he began cooking. Amateurs feel less bound by traditions and often embark upon flights of imagination; fine French cooking needs them in order to be revitalized. Manière must have learned fast since he soon got a job in the kitchen of Lapérouse and later at Chez Max, where he ac-quired the necessary technique. Six years ago he left the suburb of Pantin and opened his small place, just forty seats, named after Pacto-lus, the river in ancient Lydia in which Midas bathed, leaving gold dust in the sands.

That's a good joke, since the Midas touch is one thing Manière doesn't care about. He considers fine cooking an art and himself an artist, with a right to artistic license. He likes difficult customers pro-vided they are enthusiasts and has no use for people who come to his place "to nourish themselves." He makes no compromise with quality. He gladly spends extra hours to please a demanding connoisseur; he expects his habitués to be as devoted to eating as he is to cooking. The principle isn't new. Fernand Point used to say that great cooking was "the finest butter and lots of time." Unfortunately some modern chefs don't want to take the time and spend the money. Manière respects the Old Masters but knows that French cuisine must not stand still. Today the trend is toward lighter dishes and subtler flavors. Even Escoffier couldn't (and wouldn't) cook today as he did sixty years ago.

Thus Manière's only problem is "the human factor." Just two dedicated young men work with him in his kitchen. They start at nine in the morning and sometimes are still there at eleven at night. The five people working in the dining room are also under pressure. Sixteen hours' work a day. (To show his appreciation, Manière stays closed on Sundays, throughout February, and for most of August.) It's always difficult to get a reservation. Someday, when he no longer finds people willing to work such long hours, he will limit the number of guests and work all by himself in the kitchen. That's the true spirit, and money be damned.

Manière's creations have that special quality of having been prepared especially for the diner. If I were a Rothschild I would try to hire him as my personal cook, but of course he wouldn't accept, and why should he? An artist needs absolute freedom to create. He hates routine and likes to experiment. "You make the same dish every day, and after a while, unless you are very careful, you may wind up in the valley of mediocrity," he says. "France lost her colonies, but she is still the empire of *la grande cuisine.*"

Once a couple of friends asked Manière to create something new in a few minutes. He made a soft-boiled egg, removed some of the liquid white, put in caviar, set the egg over an alcohol burner on a tripod, and reheated the egg with Armagnac. "Amusing but hardly gastronomy," he says with perfect frankness. But the *terrine de poisson* with a *mousse de cresson* is close to gastronomy, and the *coquilles Saint-Jacques au beurre blanc* are gastronomy, and so are the *ris de veau à ma façon* and the *poularde de Bresse à la vapeur, beurre de cerfeuil.* Manière knows the secret of preserving the original flavor and the freshness of the products he uses. Even his desserts, such as his pear sherbet with a light *tarte aux pommes,* testify to that secret. The wines are unpretentious but honest, as honest as everything else in his restaurant. The prices are moderate by present-day standards, but gastronomy can never be inexpensive. Don't bother to admire the paintings on the wall. The masterpieces at Au Pactole are on the plates, where they belong. One can't eat paintings.

It so happened that the evening before I visited Au Pactole, I had been at Lucas-Carton, once one of the most celebrated restaurants of

Paris. Some greatness was still there—the fin de siècle décor, the Limoges china, a number of distinguished older people, and also the cooking. The *potage Saint-Germain* was a chef d'oeuvre, and so was the *salmis de faisan,* aptly named after Lucullus. The *bécasse flambée* remains one of the great creations of French gastronomy. But that night the service was lackadaisical, the waiters were conversing with each other in front of the guests (and possibly about them, judging by their amusement), and the spirit of dedication was completely lacking. Lucas-Carton still has a great chef, a fine wine list, a beautiful décor, but today it seems to rely mainly on the glory of its past, and unless something is done, it may become a museum of *la grande cuisine.* I thought of it the following night when I sat in Jacques Manière's unpretentious restaurant, where an enthusiastic artist creates the glory of the future.

April 1973

YOUNG CHEFS OF PARIS

Naomi Barry

The food was beautiful, with tantalizing tastes and thought-provoking textures. Out of the kitchen to take a bow came the chef, baby-faced and boyishly slim. It was disconcerting. He is as young as he looks. And he is not alone. Artists tend to congregate in schools. Right now Paris counts at least a dozen culinary virtuosos in their twenties or just turned thirty. (Not by chance does French kitchen lingo refer to the stove as a piano, an instrument for artists.)

La nouvelle cuisine, la nouvelle vague. The youth brigades have their hands on some of the most dazzling restaurants of Paris—serious big houses and experimental little bistros requiring three days' advance booking. At issue is not Young Toque versus Old Hat, or Today supplanting Yesterday. Every currently successful Paris Young Toque worth his salt has in him a little bit of Carême and Escoffier, of Fernand Point and Alexandre Dumaine. If *la bande de Bocuse* has moved to the position of honorable Older Guard, it still takes a turn at the keyboard. "We owe Bocuse a lot," said Jean-Jacques Jouteux of Les Semailles, one of the present crop of dazzlers. "Before him, a chef was a laborer. Now he is respected as a professional man."

The new boys, bubbling with creative ambition, are busily inventing, innovating, improving, refining, and reviving with new twists classic French cuisine, which for the past few hundred years has been passed down from stirring spoon to saucepan. The process is not dissimilar to that of the Comédie-Française, where Molière's gestures and directions have been transmitted by one generation of actors to another, each of whom has added touches and variations.

Among today's bright young chefs there is both competition and camaraderie. It is not unusual to spot one of them on his closing day enjoying a meal in a colleague's establishment, testing his own performance by comparison and gaining a bit of inspiration for a culinary takeoff when he gets back to his own kitchens.

The track is flashy with talents: Jouteux, Denys Gentes of Clodenis, Gilbert Le Coze of Le Bernardin, Alain Dutournier of Le Trou Gascon, Daniel Metery of Le Lord Gourmand. From the field we have selected a yeasty quartet who reflect the tone of contemporary gastronomic Paris: Patrick Lenôtre of Le Pré Catelan; Dominique Bouchet of Jamin, Robert Vifian of Tan Dinh, and Jean-Michel Bedier of Chiberta.

—

Le Pré Catelan is a gorgeous folly in the Bois de Boulogne. Despite the pretty building in a stage setting of gardens and trees, it was a consistent flop. A few years ago it was taken over by Gaston Lenôtre, who saw in it an ideal ambience for the parties and receptions he caters.

Gaston is a clever Norman, and he was determined to float the derelict Pré Catelan to success. A comparatively small luxury restaurant was developed within the complex so Parisians would get in the habit of taking the road through the Bois. Wife Colette was detached from directing the Lenôtre pastry shops in Auteuil and Boulogne and entrusted with the refashioned dining room of Le Pré Catelan. For the important post of lord of the kitchen, Gaston chose his nephew Patrick Lenôtre, whom he had been grooming since the latter was eighteen years old, in 1968. For three years Patrick was thoroughly trained as a pastry chef and then graduated into catering. He left the family fold to work in big-time houses such as Paul Bocuse's, Roger Vergé's, Michel Guérard's, and the Haeberlin brothers' before returning to Uncle Gaston's catering headquarters at Plaisir, thirty-seven kilometers west of Paris. In 1976, when he was twenty-six, Patrick was given responsibility for Le Pré Catelan. This year the former white elephant was awarded its first star from the *Guide Michelin*.

Le Pré Catelan is about a fifteen-minute taxi run from the Étoile, but that scant quarter of an hour is equivalent to a trip far, far out of town. The route through the Bois is well marked, for Le Pré Catelan benefits from the same sort of official signposts as Bagatelle, the Polo, and the racecourses of Auteuil and Longchamp. The last stretch of road is a spur, leading only to the restaurant. Peace and Privilege might be the passwords.

The first impression is that of an estate: neoclassic main hall and rustic outbuildings, gardeners busy on the fringes, and polite welcomes from "family retainers." A house-proud quality is immediately apparent. Birds amid the bucolic setting and a sparkling glass of Champagne bring instant serenity to those in jangle (the usual state of escapees from the Champs-Élysées area). And the businessman hitched to his second-hour-day-month wristwatch suddenly decides that a two-hour lunch there is just the felicity he owes himself. In good weather tables are set up on the terrace with a backdrop of forest and the blissful quiet of no cars.

There is no skimping on details. The table bouquets are thoughtful, and all the arrangements are stylish. Typical of Le Pré Catelan's small touches are the Limoges ashtrays painted with a pastel of the restaurant. (I wonder how many of these are pocketed each year.) The *amuse-gueule* that accompany apéritifs are deluxe ministarters. Last time the assortment consisted of a poached quail's egg in a croustade, a smidgen of toast topped with red caviar, and a canapé of fresh duck liver.

Appetite aroused, one was eager for the first course, a stylish mélange of zucchini, carrots, artichokes, and asparagus bound with puréed fresh herbs to form a delightful *mosaïque de légumes.*

Patrick prefers cooking to pastry, finding the latter too inflexible in its rules, allowing little room for improvisation. "I am severe and critical," he said. "My basic structure is classical and traditional, but now I am seeking subtle expressions so that the dishes that come from my kitchen are really *les plats à moi.*"

———

Jamin has been a *gratin* restaurant of the Sixteenth Arrondissement since 1960. Over the years, Raymond Jamin, who had been maître d'hôtel at Le Grand Véfour, became known around town for his shrewd but expansive personality, his well-flavored Bordeaux accent, his prize trotting horses, and the consistently good food served in his plush but conventionally decorated establishment. The *Michelin* awarded the house two stars, the well-heeled clientele was constant, and everything seemed fine in the best of all possible worlds.

Then Gérard Besson, the chef who had brought on the stars, left to strike out on his own. The goings-on were well chronicled by the local gastronomic press. Jamin felt the thunder of impending doom, but the clouds kindly showered him with good fortune. To replace Besson, someone sent a stripling assistant chef from the Concorde Lafayette, a giant modern hotel near the Porte Maillot. Dominique Bouchet was twenty-five, good-looking, modest, conscientious. In near-panic, Jamin tossed him the responsibility of his kitchen.

Eighteen months later, Jamin is in a state of near-euphoria. "I'm having a second youth," he says, his wily face creased with smiles. The correct banality of the vermilion velvet interior remains, but the atmosphere has the fizz of gaiety. Dominique grasped the helm with such authority that Jamin retained its two-star status, despite the fact that *Michelin* customarily marks a major change by ripping off a star to make restaurateurs earn it back.

Dominique, a native of the Charente, is as happy about his position as the boss. "My dream was to work like this, with my hands, paying attention to every detail. I love to start with everyday things from everyday life—a little watercress, a potato, an olive—and transform them into beautiful things. I wouldn't change my profession for anything in the world.

"When I was seven or eight making mud pies, I already wanted to be a chef. I became an apprentice at fourteen. They gave me a dark blue apron to wear, and I was heartbroken. For me the white uniform represented the nobility of the profession. In three months I was handed a white apron. It was my recompense, and I was proud."

Raymond Jamin has always been punctilious about service, and he himself is a master of affable customer relations. Currently the Jamin service is hitting a high, a cunning blend of unobtrusive traditional care and informal enthusiasm about the dishes to be selected and served. The good humor is infectious. Your mood is lifted before the actual performance starts by the charm of the overture as the waiter helps you compose your menu. The dining room's staff, as young as the kitchen's, has the good sense to know that adopting the supercilious air of the old-fashioned maître d'hôtel would be plain silly.

Jamin's menu operates on merit without resort to headline-grabbing tricks. A second meal within a week confirmed the level of excellence. Scallops are a current darling with the top Paris chefs. Dominique features them in two guises. Cold, they are a first course enhanced with a dressing of walnut oil. Hot, they are a main course teamed with cooked endive.

A Jamin signature hors d'oeuvre since the restaurant's inception has been a plate of creamy scrambled eggs incorporating some edible luxury. For years the eggs were coupled with a fortune in black truffles. This season's note has been a generous dose of minced crayfish.

Time-consuming touches give the house its finesse. The noodles that accompany the fillets of sole are freshly prepared. The nut-bread rolls presented with the cheese platter are baked on the premises. The sherbets, the caramel and coconut ice creams, the petits fours—all are made out back.

When it is suggested at the beginning of your meal that you order a *tarte fine chaude aux pommes* for dessert, heed the suggestion. This open-faced honey-glazed apple tart constructed on a wisp of buttery crust is served warm, and it is the best of its genre I've yet encountered.

———

Robert Vifian, thirty-one, of Tan Dinh was born in Saigon. Just as the Spaniard Picasso, the Italian Modigliani, and the Japanese Foujita were all luminaries of the École de Paris, the Vietnamese Vifian is an integral member of today's Cooking School of Paris.

Robert works within his own Oriental tradition, although nowhere in the Far East will you find such dishes, for he has used his background as a springboard rather than a straitjacket. The style is Vietnamese, but the flavors transcend national frontiers. An impressive list of French-born chefs regard Tan Dinh's as a cuisine that merits critical scrutiny. After a bowl of his frogs' legs soup, Alain Senderens exclaimed, "Worthy of l'Archestrate."

There are a number of initial surprises. The restaurant, with its coral fabric walls and sober chandeliers, is far removed from the clichés of paper lanterns and dragon motifs. The wine list is connoisseur. The chef speaks fluent French and English and was graduated from the Sorbonne. His kitchen costume is blue jeans and tennis shoes.

In the evenings the service is handled by a white-coated waiter and three men in business suits coming after their day's work is done— father, brother, and uncle. Family solidarity. Father is a director of marketing for Citroën. Brother is a graduate student of pharmacology. Uncle has an office job.

In Saigon the Vifian family on both sides was well-to-do. Robert's maternal grandfather owned a shop selling imported delicacies that was the local equivalent of Fauchon. From the age of eleven the boy was given sips of French vintage wines to develop his palate. Grandpa had hired Saigon's best chef to come to the house and give lessons to his four daughters as part of their preparation for important marriages.

This girlhood training helped Robert's mother when the family came to Paris to begin life again. She did all the cooking in the bistro in the Fifth Arrondissement that they named Tan Dinh, meaning New Town. The boys were still in school. Robert did his homework in the restaurant. Because of his interest in food and wine, he began helping his mother.

Vifian *père*, a nimble, tennis-playing *bon vivant*, is planning to buy a pharmacy for older son Freddy. "We certainly had to do as much for Robert," he says, explaining Tan Dinh's move to larger quarters in the summer of 1978. Now Robert directs the kitchen with the aid of mother, aunt, and two helpers.

First-timers to Tan Dinh experience a tremor of surprise upon entering, fearful they have strayed into a French restaurant. The tasteful, subdued interior is neither an accident nor a holdover from a previous tenant. The Vifians were not out to capitalize on folklore. They wanted to be judged by the same standards as a comparable French restaurant. Paradoxically, the soft sell of the décor prepares the client for the out-of-the-ordinary. Furthermore, the understatement discreetly indicates that prices will not be Oriental-bargain but going-rate-Parisian.

In addition to Robert's personalized contributions, a few traditional dishes are always available, prepared with the care they once received in Mrs. Vifian's home. They are unusual to those not familiar with Vietnamese cuisine. *Cha gio* (pronounced "cha yo") is Vietnam's version of the Chinese spring roll. At Tan Dinh it is called *pâte impériale.* The crisply deep-fried rolls are presented surrounded with their fixings. You go to work making neat packets: first a *cha gio,* then a wee slice of pickled carrot, perhaps a bit of cucumber, a sprig of mint, then the careful wraparound with a salad leaf (romaine is good) and a dip into the sauce. Forget the chopsticks. This is irresistible finger food.

Noodles are a specialty of the Orient. At Tan Dinh an individual portion adds up to three rice bowls full. Topped with an exquisite sauce of shrimp and vegetables, they are good to the point of soul satisfaction. No doubt a similarly seduced Marco Polo brought back the noodles of the East to inspire the pasta of the West. Typifying Robert's interchange between the two worlds, his fillet of beef, the most tender and flavorful imaginable, is a Western dish treated in an Oriental manner.

———

The topography of the Champs-Élysées is like the backbone of a fish, the main thoroughfare with small vertebrae leading off from either side. The Champs are now as populous as the Grands Boulevards and no longer fashionable; the *haute couture* and the class restaurants are all in the side streets.

Chiberta is located on the short rue Arsène-Houssaye at the Étoile end of the Champs-Élysées. It is the most New York–in–spirit restaurant in Paris, even though most of the customers speak French and the acme of French crystal, flatware, and porcelain is laid on the shrimp-bisque tablecloths.

Detractors criticize the place as too glitteringly perfect, not that anyone can fault the supermodern air-conditioning system that can aspirate every curl of smoke within seconds. The admirers who keep Chiberta sold-out represent a slice of successful Paris in the arts, politics, communications, and big business. If the atmosphere suggests Manhattan's The Four Seasons, that is fine with the local customers. The Concorde set is not attracted to Quaint on its home grounds.

Chiberta has had a meteoric career since it appeared on the Paris scene at the end of 1976. Within a few months it had won the annual prize given by the Académie-Kléber-Colombes. The epitome of sleek chic contemporary, Chiberta has a superlative host in Louis-Noël Richard and an interesting young chef, Jean-Michel Bedier.

A round-faced, ginger-haired Burgundian, looking younger than his thirty-two years, Bedier claims no mystic vocation, saying only, "I was a dunce in school." Homework may have been torture, but helping *maman* and *grand-mère* in the kitchen was a pleasure. For the past twelve years he has been a Parisian, beginning as low man on the totem pole at the Relais Paris-Est. From there he moved to the kitchen of Georges Garin, then the most famous chef in Paris. Next step was Le Camélia in the suburb of Bougival, regarded as a top training ground.

Sticking to the periphery, Bedier went to the dreary northern suburb of Gennevilliers and earned a *Michelin* star for a restaurant there called Julius. Chiberta was his return to the heart of the capital. The stars were right.

He had a free hand in a splendidly equipped kitchen. His recipes are evanescent. It is rare for tomorrow's dish to be precisely like today's. He likes to play the market. What looks good to him when buying determines an alteration here or an adjustment there.

He likes his sauces short, his recipes provocative, and his primary ingredients barely transformed by heat. A gentle shock of surprise is fun, but his personal rule is demanding: A Jean-Michel Bedier dish must be *bon et beau.*

Because the proof of this pudding is in the eating, here is a sampling of recipes from four bright young chefs of Paris Present.

BAVAROIS DE SAUMON FUMÉ CHIBERTA
(*Smoked Salmon Molds*)

Line 4 timbale, charlotte, or other deep molds, each 3 to 4 inches in diameter at the top, rinsed, with ¾ pound very thinly sliced smoked salmon. Trim any overhanging salmon and in a food processor fitted with the steel blade purée it.

In a small bowl beat ½ cup crème fraîche until it holds soft peaks. In a bowl combine the puréed smoked salmon, 4 teaspoons red salmon roe, preferably Russian, and ¼ teaspoon cayenne. Gently fold in the crème fraîche, divide the *bavarois* mixture among the molds, and chill it for 1 hour. Run a thin knife around the inside of each mold and invert each mold with a sharp rap onto a plate. Nap and surround each mold with *coulis de tomates frais* and sprinkle it with snipped chives. Serves 4.

COULIS DE TOMATES FRAIS CHIBERTA
(*Fresh Tomato Purée*)

In a blender or in a food processor fitted with the steel blade purée 4 tomatoes, peeled, seeded, and chopped, and force the purée through a fine sieve into a bowl. Season the purée with salt and pepper and chill it. Makes about 1 cup.

TERRINE DE RAIE JAMIN
(*Skate Terrine with Scallop Mousse*)

In a large flameproof baking dish combine 4 pounds skate with water to cover, 2 tablespoons vinegar, 1 tablespoon salt, and a cheesecloth bag containing 6 sprigs of parsley, 6 peppercorns, 1 teaspoon thyme, and 1 bay leaf. Bring the liquid to a boil and poach the skate over low heat for 5 minutes. Let the skate cool in the liquid, transfer it with a slotted spatula to a cutting board, and skin and bone it.

In a small heavy saucepan reduce 1 cup white fish stock over high heat to 2 tablespoons. In a food processor fitted with the steel blade or in a blender in batches purée 1 pound sea scallops, rinsed, with 2 teaspoons salt and ½ teaspoon white pepper. Transfer the purée to a metal bowl, set the bowl in a larger bowl filled with cracked ice, and beat the purée until it is cold and thick. Beat in 3 egg whites, 1 at a time, and the reduced fish stock. Beat in 1⅓ cups crème fraîche, about ¼ cup at a time, until it is incorporated and the mousse is fluffy. Chill the mousse, covered, for 25 minutes.

Spoon one third of the mousse into a buttered 1½-quart rectangular ceramic or glass terrine, cover it with half of the skate, and continue to layer the mousse and skate, ending with a layer of mousse. Rap the pan sharply to expel any bubbles and smooth the top with a spatula. Put the terrine in a baking pan, add enough hot water to the pan to reach halfway up the sides of the terrine, and bake the terrine, covered with a buttered sheet of wax paper and a triple layer of foil, in a preheated moderately slow oven (325°F) for 2 hours. (The water in the baking pan should be just hot.) Remove the terrine from the baking pan, let it cool, and chill it for at least 12 hours, or longer, if possible.

Remove the foil and wax paper and run a thin knife around the inside of the terrine. Dip the pan in hot water for 2 to 3 seconds and invert a platter over it. With a sharp rap, invert the terrine onto the platter. Blot up any liquid with paper towels. Slice the terrine with a serrated knife and serve it surrounded with *sauce tomate froide*. Serves 6 to 8.

SAUCE TOMATE FROIDE JAMIN
(*Cold Tomato Sauce*)

In a food processor fitted with the steel blade or in a blender purée ¾ pound tomatoes, peeled, seeded, and chopped, and force the purée through a fine sieve into a bowl. Stir in 3 tablespoons white wine vinegar and add 2 tablespoons olive oil in a stream, beating the sauce until it is well combined. Add 1 tablespoon minced tarragon and 2 mint leaves, snipped. Makes about 1 cup.

ASPERGES ET SAUMON CHIBERTA
(*Salmon with Asparagus*)

Purée 4 tomatoes, peeled and seeded, through the fine disk of a food mill into a saucepan and cook the purée over moderately high heat, stirring, until the liquid has evaporated completely. Season the purée with salt and pepper, measure it, and chill it.

In a ceramic or stainless-steel bowl combine the purée with twice its volume in whipped cream, folding in the cream a little at a time until it is well incorporated. Add Worcestershire sauce, salt, and pepper to taste, transfer the sauce to a sauceboat, and garnish it with mint leaves.

In a large skillet cook a ½-pound salmon steak, skinned, boned, sliced into 8 scallops, and flattened between sheets of wax paper, in ¼ cup clarified butter over moderately high heat for 5 seconds on each side, or until it is firm.

Remove and discard the coarse stems from 2 bunches of watercress, rinsed and patted dry, sprinkle the watercress with olive oil and salt to taste, and divide it among the lower third of 4 plates. Put 2 salmon scallops over each mound of watercress, sprinkle them with snipped chives, and on the upper two thirds of each plate arrange 4 cooked asparagus in a fan design. Serve the dish with the tomato sauce. Serves 4.

BAR AU BEURRE BLANC JAMIN
(*Sea Bass with Vegetables*)

Have the fishmonger skin and fillet a 5- to 6-pound sea bass and cut each fillet into 3 scallops.

In a saucepan cook ½ pound carrots, cut crosswise into 1½-inch lengths and each length trimmed into a neat oval, in 1 quart boiling salted water over high heat for 7 to 8 minutes, or until they are just tender. In another saucepan cook ½ pound small white onions in 1 quart boiling salted water over high heat for 5 to 6 minutes, or until they are just tender. In a small enameled or stainless-steel saucepan cook 6 mushrooms, trimmed, in 2 cups water with 1 tablespoon lemon juice and 1 teaspoon salt over moderate heat for 5 to 6 minutes, or until they are just tender.

In a large enameled or stainless-steel roasting pan combine 1 cup each of dry white wine, white fish stock, and thinly sliced fennel and ½ cup chopped shallots. Bring the liquid to a boil over high heat and reduce it for 5 minutes. Add the fish and cook it for 1 to 2 minutes on each side, or until it just flakes when tested with a fork. Transfer the fish with a slotted spatula to a platter and keep it warm. Reduce the cooking liquid over high heat for 3 to 4 minutes, or until it is syrupy. Add ⅔ cup heavy cream and reduce the mixture over high heat for 3 minutes. Whisk in 1 stick (½ cup) firm but not hard butter, cut into 6 pieces, 1 piece at a time, adding each new piece before the previous one has completely melted. Strain the sauce through a fine sieve into a bowl and season it with salt and white pepper. Divide the sauce among 6 heated plates, put a bass scallop in the center of each plate, and arrange the vegetables decoratively around the fish. Serves 6.

FRICASSÉE DE HOMARD CHIBERTA
(*Lobster Fricassee*)

In a kettle bring 4 quarts salted water to a boil with 2 tablespoons vinegar, add two 1½-pound lobsters, and cook them over high heat for 2 minutes. Transfer the lobsters with tongs to a cutting board and shell them. Force the coral, if any, through a fine sieve into a small bowl.

In a saucepan cook ½ cup each of diced carrot, diced celery, and diced turnip with salt and pepper to taste in 3 tablespoons butter, covered, over moderately low heat for 10 minutes, or until the vegetables are just tender. Transfer the vegetables to a bowl.

In another saucepan cook ½ cup green beans, trimmed and cut into 1½-inch lengths, in 2 quarts boiling salted water over high heat for 3 minutes. Add ½ cup each of snow peas, trimmed, frozen green peas, and frozen lima beans and cook the vegetables for 3 minutes more, or until they are just tender. Drain the vegetables in a colander, refresh them under running cold water, and transfer them to the bowl.

In a large skillet combine the lobster meat, 4 teaspoons dry sherry, and curry powder, salt, and pepper to taste and steam the lobster, covered, over moderately high heat for 1 minute. Add ½ cup heavy cream and reduce the sauce over high heat for 2 minutes, or until it coats the back of a spoon. Add the vegetables, the puréed coral, if any, and salt and pepper to taste and simmer the fricassee for 1 to 2 minutes, or until the vegetables are heated through. Stir in 2 tablespoons softened butter. Transfer the fricassee to heated plates. Serves 4.

FILET DE BOEUF AU CITRON TAN DINH
(*Marinated Fillet of Beef*)

In an enameled or stainless-steel saucepan combine ⅔ cup each of chicken broth and Asian soy sauce, ⅓ cup lemon juice, ¼ cup sugar, 1 tablespoon each of salt and *wasabi* (Japanese horseradish, available at Asian groceries), ¼ teaspoon each of pepper, cinnamon, and ground star anise, and freshly grated nutmeg to taste. Bring the mixture to a boil over moderately high heat, skim the froth that rises to the surface, and let the marinade cool.

With the point of a sharp knife make several small incisions in a 1½-pound fillet of beef, well trimmed. Divide 2 teaspoons each of minced lemon peel and peppercorns among the incisions, add the meat to the marinade, and let it marinate for 30 minutes. Transfer the meat with a slotted spatula to a cutting board, pat it dry with paper towels, and halve it crosswise. Strain the marinade into a bowl and reserve ½ cup of it.

In a small saucepan combine the reserved marinade, ½ cup chicken broth, and 1 tablespoon potato starch. Bring the liquid to a boil over moderate heat, cook the sauce for 1 to 2 minutes, or until it is slightly thickened, and keep it warm, covered.

Broil the meat on a broiler rack under a preheated broiler about 4 inches from the heat for 3 minutes on each side for rare meat. Trans-

fer the meat to a cutting board, let it stand for 2 minutes, and cut it into
¼-inch slices. Divide the meat among 4 plates, nap it with the sauce,
and sprinkle it with snipped chives. Garnish each plate with soft-leafed
lettuce and slices of tomato and lemon. Serves 4.

PÂTES FRAÎCHES DU TAN DINH
(*Noodles with Shrimp and Vegetables*)

Put 3 cups flour in a bowl, make a well in the center, and add 3 eggs,
lightly beaten, ¼ cup cold water, 1 teaspoon baking soda, and a pinch
of salt. Combine the mixture well, adding more water if necessary, several drops at a time, to form a firm ball of dough. Let the dough rest,
covered with an inverted bowl, for 1 hour. Knead and roll three fourths
of the dough, reserving the remaining dough, covered and chilled, for
another use, and cut it into noodles.

In a kettle bring 6 quarts water to a boil with 2 tablespoons salt.
Arrange the noodles in a wire basket, lower the basket into the kettle,
and cook the noodles for 30 seconds, or until they are *al dente*. Lift the
basket from the water, drain the noodles, and transfer them to a bowl.
Toss them with ¼ cup peanut oil.

In a large skillet stir-fry 1 large green pepper, halved lengthwise and
thinly sliced crosswise, in 3 tablespoons peanut oil over high heat for
10 seconds. Add 1 cup thinly sliced onion, 1 large zucchini, scrubbed,
trimmed, halved lengthwise, and cut crosswise into ¼-inch slices,
4 teaspoons tomato paste, and 2 teaspoons minced garlic and stir-fry
the mixture for 10 seconds. Add ½ pound shrimp, shelled, deveined,
and halved lengthwise, and stir-fry the mixture for 10 seconds. Add
1 cup canned chicken broth and the noodles and stir-fry the mixture
for 15 seconds, or until the noodles are heated through. Divide the
mixture among 4 heated bowls and garnish it with coriander leaves.
Serves 4.

TO KNEAD AND ROLL PASTA DOUGH
Set the smooth rollers of a pasta machine at the highest number (10 on
many machines). (The rollers will be wide apart.) Divide each pound
of dough into 6 pieces and flatten 1 piece into a rough rectangle. Cover
the remaining pieces with an inverted bowl. Dust the dough with flour
and feed it through the rollers. Fold the dough in half and feed it
through the rollers 8 or 9 times more, folding it in half each time

and dusting it with flour if necessary to prevent it from sticking. Turn the dial down one notch (to 9 on many machines) and feed the dough through the rollers without folding. Continue to feed the dough through the rollers without folding, turning the dial one notch lower each time, until the lowest or second-lowest notch is reached. The pasta should be a smooth, long sheet 4 or 5 inches wide and about ⅟₁₆ inch thick. Knead and roll the remaining dough in the same manner.

TO CUT NOODLES

Use the blades of a pasta machine that will cut dough into ¼-inch-wide strips. Feed one end of a sheet of dough through the blades, holding the other end straight up from the machine. Catch the strips from underneath the machine before the sheet goes completely through the rollers and put the cut strips lightly across floured jelly-roll pans, or let them hang over the tops of straight-backed chairs. Let the strips dry for 30 minutes.

CRÈME CARAMEL AU GINGEMBRE TAN DINH
(*Caramel Custards with Ginger*)

In a heavy saucepan combine ½ cup sugar and ¼ cup each of peeled and grated gingerroot and water and boil the liquid, washing down any sugar crystals clinging to the sides of the pan with a brush dipped in cold water, for 7 minutes. Transfer the ginger with a slotted spoon to a bowl and reserve it. Cook the syrup over moderate heat, undisturbed, until it is a deep caramel. Divide the caramel among four ¾-cup lotus-shaped bowls or ramekins and coat the bottoms evenly.

In a saucepan scald 2 cups milk with ½ cup sugar and the reserved ginger. In a bowl beat 4 egg yolks and 2 whole eggs with a pinch of salt until they are just combined. Strain the milk into the egg mixture, stirring, and discard the ginger. Skim the froth from the surface and divide the mixture among the bowls or ramekins. Put the bowls or ramekins in a baking pan and add enough hot water to the pan to reach halfway up the sides of the bowls or ramekins. Bake the custards, covered with a baking sheet, in a preheated moderately slow oven (325°F) for 35 to 40 minutes, or until they are just set. Remove the custards from the pan, let them cool until they are room temperature, and decorate each one with a small piece of crystallized ginger. Serves 4.

TARTES FINES CHAUDES AUX POMMES JAMIN
(*Hot Apple Tarts*)

Make puff paste and give it 2 more turns. Roll the dough into a ¹⁄₁₆-inch-thick round on a floured surface and with a 6-inch round cutter cut out 6 rounds. Invert the rounds onto a moistened baking sheet and chill them for 30 minutes.

Divide 6 Golden Delicious apples, peeled, cored, and very thinly sliced, decoratively on the dough, sprinkle them with ½ cup sugar, and dot each tart with 1 tablespoon butter, cut into 3 pieces. Bake the tarts in a preheated hot oven (425°F) for 20 to 25 minutes, or until the apples and pastry are golden. Brush the tarts with honey and serve them warm with crème fraîche. Serves 6.

GRATIN DE FRUITS ROUGES LE PRÉ CATELAN
(*Strawberries with Sabayon Sauce*)

Divide 1 pint strawberries, hulled, among 4 individual gratin dishes and sprinkle each dish with 1½ teaspoons sugar, or to taste. In a small heavy saucepan cook 2 egg yolks, ¼ cup sugar, and 1 tablespoon cold water over low heat, whisking, for 5 to 7 minutes, or until the mixture is thick. Whisk in 1 tablespoon heavy cream and 1 teaspoon *eau-de-vie de framboise* or *eau-de-vie de fraise*. Divide the mixture among the dishes and put the dishes under a preheated broiler for 1 to 2 minutes, or until the sabayon is golden. Serves 4.

November 1979

WHEN I WAS GREEN

Patric Kuh

A certain solidarity exists among the younger cooks and assistants in good Parisian restaurant kitchens. They all work the same grueling double shifts. They all disdain the high-rent neighborhoods where the restaurants are located. Even their skin seems to break out in unison, from jobs that essentially require them to stand before an open furnace for twelve hours a day. I once was proud to be part of such a tight, gritty fraternity. My rite of passage? The cooking of asparagus.

The year was 1984. The setting, Restaurant Guy Savoy (then with one *Michelin* star, on the rue Duret; today with two, on the rue Troyon). The dish was a delicate appetizer called *huîtres aux asperges* (oysters with asparagus). Each day before service began, the oysters were opened and the asparagus stalks cooked, then puréed. Their tips were blanched separately. Just before the dish was delivered to the table, the purée was heated and the tips and oysters warmed in oyster water. Everything was then plated and crowned with a sprig of chervil in an arrangement that suggested both the pastoral and the maritime. The slightest variation in temperature or presentation would send the dish from the domain of the sublime to that of the absurdly simple—a fate that seemed to loom especially large when I, a student recently promoted from cleaning wild duck in the basement, came upstairs to the kitchen to be in charge of cooking the asparagus.

"You're not in California now," my immediate supervisor, Gaetan, a nineteen-year-old from the Vendée, would say each time I gave him yet another underdone asparagus tip. (Never mind that, as yet, I'd never been to California. To him, the state had an obvious connection to underdone vegetables.) Or I'd cook the tips a second too long, and his eyes would make stabbing motions toward the blender, as if to command, "Get those puréed before anyone *else* tastes them!" I'd jump on that blender like a manic soda jerk. I knew the score. The chef wouldn't go off on *me*; he'd go off on Gaetan. For if I couldn't cook an asparagus, then Gaetan couldn't cook an asparagus. In fact, if *I* couldn't cook an asparagus, then *Gaetan* would never be a chef.

The different levels of pressure under which we at the bottom rungs worked were clearest during the *coupure*, the break between lunch and dinner. In the winter, few of us ventured farther than the café on the corner, where we'd stand at the zinc counter, too poor to sit down. But there the unity ended. At one end of the counter converged the unpaid students and *stagiaires;* at the other, clustered around the pinball machine in a cloud of Gitane smoke, were the *real* cooks—the ones who'd already had their mettle tested. They had to put up with us greener hands in the kitchen—but not here, not on their own time. They needed a good reference to move on to the next great kitchen; we rookies were just in it for the recipes. ("You know when they start taking pictures of the food, they're fixing to leave," our bosses liked to quip.) If any one of us hoped to make it over to their end of the zinc, we had to prove ourselves first.

My opportunity came during a particularly busy lunch. To my growing dismay, every second order that was called out (to an immediate *"Oui, chef"* response) was for *huîtres aux asperges.* Standing beside me, furiously working the vegetable station, Gaetan whispered urgently, "Got enough?" I didn't—but there were crates of asparagus downstairs in the cold room. I'd have to cook them in the middle of the service. "I will," I answered.

I placed a pot of salted water on the hottest part of the flattop and raced downstairs. I grabbed the asparagus, lined them up, and cut them. Back upstairs the water was at a rolling boil. I threw in the asparagus tips, and with a metal bowl in hand, ran to the ice machine, body-checking a waiter on the way. On my way back to the stove, I seized a slotted spoon and plunged it into the pot, without even tasting one asparagus. In two swift moves, I had all the tips in the ice bath, the cooking stopped dead.

Not thirty seconds later, the chef said, *"Asperges,"* like a surgeon asking for a scalpel. Gaetan set the warmed tips beside him. But the chef didn't plate the orders immediately. First, he took a tip from the pan and, with the eyes of the kitchen on him, bit into it. Gaetan swallowed. I swallowed. Everyone, even Hassan the dishwasher, swallowed. There was more swallowing going on in that kitchen than in the dining room. Then, without saying a word, the chef resumed assembling the orders. I exhaled. No comment. That was as good as it got here.

And so it was, wordlessly, that afternoon that Gaetan waved me over from the other end of the zinc, and I joined the other young cooks around the pinball machine.

ASPARAGUS AND GRUYÈRE TART

Serves 8 (lunch main course)
Active time: 1¼ hr   Start to finish: 2¾ hr
  Black pepper and sour cream pastry dough (recipe follows)
  3   lb thick white or green asparagus, trimmed to 6 inches and
      peeled
  ½   teaspoon kosher salt plus additional for sprinkling
  1   cup heavy cream
  2   large eggs
  ¼   teaspoon freshly grated nutmeg
  1   cup finely grated Gruyère

  Special equipment: a round pizza pan (13 inches in diameter, not including rim) and pie weights or raw rice

Make crust:
Roll out pastry dough on a floured surface into a 15½-inch round. Transfer to pizza pan by rolling dough around rolling pin and unrolling it across pan. Trim edge just enough to make even, then fold

over and pinch to form a ½-inch-high, double-thick side. Prick bottom of shell all over with a fork and chill until firm, at least 30 minutes.

Preheat oven to 375°F.

Line shell with foil and fill with pie weights or raw rice. Bake in middle of oven until sides are firm, about 20 minutes. Remove foil and weights carefully and bake shell until golden, about 10 minutes more, then cool.

Prepare filling while shell cools:
Layer asparagus on a steamer rack, sprinkling each layer with kosher salt to taste. Steam, covered, over boiling water until completely tender but not mushy, about 8 minutes for green asparagus or 12 for white, then transfer to a bowl of ice water to stop cooking. Drain well and pat dry with paper towels.

Whisk together cream, eggs, ½ teaspoon kosher salt, and nutmeg, then season lightly with pepper. Pour custard evenly in tart shell.

Top filling and bake tart:
Sprinkle custard with two thirds of cheese, then arrange spears in custard, tips out (like the spokes of a wheel). Sprinkle remaining cheese over top.

Bake tart in middle of oven until custard is set, about 20 minutes. Then broil tart 2 to 3 inches from heat until golden, 1 to 2 minutes.

Cooks' note:
If you don't have a pizza pan, you can use a 12-inch tart pan (you'll need to trim asparagus to 5½ inches).

BLACK PEPPER AND SOUR CREAM PASTRY DOUGH

Makes enough for a 13-inch tart shell
Active time: 30 min   Start to finish: 1½ hr

This dough would make a delicious crust for any kind of savory tart, such as a quiche.

2¼ cups all-purpose flour
1   teaspoon salt
¾   teaspoon black pepper
⅛   teaspoon sugar
1¼ sticks (10 tablespoons) cold unsalted butter, cut into bits
⅓   cup cold vegetable shortening

3 tablespoons sour cream
3 tablespoons ice water

Blend together flour, salt, pepper, sugar, butter, and shortening with your fingertips or a pastry blender until most of mixture resembles coarse meal with remainder in small (roughly pea-size) lumps. Stir together sour cream and ice water, then stir into dough with a fork until incorporated. Gather dough into a ball.

Flatten dough into a 6-inch square on a lightly floured surface. Roll out into a roughly 18-by-6-inch rectangle and fold into thirds (like a letter) to form a 6-inch square. Turn dough so an open-ended side is nearest you, then roll out dough into an 18-by-6-inch rectangle again, dusting work surface with flour as necessary. Fold into thirds same as above.

Repeat rolling and folding 1 more time, then chill dough, wrapped in plastic wrap, at least 1 hour.

Cooks' note:
Dough can be chilled up to 1 day.

ROAST CHICKEN WITH ASPARAGUS, MOREL, AND PEARL-ONION RAGOUT

Serves 4
Active time: 1 hr   Start to finish: 1¼ hr
   10 oz pearl onions
   1 (3- to 3½-lb) chicken, excess fat removed and legs tied
   1 tablespoon olive oil
   4 tablespoons unsalted butter (2 tablespoons cold, 2 tablespoons softened)
   1 lemon, halved
   1 oz small dried morel mushrooms
   1 cup warm water
   1 lb medium green asparagus, peeled and trimmed
   Kosher salt to taste
   ¼ cup dry white wine

Preheat oven to 425°F.
Blanch onions in boiling salted water 1 minute. Drain in a colander and rinse under cold running water to stop cooking. Trim root ends and peel.

Pat chicken dry. Coat a 17-by-12-inch flameproof roasting pan with oil and put chicken in pan. Rub 2 tablespoons softened butter into skin over entire chicken. Season chicken inside and out with salt and pepper. Put 1 lemon half in cavity and squeeze remaining half over chicken.

Roast chicken in middle of oven 20 minutes. Baste chicken, then continue to roast, basting about every 7 minutes, 20 minutes more. Scatter onions around chicken and continue to roast, turning onions and basting every 7 to 8 minutes, until chicken is golden and a thermometer inserted into fleshy part of a thigh registers 170°F (juices will run clear), 25 to 35 minutes more.

Once chicken begins roasting, soak morels in warm water 20 minutes. Lift mushrooms out of water, squeezing excess liquid back into bowl, and reserve liquid. Rinse morels thoroughly to remove grit and squeeze dry. Trim any tough stems. Pour reserved soaking liquid through a sieve lined with several layers of cheesecloth or a paper towel into a small bowl.

Cut asparagus diagonally into 2-inch lengths. Arrange on a steamer rack and sprinkle with kosher salt. Steam asparagus, covered, over boiling water until crisp-tender, about 5 minutes, then transfer to a bowl of ice water to stop cooking.

Transfer roast chicken to a platter, then discard string and cover chicken loosely with foil. Transfer onions and pan juices to 2 separate small bowls (do not clean roasting pan). Skim and discard fat from juices. Set roasting pan over a burner. Add wine and deglaze by boiling over high heat, stirring and scraping up brown bits, until reduced to about 2 tablespoons. Add pan juices from bowl, any juices that have accumulated on platter (from chicken), mushroom-soaking liquid, and morels, then boil until liquid is reduced to about ⅓ cup.

Cut remaining 2 tablespoons butter into pieces and add to morels with onions and asparagus. Cook over moderately high heat, shaking pan, until butter is just incorporated and vegetables are glazed. Season vegetables with salt and pepper and spoon around chicken.

White Asparagus with Truffle Vinaigrette

Serves 4 (first course)
Active time: 30 min   Start to finish: 45 min

White asparagus has a delicate flavor that works especially well with our truffle vinaigrette, but try the dish with green asparagus, too.

1½ tablespoons sherry vinegar
1½ teaspoons fresh lemon juice
1   (15-gm) bottled black truffle (1 inch in diameter), finely minced
½   teaspoon kosher salt plus additional for sprinkling
4½ tablespoons hazelnut or walnut oil
1½ tablespoons chicken broth or truffle liquid from bottle
1½ lb white asparagus, peeled and trimmed

Garnish: fresh chervil sprigs or chopped fresh chives

Whisk together vinegar, lemon juice, truffle, kosher salt, and pepper to taste. Add oil in a slow stream, whisking. Whisk in broth and season with more salt and pepper if necessary.

Arrange asparagus on a steamer rack and sprinkle with kosher salt to taste. Steam asparagus, covered, over boiling water until tender, about 10 minutes for white (4 to 6 for green).

Transfer asparagus with tongs to paper towels and pat dry. Divide among 4 plates, then spoon vinaigrette over and serve warm.

CRÈME D'ASPERGES
(*Cream of Asparagus Soup*)

Serves 4
Active time: 20 min   Start to finish: 50 min
2   lb green asparagus, trimmed
1   large onion, chopped
3   tablespoons unsalted butter
5   to 6 cups chicken broth
½   cup crème fraîche or heavy cream
¼   teaspoon fresh lemon juice, or to taste

Cut tips from 12 asparagus 1½ inches from top and halve tips lengthwise if thick. Reserve for garnish. Cut stalks and all remaining asparagus into ½-inch pieces.

Cook onion in 2 tablespoons butter in a 4-quart heavy pot over moderately low heat, stirring, until softened. Add asparagus pieces and salt and pepper to taste, then cook, stirring, 5 minutes. Add 5 cups broth and simmer, covered, until asparagus is very tender, 15 to 20 minutes.

While soup simmers, cook reserved asparagus tips in boiling salted water until just tender, 3 to 4 minutes, then drain.

Purée soup in batches in a blender until smooth, transferring to a bowl (use caution when blending hot liquids), and return to pan. Stir in crème fraîche, then add more broth to thin soup to desired consistency. Season with salt and pepper. Bring soup to a boil and whisk in remaining tablespoon butter.

Add lemon juice and garnish with asparagus tips.

Cooks' note:
Soup keeps, covered and chilled, 2 days. If making ahead, add last tablespoon butter and lemon juice after reheating.

March 2001

AMERICANS IN PARIS

A Memory of Alice B. Toklas

Naomi Barry

The most memorable table I have known in Paris was in an apartment over a printing plant at 5, rue Christine. The entrance was little better than a slum, but in the old quarter of Paris the entrance tells little. Once you were inside, the rooms were spacious and the furniture, the *objets d'art*, the bold individuality of taste, the reflection of strong personalities made you feel as though you had gone straight through the looking glass.

Invitations to lunch or dinner were precious affairs and hard to come by until you were accepted. There was no dropping in. The owner, a lady of unmistakable appearance, was quite likely to tell any unfortunate who rang the bell without an invitation that the *maîtresse de maison* was not at home.

This year those of us privileged to have been admitted have been musing a lot about those exquisite meals, because there will never be any more. They belong to an iridescent history. The hostess, Miss Alice B. Toklas, who was an integral part of the Paris of art and literature and *esprit* for sixty years, died in March.

Alice Toklas was the first true gourmet I ever met. She knew how to grow, to buy, to prepare, to cook, to savor, to serve—and how to put food in its proper place. She understated flavors so that you were deliciously tormented trying to grasp them. A lunch at the rue Christine lasted three hours if you broke away brusquely, but it was more likely to be a leisurely four hours, for the meal was meant to be a trampoline for conversation and pithy criticism.

The first time I was brought to lunch was in the spring of 1947. It was a splendid year with lovely weather, and though there still was hardship—although nothing, they say, like 1919—there was lots of gaiety.

She opened the door herself. I was a little taken aback by the Dantesque profile on the very small, thin hunched figure. She was wearing an apron and the tan leather sandals that she had custom-made. "Oh, dear," she said, "the lunch will be late. I should have gotten up at five instead of six."

I laughed nervously, assuming it was a pleasantry, not realizing that she meant it. She had been to Les Halles herself to choose the eel that she was serving in a *sauce verte*.

I didn't know what to say, and I didn't know how to look, and I ate too much of the first course, which was a spaghetti au gratin, golden rich and sticky with cheese. When it came a second time, I thought it was the main course and helped myself again. Whenever you had lunch at Alice's, you automatically canceled all plans for dinner.

Later, much later, she confessed to me that each time Thornton Wilder came—and she adored Wilder—she felt she was walking on eggs because he was so *fin*. That comforted me a little. And though I had the opportunity to see her many times over the years and I loved her, I never got over feeling a clod, fearful of making some observation she would dismiss as banal.

The apartment was unlike anything I had ever seen before. The salon was paneled in white. "After white," she explained, "all colors are vulgar." The sun streamed through long French windows. Basket, the royal white poodle who appears in the paintings by Marie Laurencin and Dora Maar, raced up and down the flat roof that formed his private terrace. The flowers were set in vases of romantic, unexpected shapes. Usually, Alice B. Toklas sat deep in her armchair, quite likely to be dressed in a suit of Irish tweed made for her by Pierre Balmain, a tremendous oval of yellow diamonds on her forefinger.

Much of the furniture in the room was dark and massive. Later, I realized it was magnificent.

"Buy your antiques well," she said, "and they will always go up in value."

The hexagonal dark-oak table nearly filled the tiny dining room. The chairs were so high, she always used a footstool. There was a huge cupboard which she said was rare American Federal. An eagle was sculpted atop the pediment.

The salon was divided in half by a long Italian Renaissance table, which Gertrude Stein had bought in Florence for a good price because in those years it was not in fashion. The table was a worktable, laden with piles of letters, memorabilia, a few books that had come in the recent post, an opulent bouquet of flowers. On the far side was a brown satin horsehair couch, a companion armchair, a tufted brown satin side chair.

"We had our bottoms measured before they were made," explained Miss Toklas.

I recall a small occasional table inlaid with French Revolutionary symbols like the Phrygian bonnet, and a collection of silver miniatures of furniture and windmills on another table. My taste, which had been formed in White Plains, New York, didn't know what to make of stiff Mallorquin dolls made of shells, a reclining baby Saint John resting his head on a skull, the faience jars, the pedestaled silver ashtray lifted by a handle in the form of a cherub. But now, if I were to have a covetous dream, this might be the interior.

"Much has been repaired," she explained. "If it had been in perfect condition, we would never have been able to afford it."

This lesson has remained with me. Today I look at a green Ming vase with a partial oxblood glaze that I bought in Macao a few years ago. The imperfect side faces the wall. The visible good side provides me with enormous pleasure.

In the apartment on the rue Christine the corridor and the bedroom were lined with a blue paper patterned with large white pigeons. Curiously, there were no books visible except on the worktable or the night table. Apparently, it was a conviction. Books were for reading, not for decoration.

But there were pictures, mounting the walls two, three, five deep, even covering the mirrors. One afternoon tea when Alice went to the kitchen (a miserable, ill-equipped kitchen by *House & Garden* standards), I counted thirty-seven Picassos on the salon walls. There were trees and rocks of a green period I had never seen before. There was his first cubist painting, a village in Spain of only seven (or was it nine?) buildings, which gave the impression of a huddled metropolis. There was a rose-colored painting, a full-length nude that suggested a Chinese lady. There was an adolescent nude holding a basket of flowers (certainly the most touching of all Picassos of the early years in Paris).

The Louis XV chairs had tapestries designed by Picasso, a present because one day she said she felt like doing some needlepoint.

It was astonishing to me that all the paintings, the incomparable Juan Grises, the Picabias, the Picassos, the Dora Maars were without frames, the canvases held taut by simple, narrow wood moldings.

Several years ago, while Miss Toklas was away on a visit to Rome, the paintings were removed from the rue Christine. When someone commiserated about the accusing vacant patches on the walls, she merely said, "It makes no difference. My eyesight is failing. Besides, I have them all here," and she pointed to her forehead.

Now all this may seem a long way from *boeuf bourguignon* and Singapore ice cream, but in Miss Toklas's apartment the food always fitted into the surroundings and the company. In its preparation, she was always painstakingly finicky about every detail. It was part of the old-fashioned scheme that decreed that an educated lady penned a Spencerian hand and embroidered an invisible seam.

Once she spent a summer month with me in the country because I had a spare bedroom with two windows for cross-ventilation, an indispensable requirement. Occasionally, when we had company, she would move into the kitchen, employing me as a tweeny. She once gave me some celery "to string." After ten minutes, I handed it back satisfied I had removed every fiber. She simply returned it, saying tersely, "I said string it."

She made an incomparable apple pie, setting whole poached apples into a puff paste crust, causing one of the guests to remark, "How is it that I never eat like this in restaurants?"

Alice B. Toklas's childhood and her first lessons in the culinary arts occurred in San Francisco, which she left in 1907. In her memories, California was a glamorous place where everyone who was at all brought up knew how to whack off the top of a Champagne bottle at the neck. "You had to know for picnics." There were many French people in San Francisco, and she always claimed that France was a bit of a letdown because no one was as marvelously French as those people she knew in San Francisco.

"After their parties, the maids would sweep up, keeping a sharp eye for the diamonds," she reminisced.

Her first party meal was prepared in San Francisco when she was seventeen. It was a lunch of game for her father and a group of his friends. The cayenne was forgotten at the appropriate moment but tardily served a few minutes later. Her father's cold comment afterward always stayed with her. "Don't apologize. There should be no occasion for apology."

In her fluent French—tinged with a strong American accent of which she was proud—Miss Toklas expressed her own decisive views. She was a sharp opponent of "the whole school of economizing time, advertising quick ways to glamorous food. If you want to be a good cook, you should go at it as a daily pleasure. And if you don't have time, you should be a Sunday cook like a Sunday painter, who makes nice little pictures for himself and his friends."

She objected to everybody's trying to become a short-order cook. "When everybody cooks, there is no cooking. Cooking, like any art, is not for the millions.

"It is as though there has been a shock of discovery and women have plunged in too deeply. They feel they must try everything, and then add little fancies—spices, condiments, and a drop of wine to anything," she said.

Yet her own little grace note was to add a careful drop of Drambuie to whipped cream.

"At the same time most women today cheat in cooking. I call using ready-made tins cheating. They substitute cornstarch and flour instead of thickening with eggs and butter. They put gelatin in their puddings. You should never economize in the kitchen. Once the menu is established, the materials should be the very best. American women won't buy butter, but they will buy expensive tins."

There was no stint in her nature. Once, Dorothy Schiff, publisher of the *New York Post*, had taken another woman to lunch at La Tour d'Argent. Mrs. Schiff was shocked recalling the price, and added, "We didn't even have dessert."

When she heard about it, Miss Toklas was enchanted. "If that's all it costs," she said to me, "let's go there for lunch tomorrow." We had a spectacular time, although I really don't like that over-celebrated pressed duck.

Attitude and principle played a big part in her approach to food, as they did to any other creative aspect of her life. A young American journalist who fancied himself the possessor of a keen palate invited her to a restaurant that he had discovered in the neighborhood of the Bourse. He was very pleased with it, but wanted her approval. Midway through the meal, she shook her head negatively. It seemed like a judgment of Madame Lafarge.

"What's wrong?" asked the young man defensively.

"They put too much on the plate at one time," she said, indicating that the restaurant had offended all sensibilities except that of gourmandise.

Actually her appetite and capacity were astonishing for such a tiny creature. "I can eat more than you at any single meal," she said to me, "but it adds up to less in a day because I have only fruit for supper."

Largesse was a principle but each plate had to be a delicate presentation. When a fourth or fifth cup was poured from the elaborate silver teapot, it was never, "Have another cup of tea," but always, "Have a cup of tea," as if it were the very first.

She was extremely French in her treatment of guests. Potluck even for close friends was absolutely alien to her.

At Bilignin, in southeast France, where she and Gertrude Stein spent the summers between the two wars, she grew Saint-Antoine strawberries.

"They were a little bigger than *les fraises des quatre saisons,* and they grew on a stronger plant, straight up. They were more delicate in flavor and full of juice. It took an hour to gather a small basket, enough for a man's breakfast. Of course I picked them. Who else? By the time everybody got up, my breakfast was long past."

I recalled a cheese that seemed familiar, but so vaguely that I was moved to ask her about it.

"It's a West Coast recipe," she replied. "Begin with an excellent Camembert soaked for twenty-four hours in a good white wine. Scrape away the crust. Mash the cheese with a cup of softened butter. Use a wooden spoon; a metal spoon leaves its own taste. Reshape the mixture and place for one hour in the refrigerator. Remove before hardened, roll in finely crushed nuts, and set back in the refrigerator until firm enough to hold its shape."

The result—a velvet texture and a tantalizing taste.

For holidays, she would give sweetmeats. These were dates that she had pitted, filled with a walnut and a butter cream, and then powdered with confectioners' sugar. They were set on some sort of carefully chosen plate or dish which you were happy to keep as a treasured memento.

The dates were a trademark, like the little mushroom sandwiches that were a specialty at teatime. The mushrooms were cooked in butter with lemon juice. After eight minutes of cooking, they were removed from the heat, chopped, and then pounded into a paste in a mortar. Salt, pepper, a pinch of cayenne, and an equal volume of butter were thoroughly amalgamated with them.

"I'd like to write a millinery book," she said to me one day. "I have a very strong feeling about hats. I know a lot about them and I have had some hats which should have gone under glass. Millinery is quite a lot like cooking. It should be approached with the same care, taste, and imagination." Miss Toklas's hats were as unique in their way as those of Queen Mary. They were made for her by a modiste of the Place Vendôme, and the trimmings were worth a fortune.

The millinery book never came into being. But I'm glad the lady who didn't write *The Autobiography of Alice B. Toklas* nonetheless managed to leave *The Alice B. Toklas Cook Book.*

August 1967

Noël à Paris

Judith and Evan Jones

Rue Vaneau is not one of those Left Bank streets that are stuccoed with the imprints of celebrated Americans, nor does it teem with young people tempted to become expatriates. It stretches a few blocks from the *métro* station Vaneau on the rue de Sèvres northward to the rue de Grenelle and is lined with apartments of diplomats and affluent Paris folk as well as with an occasional nineteenth-century residence hiding behind a gated wall.

Long ago when we rented the attic of a carriage house just inside a wide iron gate, one of us each morning would preface breakfast with a quick jaunt around the corner to pick up freshly baked croissants or brioches in the rue de Babylone. This street, running toward the Invalides to the west, was our neighborhood marketplace, and close to the bistro on one side was the butcher and a cheesemonger who taught us the meaning of such fragrant words as Livarot, Gaperon, and *chabichou*. A few doors from the *pâtisserie* was the Jardin de Babylone—a dimly lighted space pungent with the smell of damp leaves, where we bought vegetables and other groceries.

Not much had changed when we returned last December to rue Vaneau. We were again in the *quartier* we loved, the heart of the Seventh Arrondissement, or Palais Bourbon district, and we seemed to be turning back the clock to a time that might have become no more than a packet of faded letters home or a scrapbook of snapshots.

By one of those extraordinary coincidences that offer no explanation, a rental agency, Paris Accueil, had made available a studio directly across the street from the gate behind which we had lived. We could step out each morning, just as we used to do, to buy the still-warm breakfast croissants around the corner. From the studio's upper level we could see, across rue Vaneau, the roofline of the familiar small garret poking over the wall. The neighborhood, which had dimmed for us with time, reasserted itself. Almost at once we felt at home again on the Left Bank, as eager for Christmas to come to Paris as when we had lived there on a leaner budget, though the lack of affluence hadn't seemed to matter: As is often said of the French themselves, no matter how strapped, we were never too poor to eat well.

In our early days we had observed the advent of Christmas as the French do, quite by chance having our first Paris lunch together in a restaurant that offered the seasonal treat of *boudins blancs*. We knew nothing then of the traditions nor even the mysterious ingredients of the white sausages that were served so commonly as a holiday specialty. These pale meaty sausages, we learned from the waiter, were actually studded with truffles; their delicate interior was composed of puréed chicken breast, sweetbreads, bread crumbs, and seasonings, in the manner of Avranches.

To learn what Christmas meant to the French in that time of recovery after the war was to observe the women who stood in line in worn-out carpet slippers to buy *boudins blancs* and other such delicacies for their families, to see them spending what seemed like large sums for the best of pâtés and pastries . . . and to listen one day to the delighted cries of customers in a *boulangerie* when one of them broke into a baguette and discovered it was made of pure white flour instead of the coarse, dark, "inferior" grain imposed on them by war austerities.

To mark our return engagement on the rue Vaneau, nothing would do so well for a festive first meal as *boudins blancs,* and it was Monsieur Barbet of the Jardin de Babylone who stood on the sidewalk outside his shop to point to the *charcuterie* where the classic white sausages were, as he said, *plus beaux*. He seemed to understand our yearning for all that was needed to relive Christmas memories.

We brought the *boudins* back to rue Vaneau and steamed them in a little water before lightly browning them to serve with a crunchy baguette (alas, more airy and bland than in the old days), a Côtes du Rhône, and a salad, put together at the Jardin, of *mâche* (lamb's lettuce), endive, radicchio, and chicory. We also brought back from Monsieur a four-foot *sapin du Canada* in a planting pot, and with the tinselly trimmings we found for the evergreen tree we began to feel infused with the spirit that Paris and its own magic bring to Christmas.

—

On the walk back from rue de Babylone we recalled things we had learned there when young. There we had first encountered the whiskery celery root knobs we soon transformed into *céleri rémoulade*. There we caught on to the knack of choosing handfuls of endive to braise in lemon-accented chicken stock. And just a few more steps from the Jardin was the *boucherie* where the butcher and his wife, we remembered, had taken pains to offer a basic culinary tip: It is proper fat that produces good *pommes frites*, they told us as they spooned into a container just the right proportions of rendered beef suet and pork fat.

The passage of time hadn't blunted the exhilaration we felt at the prospect of cooking again in Paris. Steps from our rented studio led down into a pristinely white *cave* with crusty plaster walls and a long galley furnished with modern kitchen equipment. There were tile floors and a round open fireplace under the low arched ceilings; a narrow refectory table, softly patinaed, turned the space of the *cave* into a handsome dining room.

As we made our way from the studio to the rue de Bellechasse, where a Santa Claus sat amid tins of tea in the window of the Tanrade *confiserie*, then zigzagged toward the ancient, angling streets near the Place Saint-Sulpice, we found it easy to believe that the French derive more pleasure from holiday food shopping than from hunting down Christmas gifts. We shared the spirit of the holiday, just as we had years before, joining hundreds of discriminating shoppers standing in line for the makings of family feasts. At Poilâne, on rue du Cherche-Midi, the line of patient, gossiping men and women waiting for "the best bread in Paris" stretched all the way to the corner. The narrow window at Au Bel Viander, just off the carrefour du Croix-Rouge, was filled with two feathered birds so lifelike that they served as implied proof of the freshness of the shop's meat, untouched by automation. A few streets on were small carved statues of the Wise Men gathered around the Mother and Child, replacing the usual objets d'art in the window of G. Thulier. At the Maison de Poupée, the puppetmaker's near the Jardin du Luxembourg, a grandparently couple stood hand in hand, awed by the marionettes poised for Christmas entertainments, while eager householders of all ages clustered in nearby food shop doorways.

Some of those shoppers, laden with overflowing plastic bags, paused on the way home to pray in the Church of Saint-Sulpice. There, in the soft gray light, the near-life-size crèche beyond the Delacroix frescoes evoked the serenity that may have been lost in the crowded streets. The Place Saint-Sulpice itself, only a couple of hundred yards from the bustle of Saint-Germain-des-Prés, gives one the feeling, so rare in Paris, of actually being in a small French town. Circling around the great fountain in front of the twin-towered church on Christmas Day was a covey of schoolchildren on roller skates.

The life of the Left Bank pulses on, much as it always did. In *A Moveable Feast* (1964), Hemingway remembered the Place Saint-Sulpice and the pigeons perching on the statues of bishops, and one hungry day his senses were alert to anything that smacked of eating. "From this square," he wrote, "you could not go further toward the river without passing shops selling fruits, vegetables, wines, or bakery and pastry shops." And he noted on his walk that only when he reached the Odéon were there restaurants. In other streets today, there are bistros that we had known years before, serving good, simple meals. It was also true, however, that not far from the church some of our former favorite restaurants had disappeared.

———

Almost in the shadow of Saint-Sulpice's towers, the rue des Canettes straggles toward boulevard Saint-Germain, unimpaired by the half dozen pizza places that give the narrow street new color. Still, halfway along is the varnished front of Aux Trois Canettes, and inside, though almost everything else looked smaller and more intimate, the dining room seemed unchanged. Nearer Saint-Germain-des-Prés, on the other hand, Le Récamier in the cul-de-sac of the same name—once a bistro we'd often been able to afford—has become posh and, like most upper-echelon hostelries, it was closed for the holidays.

Proprietors whose neighborhood shops were kept open for the Christmas crowds filled the small room at Aux Trois Canettes. Settling in among them, we ordered from a menu characterized by country food. We chose *rillettes d'oie* (shredded goose spread) and salad followed by monkfish masked by a tomato sauce as *lotte à la languedocienne*, and *colin meunière*, or sautéed hake, in a creamy tartar sauce thick with minced *cornichons*, capers, and pimientos. Such a lunch brings out one's admiration for the neighborhood eating places that still serve many old standards, among them hearty soups, delicately sauced *blanquettes de veau* (veal stew in white sauce), and simple desserts that include ungussied-up rewards like *tarte aux pommes*.

A few steps away on the rue de Sèvres, the peaceful vibrations of bistros were lost in the traffic jam of celebrants at Vigneau Demarest, a great meeting place for connoisseurs of foie gras and other Gallic culinary classics. Its window display of geese and pheasants, with ruffled necks and beaks still on, drew us inside, where every aisle was congested with determined buyers of all the treats that enhance a festive board. Most of them were shopping not only for Christmas dinner but for the midnight supper called *réveillon* that awaits most French families after Mass on Christmas Eve.

A friend from Brittany had been responsible for our first *réveillon* in France some years back. That night a cold mist coming in from the Golfe de Saint-Malo had whetted our anticipation as we came down the cobbled street from the stony chill of the village church. We had not been disappointed, for waiting on an ancient oak buffet were oysters *morbihannaises*, a steaming *cotriade* (a Breton stew of white fish with mussels, onions, potatoes, herbs, and cream) in a chafing dish, a terrine of foie gras, and babas au rhum, which were served with Champagne.

At Vigneau Demarest this time around, young waiters squeezed through the aisles full of shoppers, with trays bearing tulips of pink Champagne for everybody. Broods of ortolans and tiny quail behind the glass front of one counter reminded us of "four-and-twenty blackbirds baked in a pie." Across the aisle, in spite of the jostling, a slicer with his back to the throng used his long blade expertly on one smoked salmon after another. There were *galantines de volaille* (chicken terrines) to be bought and chanterelles among the vegetable displays. For our own holiday bird we chose precisely what was needed, as we had decided from the start that we would try to reproduce as closely as possible a Christmas dinner we had once shared with our friends Jacques and Bettina, a couple who still lived in Paris. And so, with the help of the floor manager and a crisply attendant young clerk, we ordered a handsome goose and waited as it was eviscerated and deprived of its head. (In true French fashion the head and giblets were packed up for the makings of a stock.)

It was a different sort of marketing than we had done the first time we'd cooked a Christmas goose in Paris. Our Breton friend, who now lived in Montparnasse, had demonstrated what any *bonne femme* would know by instinct: The trick of dealing with an open market is to walk the length of it, inspecting everything closely for both quality and price, then about-facing to buy only from vendors who make the best deals. Our first goose had been bought that way, but in bargaining for a cheaper price we brought upon ourselves a nasty chore. The goose had not been plucked, and the poultry seller had neglected to sever the neck, creating a kitchen dilemma that was solved only when a saw was located—the only instrument we had that was up to the challenge.

We had no similar problem this time, and the dinner itself was sheer pleasure because of the presence of the guests who had shared that long-ago feast of sawed-off goose. To prepare for the reunion we got an early start in the kitchen. The goose, stuffed with a baguette torn into pieces and mixed with onions, Alsatian sausage, green apples, and *herbes de Provence,* sizzled and spat in our kitchenette oven for two and a half hours. Meanwhile, simmering on top of the stove was a triumphant mushroom soup based on *bolets* (also known as *cèpes*), shallots, leeks, and sautéed chanterelles. Their woodland juices combined with the butter in which they cooked to produce an elixir that was poured into the soup, which was then topped with a tablespoon of *crème fraîche.* When first in Paris we had yet to learn the subtle techniques that made such a dish so good.

We'd had several culinary mentors then. The first was named

Bernadette, born in the Alsatian city of Colmar, and we found her so much on our minds on this trip that one evening, when the holiday had passed, we had dinner at La Chope d'Alsace, near the Odéon, a favorite spot for the French when in search of country classics; in her honor we chose to have the restaurant's *"fameuse"* onion tart, as well as *la demi-faisan au chou rouge* (pheasant with red cabbage). As the rich food was served, it suddenly became apparent how memory can sneak up on one: The sausage stuffing we had made is as Alsatian as a glass of gewürztraminer, and it had been Bernadette who first shared with us her knowledge of French Christmases. It was she, memory told us, who had thrown up her hands with a grimace: If one must have a *bûche de Noël,* she said, it should come from a *pâtissier* instead of being produced inexpertly in a family kitchen.

Christmas dinner had been enhanced by the lingering past. The plump goose, surrounded by quail cooked in goose fat, was a tribute to the one we had all first shared. The combination of chestnuts fresh from the Cévennes, in the center of France, and brussels sprouts was another reminder of Bernadette, who matched chestnuts more often with cabbage, as do many cooks in Alsace. Whatever else, the meal caused Bettina to exclaim that we should say grace again and Jacques to kiss the tips of his fingers as he summed up the reunion feast in a phrase: *"Ça alors, c'est fantastique!"* Yet nothing about the meal was ornate. There was a giant round brown loaf of bread from Poilâne, decorated with a wreath of sculpted dough. And there was plenty of wine to toast the past, the present, and the future. The *bûche de Noël* from the *pâtisserie* a block away in rue Vaneau was the crowning glory.

———

To cap the reunion and the end of the old year as well, we drove up the Champs-Élysées, etched with frostily lighted white branches against the evening sky, to Neuilly. There on the boulevard du Général Koenig, in their apartment next to the Seine, Bettina and Jacques had set out an exceptional celebratory repast. Except for the aromatic sorrel soup, it was a composition of marvels playfully, ingeniously, even lovingly prepared by neighborhood *traiteurs* (caterers), who everywhere in Paris make such treats easy to be had.

First there was a fine Michel Guérard creation, a fish *mousseline* in puff pastry with *beurre blanc* that needed only to be heated. Then there was the pure, rosy, unctuous foie gras in a charming little terrine. Bettina served great scoops of it, plunging a hot spoon—which she warmed between each serving—down into the interior of the chilled, lightly cooked goose liver. As Jacques poured the Alsatian Tokay he'd chosen to complement the *foie gras,* he announced with a glint of mischief that "it is known as 'little Jesus in velveteen britches,'" and it was indeed like liquid velvet. After the green salad and before dessert there were cheeses that never taste the same when eaten outside France. They included a Mimolette, an oozing Vacherin, a Camembert straight from the farm where it had been made, and a sage-seasoned crusty wheel of goat cheese. These were served with fresh walnuts, for which Jacques poured a fine Bordeaux that had long been at rest in his cellar.

So typically French, it was nonetheless a meal purchased almost entirely from food shops of impeccable repute, and it was probably superior to what the average Paris host could have prepared. Small wonder that most of the esteemed chefs can vacate Paris during the holidays, leaving no one behind in real deprivation. We understood why the *fêtes de Noël* and the *nouvel an* are so unanimously family occasions, and we applauded. Such times are cherished by chefs and restaurateurs as opportunities to sit down with their own families just as others do, and thus they prove that making money does not outweigh some of life's better moments.

———

In many parts of Paris—no surprise—there are Americans who years ago chose to lay permanent claim to the best aspects of living in France. On the day before we returned to the United States we had lunch with Warren and Jean Trabant, two former colleagues who publish the informative, stylish "Letter from Paris," with subscribers throughout the States. Its columns are filled with their current observations on the changing culture of Paris; squibs on shopping of every stripe, including food; and full reviews of books, hotels, and restaurants.

A nostalgic piece the Trabants had published on Paris's now vanished Les Halles led us to visit together the cavernous Saint-Germain Market near the Mabillon *métro* station. Jean seemed to know every vendor by name, and we stopped with her, just before going on to the Restaurant La Foux, to chat with Madame Decots, a statuesque, blond farm wife who with her husband raises free-range chickens and pigs exclusively on natural feed. They sell their meats and homemade pâtés at a spacious corner concession in the high-ceilinged market. "The *only* way to create excellent terrines," Madame said, her grin showing her affection for Jean, "is to use meat that is grown as God meant it to be—that's where the real flavor comes from."

The point was echoed by Alex Guini, a giant veteran of thousands of meals whose face, behind a wonderful mustache, is fissured with laugh lines. Born in the gastronomic shrine of Lyons, he is cook-*patron* of La Foux, the establishment he moved to rue Clément from a village southeast of Lyons. As he joined us at our round, commodious table, we were told that he features his own recipes among the plats du jour. Every Tuesday he serves *poularde de Bresse* poached in pig's bladder. *Soupe au pistou* (vegetable soup, much like minestrone) is another specialty that Alex makes his own, and we decided to have it on the recommendation of his wife, Simone. When the next course of *saucisson de Lyon* was brought, Alex confirmed that recently he had initiated a more relaxed, bistro-like menu for midday meals on Saturdays. He described this idea as his version of brunch—the white table linen is replaced by checkered oilcloth—and said that the word for it in Left Bank vernacular is *mâchon*. The lighter, less formal bill of fare sharpens the focus on the casual, easy friendliness that often exists between restaurateurs and their clientele throughout France. It's also a sign that today's more knowledgeable enthusiasm for good food among Americans is being saluted by French professionals. Parisians in earlier times were usually friendly enough with American travelers, but now they're apt to accept the more intense American interest in food as a common bond.

It became clear as our time together waned that the Trabants and the Guinis had come to exemplify that common bond. Certainly this seemed indisputable when the chef brought out an irresistible plum brandy as a *digestif*. And the degree of camaraderie between the families was engagingly certified when we understood that they were all gathering the next day for a New Year's dinner. The pièce de résistance, to be cooked at home by Alex, would be chili, as authentically American as possible. "I don't make chili because these friends are from the States," Alex said. "I try it because it is a new dish to me, and I like to master every kind of cooking."

We thought about such portents as we walked "home" toward rue Vaneau. We swayed a bit, lingering in the pleasure of our indulgent lunch and *joie de vivre*. The realization that the next day we'd be landing at Kennedy Airport seemed to heighten all the impressions of another Christmas on the Left Bank. Among them, one thing was sure: It would have been next to impossible to find a better way to say *"Joyeux Noël."*

December 1986

A LITTLE BLACK MAGIC

Ruth Reichl

The woman was ageless. Her coal-black hair was cut in a severe bob, the bangs slashing a straight line across her forehead. Her feet were booted, and the little black Courrèges dress caressed her slight frame familiarly, as if they had been intimate since the sixties.

"Bonjour," she said from the small desk in the center of the elegant shop in the Palais-Royal. The beautiful old man in the corner looked up, nodded sleepily, and went back to his newspaper. The little white dog approached, sniffed, then retreated. With an appraiser's eye, Madame surveyed me, then walked to the rack of vintage dresses and began studying its contents. "You will try this one," she said, choosing, "and this." The hangers slid, clicked, slid again. "No," she said suddenly, her voice rising with excitement, "try this one!" She reverently lifted a dress from the rack and held it aloft in triumph. "This is from Saint Laurent's second collection for Dior in 1959."

Her arms were filled with a froth of black lace that foamed briefly before settling into the shape of a huge dark orchid. "So beautiful," I breathed, as she led me to a corner curtained off with black velvet. She watched dispassionately as I removed my clothes. Then, very slowly, she lowered the dress over my head in an avalanche of lace.

Madame knelt to close the tiny hooks. It was odd and unexpectedly pleasurable; with each hook, the embrace of the dress became increasingly sensuous. At last she stood up, put her knuckles to her mouth, and gasped, *"C'est magnifique!"*

I looked in the mirror; a stranger was staring back at me. The dress had transported me to its own era, given my body voluptuous new curves.

"This dress was meant for you," said Madame. "You'll take it, of course." She was glowing proudly, no mere saleswoman but someone who has had the great pleasure of introducing strangers and watching them fall in love.

I nodded, completely in her thrall. And then I realized that I had absolutely no idea how much my dress cost. Madame glanced at the clothes I had been wearing and said, "Let me negotiate with the owner." From the dressing room, I could hear her urgent voice crying into the phone, "But this dress was meant for her!" She returned ecstatic. "He has agreed to take two thousand francs off the price!" she said happily. "Your dress is only fifty thousand francs."

I made the calculation, then sadly removed the dress. It was not meant for me after all. As I handed it over, I said, "This dress belongs in a museum."

"Oh no!" said Madame, fervently clutching it to her. "Clothes were meant to be worn. And this dress was meant to be worn by you!"

She watched me step into my own clothes, watched the magic creature I had momentarily become disappear. I was letting her down. As I buttoned my coat, she pressed her card into my hand and said seductively, "I will be in New York next month. I could bring your dress with me. Think about it."

I have thought about my dress many times since leaving that shop last fall. For one moment, I saw the person I might have been if I had been born in another time, another town.

And that, for me, is part of the wonder of Paris. For years I have been treating Paris as a movable feast, reveling in the fact that I was eating where Colette once dined and buying bread in a *boulangerie* frequented by Napoleon. But you don't have to be at the table to understand that this is a passionate city, a place where the past and the present coexist and the future is filled with possibilities.

March 2001

An Insincere Cassoulet

Michael Lewis

A few months ago my parents came to visit us in Paris, to see their new granddaughter and to see how we were getting on. They hoped to be shown around the city, of course, but they didn't need us to help them find the Louvre. They already knew how to be tourists in Paris; what they wanted to know was what it was like simply to live in Paris. This raised a question: Around which quotidian Parisian experience might I structure a week with my parents? I was able to think of only one: a cassoulet. A cassoulet is less a French dish than an athletic event capable of eating up large chunks of time. It requires at least a day and a half of scavenger-hunt-style shopping; two more days of cooking; and then another two days of digestion. To do it well, you must travel from one end of Paris to the other.

When informed that the centerpiece of their week in Paris would be the creation and consumption of a single meal, my parents had radically different responses. In forty years of marriage my father has been cooked approximately 14,600 dinners by my mother. He couldn't find his own kitchen with a map, and he tends to assume that I'd do well to follow closely in his footsteps. When he heard about the cassoulet, his face instantly became a mask of ironic detachment that as much as shouted, "What? *You* are going to cook? So how am I going to eat?"

Just as instantly my mother assumed the expression of maternal concern that typically precedes her intention to meddle.

Both reactions I fully understood. My personal culinary history has never been anything to write home about. Around ten years ago, for the first time in my life, I was seized by the desire to learn how to cook. I got over it soon enough, but before I did, I pretty well determined that I had no talent for it, for the same reasons I'm slow to learn new board games and to assemble Christmas gifts that arrive in boxes filled with parts. I take instruction poorly, especially when the instructions are written, and I have yet to encounter an oral recipe. So, you might well ask, "Why on earth did you think you should learn how to cook?" I admit, it's a good question. The answer is that I was a single heterosexual American male looking for a quick and easy way to fool single heterosexual American females into believing that I held enlightened, up-to-the-minute attitudes about gender roles—which, at the time, seemed more important than it in fact turned out to be. Also, I liked to eat.

But that's the catch. To become a cook, you not only need to be able to read instructions, you must want to cook when you don't feel like eating. It only ever occurred to me to cook when I was hungry, and by then, of course, it was already too late. Chinese takeout beckoned; Domino's whispered its deadly pickup line into my ear: *"Why bother?"* Realizing that I lacked the self-discipline to cook for myself, I took to forcing myself into must-cook situations. I invited friends to dinner and practiced on them. But my dinner parties tended to be long on the party and short on the dinner. I don't think the guests actually suffered any real harm, but I don't think they ever felt fed. Occasionally, I found them rummaging through the back of my refrigerator on their way out the door. Years later, a friend who came early and often, confessed that before he came to my place for dinner he routinely stopped at McDonald's.

In any case, six months or so into the cooking life, I abandoned it.

Then, last year, we moved to Paris. We arrived in the dead of winter with fifteen suitcases and a trunk full of assumptions. One of the assumptions was that we would learn how to cook French food. Of course, if you are the sort of person who believes that it is pointless to cook when Domino's is just around the corner, you are likely to find it even more pointless to cook when there are several dozen monomaniacal French chefs around the corner whose sense of self-worth depends entirely on the expression that crosses your face as you masticate. But it's more complicated than that. There may be no point in knowing how to cook when you live in Paris, but there is every point in knowing how to cook when you *have lived* in Paris.

———

Permit me to explain. As anyone who is honest about it will tell you, Paris is a city of vulgarians that has somehow cowed the world into believing it is the global capital of worldliness, a living and breathing arbiter of good taste. The Parisians treat each other and everyone else with a crudeness and contempt that would make a New Yorker blush. Yet for reasons as deep as they are mysterious, they retain the unique ability to convey an air of sophistication to anyone unlucky enough to experience prolonged contact with them. You don't live in Paris for the fun of it; you live in Paris to acquire, or seem to acquire, a bit of the Parisian ability to impress others with your worldliness.

Put another way, the whole point of living in Paris for a year is to let others know that you are *the kind of person who might well have lived in Paris.*

Put yet another way: Though I have arrived at the point where I can't wait to leave Paris, I don't exactly want to leave Paris behind.

To that end, ten months ago, for the second time in my life, I set out to conquer our new French kitchen. Knowing how to prepare elaborate French meals, I figured, might well inspire future dinner guests in the United States to inquire, "However did you learn how to cook this terribly classy French meal?" Whereupon I might reply, "Oh, it's just a little something I picked up while living in Paris." And my American dinner guests would just stare, slack-jawed, in awe.

Sincerity of purpose is in many respects an overrated attribute, but it is extremely useful when setting out to learn to do something new. In the ten months or so since I set out to learn how to cook French food, I have learned how to cook exactly one French dish—my cassoulet. The good news about my cassoulet is that it tastes great. The bad news is that it will do nothing to enhance your reputation as a French sophisticate. Cassoulet isn't what most people imagine when they think "fine dining" or "classy food." It's what they imagine when they hear the phrase "peasant slop." But that, in a way, is also a virtue. Perhaps because it has its origins in the peasant culture of southern France, the typical cassoulet recipe is sufficiently fault-tolerant to be passed along orally, with happy consequences. The recipe that I settled on for my parents' visit, for instance, is not so much a recipe but a few simple rules of thumb.

Rule #1: Nothing should be permitted to distract from the importance of the beans. You will spend a lot more money, and a lot more time, on the other ingredients, but you must always remember to treat the beans as the stars of your show. This isn't as easy as it sounds. The cassoulet cook is subjected to endless entreaties from his fancier ingredients; he is a bit like the director of one of those independent films in which the leading actor is a humble unknown and the walk-on parts are played by glamorous celebrities. The cook who lacks the discipline and resolve to keep these prima donnas in their assigned places will find his entire production undermined. When he shops for ingredients, when he fiddles with his recipe, when he makes those slight adjustments to taste that allow him to feel less a dutiful craftsman than an improvisational visual artist, he must keep in his mind's eye the simple white bean.

Rule #2: Do not attempt to flatter the beans falsely by juxtaposing them with inedible pseudo-foods. The French tend to ignore this rule. They include in their finished cassoulet many disgusting shards of animal fat and rind. The cassoulets you find in Parisian restaurants, in particular, are minefields of animal parts. This does not flatter the beans; it insults them. It suggests that they cannot hold their own in polite company. They can.

Rule #3: Avoid reminding your guests that they are eating meat. In my view, the well-cooked cassoulet should be able to fool a vegetarian for a bite or two. This is a radical departure from the French view of the matter, which assumes that cassoulet should be presented as a hearty meat dish. But, like many Anglo-Saxons, I am a hypocritical carnivore. I realize that there are people in this world, many of them French, who when they drive past a field of sheep, crave lamb. I am not among them. I enjoy a piece of meat from time to time, but not if I'm reminded where it came from. Of course, the English language encourages this hypocrisy—we don't eat "cow," we eat "beef." People don't say "Pass the deer" because it conjures up a mental picture that ruins everybody's dinner. But I take the hypocrisy one step further—I like meat less the more it resembles its former owner. Fat and gristle and large chunks of dripping flesh put me off, and so I keep all of them out of the pot. All meat is sliced and diced to be as un-meatlike as possible.

Rule #4: Take off your watch. The pleasure of making cassoulet is precisely that it is an unsophisticated dish, created by unsophisticated people whose lives were so different from our own that we can barely imagine them. The cooking of their dish hauls you away from modernity and its time-is-money sensibility and throws you back into eighteenth-century French peasant life. There is no such thing as instant cassoulet; when you set out to make this dish, you have to acknowledge right up front that it will require the better part of three days. The mere thought that you will be spending that much time on a single meal is annoying at first (at least it is to me). But I find that once I've settled into the cassoulet's deliberate rhythms, I lose all sense of time. For this reason and others—the main one being that I can't cook anything else—I have found that cassoulet is well suited to those special occasions when you have cut a deal with your mental diary to abandon your ordinary rushed habits.

Rule #5: If you want to preserve your authority in the kitchen, keep your mother out of it.

At some point between the vegetable stands and the butcher shops, my father simply vanished. I'm still not sure where he went, but he was gone for most of the week. The moment he did this, my mother took charge of my cassoulet. In apparent harmony, we passed from the glorious indoor market at Le Bon Marché—Paris's devastating answer to Dean & DeLuca—to the glorious outdoor market on the rue Mouffetard, but just below the surface there simmered a power struggle that will be familiar to any man who has ever tried to cook for his mother.

In addition, my mother is one of those people who do things their way or not at all. She's the only person I've ever met who becomes irritated when someone else tries to help her wash the dishes. As a result, she can't really understand what others mean when they ask her to lend a hand. She assumes they mean that they want her to do whatever needs doing for them. Often they do—nearly always I do—but whether they do or they don't, she winds up doing all the work.

———

As we ducked beneath the animal carcasses into the French butcher shops, I could feel my authority shrink. It began with seemingly harmless suggestions ("Shouldn't we really have some bacon?"; "Are you sure that's the *best* duck?"). By the time we arrived back in the kitchen with the sacks of ingredients, I realized that I was already the victim of a coup d'état. I had intended to serve the cassoulet straight, with maybe a little side salad. Somehow, my mother got her mind set on an elaborate concoction of green beans and carrots that I won't bother to describe because I can't. Once the cooking began, I became a puppet dictator in my own kitchen. In a blur of activity, the new regime rejiggered the cooking order, reduced the cooking time for the beans by 15 minutes, and restored the bacon to the pot—all of which, I admit, were improvements on my design.

Her insistence on bacon was a good example of her kitchen politics. I initially opposed the bacon. As I say, the biggest mistake that the French make in their cassoulets is their lack of discrimination about the meat. One solid chomp on a piece of loose goose rind can ruin your week. And what the French call bacon is not the light and crispy breakfast food so relished by red-blooded Americans. It's a thick, ugly wedge of ham with a repellent brownish rind and thick streaks of glutinous white fat; there's no disguising where it comes from. You could cook a piece of it for a week without rendering it any more appealing unless, of course, you're a meat fanatic.

Ignoring all these obvious objections, my mother diced the bacon and eliminated every trace of brown or white. It took an hour or so, which to my mind was a huge waste of time for a few scraps of bacon. But each time I complained she'd say things like "I'll just put in a little bit" and "I'll chop it up so you won't even notice" and "It really won't change your recipe at all." As it is impossible to cook a cassoulet and, at the same time, monitor another human being intent on taking control, the little pile of meat was ready to drop into the pot before I knew what had happened. It was all done with such subtlety that I nearly forgot it wasn't my idea.

On day four, the guests we had invited arrived, and my father finally emerged from whatever hole he had disappeared down. The cassoulet came out of the oven at just the right moment—which is the moment everyone is ready to eat. My daughter, Quinn, took the first bite—then another. Soon, everyone was tucking into seconds and proclaiming the dish a smash hit, which they always do. "This is *really* good," said my father, with something like shock. "You did a wonderful job," said my mother. I didn't, of course, but what does that matter? The cassoulet was nothing to me, the applause everything.

MICHAEL LEWIS'S CASSOULET DE CANARD

Serves 10
Active time: 2 hr   Start to finish: 2 days

My recipe was adapted from Julia Child's Mastering the Art of French Cooking. *I've changed the meats (a lot) and the seasonings (a bit). I've also tinkered with cooking times and sequence.*

2½ lb	dried white beans such as Great Northern
½ lb	fresh pork rind
2½ lb	confit duck legs
6	fresh parsley stems (without leaves)
4	fresh thyme sprigs
5	whole cloves
12	garlic cloves
1	(1-lb) piece smoked salted slab bacon, halved crosswise
3	cups chopped onion (1 lb)
1	teaspoon salt
1	lb meaty mutton or lamb bones, cracked by butcher
1	cup rendered goose fat
6	large tomatoes (3 lb)
5	bay leaves (not California)
1	qt beef stock (not canned broth)
1	(750-ml) bottle dry white wine
2	teaspoons black pepper

2½ lb fresh garlic-pork sausage (not sweet or very spicy) such
   as *saucisson à l'ail au vin rouge, saucisse de canard à l'armagnac,* or a
   mixture of the two
1½ cups plain dry bread crumbs
1   cup chopped fresh flat-leaf parsley

Special equipment: a small square of cheesecloth and a wide
   10-quart enameled cast-iron pot

DAY 1

ACT 1: NASTY WORK

1 hr

Bring 5 quarts water to a boil in an 8-quart heavy pot. Boil beans,
uncovered, 1½ minutes, then turn off heat and let them soak 50 minutes.

While beans soak, do all the really disgusting work with the meat.
Put pork rind in a 3-quart saucepan three-fourths full of cold water
and bring to a boil. Boil pork rind 1 minute. Drain and rinse under cold
running water, then do it again. (Sometimes you know it's ready because it grows nipples.) After draining, cut the truly repulsive boiled
pork rind into pieces that are big enough to identify (about 2 inches),
so you can fish them out before serving.

Scrape off and discard fat from confit duck legs and shred meat (the
more it shreds the better). [Editors' note: Those who have no problem
with identifiable meat in their food might want to keep the shredding
to a minimum.]

ACT 2: SLIGHTLY LESS NASTY WORK

1 hr and 20 min

Put parsley stems, thyme, whole cloves, and 8 garlic cloves in cheesecloth and tie into a bundle to make a bouquet garni.

First seasoning of beans: Add rind pieces, bacon halves, 1 cup onion,
bouquet garni, and salt to beans. Simmer, covered, 1¼ hours, skimming
regularly. Cool, uncovered.

While beans simmer, brown mutton bones. Do this by heating goose
fat in enameled cast-iron pot over moderate heat until it smokes, then
cook mutton bones, stirring occasionally, until browned, about 5 minutes. Set them aside on a plate. Drop remaining 2 cups onion into pot
and brown that, too. This can take as long as 15 minutes. Stir regularly.

Peel, seed, and chop tomatoes.

ACT 3: NASTY GETS NICE
1¾ hr

Flavoring the meat: Add browned bones and shredded duck to onion. Add bay leaves, beef stock, tomatoes, remaining 4 garlic cloves, white wine, and pepper. Simmer, covered, 1½ hours. Cool to room temperature, uncovered.

DAY 2
ACT 1: CRESCENDO
1 hr

Poke holes in sausage with a fork and grill it slowly in a well-seasoned ridged grill pan over moderately low heat 20 minutes (to get the fat out). (Sausage should still be slightly undercooked on the inside when you're done.) Transfer to a cutting board and cool slightly. Slice into thin (¼-inch) rounds.

Remove and discard bones and bay leaves from meat pot. Remove duck with a slotted spoon and put on a plate. Reserve cooking liquid remaining in pot.

Remove bacon from beans and cut into tiny, fat-free pieces. Put pieces on a plate and discard remaining bacon fat. Discard pork rind and bouquet garni from beans.

Julia Child says: "Now is the time to drain the beans and dump them into the ample, leftover meat cooking juices." In my experience, there is nothing left to drain. What you are looking at, when you stare into the bean pot, is a fairly solid wall of beans, with some gluey goop in between. So pour reserved meat cooking juices into bean pot. Bring to a simmer over moderately high heat, stirring occasionally, and simmer 5 minutes, skimming any scum. Then turn off heat and let sit another 5 minutes.

ACT 2: FINAL ASSEMBLY
1½ hr

Preheat oven to 375°F.

Spread a layer of beans on bottom of enameled cast-iron pot. Layer half of sausage and bacon on top, then another layer of beans, then half of duck (and any mutton), then another layer of beans, et cetera, ending with a layer of beans. Then add enough remaining liquid from bean pot until beans are submerged. Sprinkle with bread crumbs and parsley.

Bring the whole thing to a simmer, uncovered, over moderately low heat. Then stick it in oven 20 minutes. Break through bread crumbs in several places with a spoon, allowing the liquid to mess up the look of the thing. Then reduce heat to 350°F and leave it in another 40 minutes. Serve very hot.

March 2001

PARISIANS

She Did Not Look Like
an Actress to Me

Hilaire du Berrier

In point of history it was Paris's Indian summer. That venerable old eyesore, the Trocadéro, still gazed across the Seine at Tour Eiffel, and taxis were not the uniformly squat bugs they were to become at a later date.

They still had originality, snub noses, bulb horns, and high cabs with luggage racks on top and were owned by erratic drivers with handlebar mustaches.

You could linger all day on the terrace before Closerie des Lilas over a one-franc-fifty cup of coffee or a three-franc milky elixir called Pernod and see Salle Bullier hugging its memories of the Second Empire directly in the line of march of a heroic statue of Marshal Ney swinging a sword and shouting over his shoulder for shadows to follow as he leads that last great charge that is hopeless and never ended.

A bunch of violets to throw at his feet or send to the sad-eyed lady at the next table cost a franc.

A plate of borscht was two-francs-fifty in Dominique's on rue Bréa, and five hundred at the Schéhérazade, in Montmarte, but under the regime of the temperamental old general who was headwaiter at Dominique's there was a sporting element to dining there which made it doubly attractive. When you ordered borscht, you never knew what he would bring you.

On the basis that a gentleman is judged by his French, a tourist's finances by his nationality, a lady by her face, and a general by who exiled him, the pretentious Russian cabarets on Montmarte employed a sliding price scale entirely at the discretion of the waiter. On taking a seat at a table you were charged forty francs for almonds before ordering anything.

You could get a room fit to walk out of in striped trousers and carrying a cane for anything from twenty-five francs a day to ten thousand, but I did not pay anything. I enjoyed free rent in the apartment of a seventy-year-old prince who called me *fils* and regarded me as an inexpensive insurance policy, carried to assume responsibility for Maggy, his twenty-three-year-old mistress, should his estranged wife, a famous Cuban beauty with a sugar fortune, ever swoop down on the place with her lawyer.

I did not mind that. Being able to support a girl like Maggy was pure flattery, as far as I was concerned. Besides, living with Charles afforded an excellent opportunity of acquiring by osmosis impeccable manners, erudition of sorts, and an endless repertoire of fine stories. In brief, Charles taught me how a gentleman should live. Whether or not either of us would ever be able to afford it was another matter.

We lived on a short street near the Lutetia Hotel in an apartment that was small but had a certain slovenly elegance about it.

Tags from the Jockey Club, the Club des Cent, and half a dozen others that he had not frequented since his wife left him and his dues lapsed hung from the binocular case to which he had lent distinction in those days as he raced horses at Longchamp.

A ponderous oil painting of one of his ancestors stood on the floor because the ceiling was too low to hang it. A gun and a sword leaned against the wall in a corner. Attached to the gun was a whistle. If he touched either, Chaupette, an aged and woebegone cocker spaniel, went crazy. Then a restlessness would come over both of them who would never hunt again.

After a time my dinner conversation, when I contrived to get invited out, consisted of anecdotes from Maxim's and Longchamp, and scandals that took place at the turn of the century. The menus I knew by heart and recipes I had memorized would have shamed Lucullus.

Mornings we had coffee, cheap Champagne from a Nicolas wine store on the corner, and a brown sack full of ladyfingers for breakfast, accompanied by stories that were wonderful, of meals and wines that had cost thousands.

The prince had a small group of cronies of his own age who for years had moved in similar, respective cycles as regularly as planets in their prescribed courses. Coffee and croissants in the morning, a particular point where their paths touched for apéritifs before shooting off in divers directions toward an ultimate *déjeuner*. Afternoons and evenings were designed by a gentleman's deity to be spent over liqueurs and coffee after a certain age. It was a life that was leisurely and dignified and gracious.

At any hour any one of them knew where to find the others.

Of the five of us that drifted of an afternoon toward an appointed bistro with its stone-topped tables, four had an average age of seventy-one. The next youngest was your servant, twenty-four, the most attentive listener at the table and probably the one whose opinions were most respectfully deferred to, because at least they were flattering.

Charles and I generally arrived first, since we were nearest. Besides, we had nothing else to do after Maggy disappeared to go to the hairdresser's or to some other vague appointment.

While waiting for the others, Charles told stories ranging from his grandfather's fight to save the empire that famous Sunday of September fourth, after Sedan, when the Leftists shouted down the assembly, to the most intimate details of the untimely demise of Félix Faure. His story of Boulanger, *le brave général,* whose love for Madame de Bonnemain was greater than ambition or party or *la patrie,* may not be the published version but it would make better reading.

Baron Roodenbeke, a jolly little red-nosed Fleming, had to come all the way from No. 5, rue Chomel for these sessions, so he was sometimes late.

Commandant de Marolles lived in Versailles, so he came only once a week. His army post had been in Peking at the time of the Boxer uprising, but he was still meticulously addressed by his rank.

An old gentleman who lived over near Les Invalides and another from a side street near La Madeleine were the other members of our circle.

Along about three o'clock I imagined them eyeing a clock in the respective retreats they maintained for collecting souvenirs and sleeping, preparatory to sallying forth and converging on the shabby café where they did their living. Here all conversations were prefaced with "Do you remember—?", and the amenities strictly observed.

The other old men knew about Maggy, but the only time I ever heard her mentioned was when Baron Fouquier, of the Académie des Oenophiles, joined us one day and observed, "I can't see why Charles goes on with Maggy; she is stupid and she has no charm."

With a deprecatory wave of his hands that expressed complete incomprehension, he added, "A man marries anybody; but a mistress, she has to have something!" It was beyond him.

Whether the others had a Maggy or not I never knew, but Charles took a great deal of pleasure in divulging nothing to either Maggy or his old cronies about the other. It gave him the satisfaction of feeling that he was leading a double life, in a way, and I suppose they did the same.

Over a *ballon* of red wine or a *tasse de café*, one of them would set a course.

"Do you remember the hunt, Prince, in the *forêt de X*, in 1905? You were master of the *chasse*. Remember?"

"*Oui, oui, oui, oui! La duchesse d'Uzès était là!* It was like this—"

Charles folded his hands over his mouth and, ever so softly at first, started sounding subdued approach to a hunting horn.

"To-torro, to-torro, to-torro-oo!"

"Yes, it was like that." Baron Roodenbeke had a faraway look in his eyes.

"And now the deer is in the water," Charles continued, a little louder this time, "to-torro, to-torro, toroooo."

Between renditions of the horn, Charles paused to recall the turn they had taken and the landmark marking it. By now, completely carried away in the excitement of the hunt, his sounding could be heard all over the café.

A few red-faced gentlemen at the bar and a sprinkling of peaceful clients investing tables looked up tolerantly from drinks or a current issue of *L'Illustration* but saw nothing unusual in four old men rising up and down in their chairs with the movement of men on horses as Charles folded his hand over his mouth and bellowed on an imaginary horn, "To-torro, to-torro, *toroooo!*"

They were starry-eyed and oblivious to the rest of the world.

About the time the last detail of the kill was exhausted, someone would hear a newsman calling *"Paris-Soir!"* on the street and dispatch me with five sous to buy a copy. The others sipped wine and rested while Baron Roodenbeke read the headlines aloud.

There was never a reading of that paper that did not lead into another story. The obituary column provided most of them; what England and Germany and the rest of the world were doing did not make sense, so they did not bother to read about it.

A hush fell on the table the day the Baron solemnly announced that Boni de Castellane was dead.

The loss of any name known to clinking glasses and the cancan at Maxim's leaves a gap in the lives of old men, but Boni de Castellane's passing meant more than that.

He was one of the pivots that memories and stories swung on. He was not as other men; he was a legend and a spirit, a symbol, like Tour Eiffel and swallow boats on the Seine. He was used to reckon dates by. Now only Tour Eiffel remained.

They had drifted away from him in his later years, like everyone else, but when he died they regretted it.

The man I have pictured Boni de Castellane as being since that afternoon was a dashing young noble who laughed and drank and dined. He was Paris's sweetheart, born to be tossed roses by women on balconies, to wear high red heels and die young from too much Olympian affection. Their eyes lit up as they talked about him.

He never squandered life in sleeping. At night he danced and drank Champagne. Instinctively you associated him with duels in Parc au Prince, Bois de Boulogne bridle paths, and dinners where men wore their decorations and women their tiaras without fear of inciting a revolution. He represented a way of life where men ate well, drank well, and knew how to live.

Also his was the gift of going through large sums of money with grace and rapidity. But it was taken for granted that Boni de Castellane deserved the best. That it was a shame to see such a man hampered for want of money was the opinion of everybody, including his tailors. Before long he was in debt for a fortune.

According to gossip, his creditors formed a corporation and pooled enough to send him to America to look for an heiress, as their only means of retrieving their investment.

Be that as it may, he arrived in New York in a day when mere millionaires were regarded by the Four Hundred much as middle-class Britishers in Hong Kong look at a Eurasian, and in a whirlwind courtship he won and married Anna Gould.

The bride's dowry, stated to run into three millions, was, so her father believed, sewed up to protect the principal; but in the years that followed, the arrival of Boni de Castellane's yacht in any port in Europe was cause for more excitement among resident nobility than the *Polar Star* of the Czar of Russia.

On the edge of Bois de Boulogne he built a home for his wife, a copy of Marie Antoinette's Petit Trianon, out of red marble, and he amassed art objects like a looting mogul. His taste was exquisite; landscape gardeners moved trees as though they were chessmen and changed the whole grounds to suit his plans for a party. Carpets of out-of-season flowers to match Anna's gowns were the order. He was a snob in the grand manner, *ce sacré jeune comte de Castellane.*

Naturally, Anna loved it while it lasted, but as Charles philosophically pointed out, Oenone has received a great amount of wholly unmerited sympathy through the centuries, simply because Paris ran off with Helen.

Had Paris been a penniless young ne'er-do-well without a sou in his pockets, instead of prince of the horse-taming Trojans with a father like Priam and a brother like Hector to whom he could always take a woman home, she would have left him without a tear and Homer would not have given him a paragraph.

One day Boni de Castellane's money ran out, and, so the story goes, Gould wrath and indignation rose to high heaven. Parental investigation disclosed, among other things, a tidy sum spent to provide annuities for some half dozen ex-mistresses.

The Goulds did not understand the code of a gentleman, that was all.

When he was young and impecunious, and their time might have been more profitably spent elsewhere, these women had been kind to Boni de Castellane. He was only a handsome, futureless young *vicomte* then.

About the time he was at his peak they were poor and passé, and he felt responsible for them. Their affection for him had amounted to improvidence in a way. In their declining years he took this into consideration and showed his gratitude.

Nevertheless, Anna, too young and headstrong to realize that a woman is better off sticking to a likable man she has tried and found wanting than being disappointed in a new one, divorced him and married his cousin, the Duc de Talleyrand.

Boni moved into a modest house on rue de Berri and, without the large sums necessary to his way of life, gradually dropped out of sight. Soon the art objects and paintings began to go. Of those who had known his brilliant dinners, only a few old servants remained, but these went down with their master, in the grand manner. They wore livery to the last, shiny at facings and elbows but with gold buttons bearing the Castellane arms as proudly as ever.

He had a stroke and was confined to a wheelchair, but each day, carefully dressed, meticulously groomed, and with waxed mustache, he was wheeled to a window where for years he sat in a chair and looked out on rue de Berri, watching Paris pass.

Sometimes a heavily veiled woman came to see him, but rarely a man. When the art objects and paintings were gone, dealers started filling his home with new ones, which they brought newly rich clients around to buy. It was worth something to see the inside of that house and be able to point to a vase and say, "It came from the Castellane collection."

Boni's observations on his cousin are said to have been bitter those years; what Anna thought, if anything, about the dark house on rue de Berri is unknown, but I have always had a sneaking suspicion that anything, after life with Boni de Castellane, must have been boring and humdrum. His chef must have thought so, too, for he stayed with his master.

The New York girl who had risen from *vicomtesse* to duchess and princess still had her money, her titles, and a pink marble palace in the Bois de Boulogne, which became more conspicuous year by year as monstrosities of an opposite extreme sprang up around it to make it appear like some hangover of a bygone age, as indeed it was. The shuttered house on rue de Berri was only a few minutes away by taxi.

As the old prince and the baron discussed the relative latitudes of both residences in terms of happiness, they gravely agreed on one thing: We would have to go to the funeral. Everyone remembered then.

So, in due course of time, along with many others, we traversed a narrow street and passed through the shopping district that has crowded in on the old church of Saint-Philippe-de-Roule.

Its somber pillars were covered with black drapes on which the Castellane arms were embroidered in gold thread, and aside from the depressed feeling a church always gives me, I felt a wistful regret for having been born too late. The old man beside me was mourning his youth; Boni de Castellane was only a rather imposing knickknack in it, a symbol of impeccable taste and wines and dinners.

He pointed out people as they entered. Paris and the great names of France came to the funeral. It sounded like a roll from the pages of *Almanach de Gotha*. Marshal Lyautey was present, and Paderewski.

Charles's underlip protruded like a pouting boy's as he recalled memories through which the man in the coffin surrounded by ugly wreaths had walked: the dinner where Duc de la Rochefoucauld met Mattie Harris, Countess de Montesquieu's parties, and riding to hounds at Gros Bois.

Baron Fouquier took his place at the left of us, and Charles was jarred from his reverie. In a whisper more carrying than a shout he complained to me, "*Regardez*. He has the rosette of the Legion of Honor, and I haven't even the ribbon. I don't know how he trafficked it. When we were young, he arranged the rendezvous with actresses for all of us, *tous les ducs et tous les princes*. Castellane and Rochefoucauld and all of us. He took our cards to their dressing rooms—and now, he has the *Légion d'honneur* and I have nothing."

His lower lip protruded still farther and his words trailed off. As he finished speaking, a little old lady walked down the aisle and quietly seated herself toward the front, near the family.

Her face was white with powder and she wore a high lace collar. Her knitted gloves were darned at the fingertips, and you pictured her stepping out of an electric car steered by a handle. Charles knew nothing about her and neither did anyone else, apparently. When the rest filed out to go to the cemetery, the frail old woman stayed behind in the church. I suppose she had no way of going, and no one offered to take her.

Boni de Castellane's funeral provided conversation for days in our bistro as the old men talked about Marshal Lyautey and the Duc de Broglie and la Marquise de Clement Tonnerre and everyone else.

The Duchess of Talleyrand, née Anna Gould of New York, did not come. She had a cold, so she stayed home in a pink Petit Trianon where the garden was never changed on a whim anymore.

Major Pollock, of La Fayette Escadrille, made a blasé observation to a group of Americans that Boni de Castellane's death marked the passing of an era that in its decadence had the sweet, heavy odor of tuberoses. This was carried back to the café as my contribution, a sort of report on foreign reaction to the obsequies.

The only part of the whole proceeding to have any effect whatever on Maggy, who was a hopeless romantic and an avid reader of cheap novels, was the story of the unknown little lady with hatpins in her hat and gloves with the fingertips darned. It appealed to her, the idea of a frail old woman in clothes dug out of a lavender-scented trunk, coming to put the period to the last line of her own story of Boni de Castellane.

Maggy was sure it must have been one of the actresses he pensioned off. Charles seemed to feel that his old friend had let him down by establishing a precedent he could never live up to, which made it rather bad taste to pursue the subject with Maggy.

For my part, never having had an affair with an actress, nor any prospects of putting one out to grass, if I did, I preferred to think of her as some ordinary *bourgeoise* housewife who had the beauty of youth once and nothing else; and for a brief space of time, probably only a night, as his romances were reputed to have been reckoned, Boni de Castellane at least pretended to love her. Maybe he did at the time. And forever after, that memory was her high spot.

I liked to imagine her raising children for some minor official of the

Crédit Lyonnais, while reading of Boni de Castellane's marriage and cruises and parties; following, in some dowdy, middle-class parlor, the down-graph of his divorce and stroke and death notice.

He probably wouldn't have remembered her either, but I'd like to have heard her story also. If she had known Boni de Castellane well enough to weep at his funeral, her life could not have been wholly drab.

I tried to start the other old men off on her during one of our afternoon meetings. Usually they would rise to something like that and pursue it to the end, but here I ran into complete disinterest. They loved small talk and gossip, particularly if it touched on the bar sinister of someone's escutcheon, or romantic dallying, but they did not want to see any story in this, it seemed.

They would talk for hours about how Escoffier, the king of chefs, worked to carve a swan out of a block of ice and fill it with ice cream topped with sliced peaches for Madame Melba, then called it *pêche Melba,* because he knew she loved peaches. They would go to great lengths to unearth the menu of some long-dead dinner, or discuss the effect of an August rain on a particular vintage. The way their eyes sparkled and drew into crow's-feet at the corners when they talked of beauties long since wrinkled and balls and *bons mots* under ceilings that dripped chandeliers attested to the truth of the old Persian's saying, "Somewhere in space such spells survive, for their delight is deathless." But when it came to surmising about the private affairs of the strange woman at the funeral, they became reticent, as though they were afraid of ghosts. Maybe some mutually understood and shunned memory among themselves was involved, or a clause in the code of a gentleman.

I'll always wonder. Probably so will Maggy.

September 1949

THE CHRISTENING

Lillian Langseth-Christensen

There is no celebration of any kind in Paris without food and wine, and the greater the occasion, the larger and more elaborate the menu. In a city in which two friends who meet on the street instinctively turn into the nearest restaurant to do honor to the happy occurrence, the mind naturally turns to veritable dream castles of food when the occasion is a christening. Expectations are especially great when the devil is about to be dispelled from a dimpled boy who is not only the first child of well-situated parents, the de la Chesnayes, but the first grandchild of a substantial banker and a professor, and the great-grandchild of *une veuve de général*, a general's widow.

The christening feast always has the added advantage of finally putting to rest all the whisperings and excited speculations that run riot among friends and relations whenever a lady is *enceinte*. Some of the de la Chesnaye guests, with true French acumen, had been looking forward to their invitations to the christening dinner for several months. Others, with a stronger sense of fateful consequence, had been counting on it ever since the wedding. Everyone hoped for a boy, since boys had a way of producing more Champagne and older brandies than girls. Considering the magnitude of the de la Chesnaye celebration, there was no doubt in anyone's mind that the birth of their son was an event calling for the very best wine, for the heirloom recipes, in sum, for the *effort suprême*.

Even if superstition and custom did not forbid detailed advance preparations, the last month before the birth of the infant (as all mothers will testify) is hardly the time for her to plan a suitably splendid menu for the christening party, and very few Parisian ladies retire to their labors with this work behind them. Madame de la Chesnaye, for one, took her party lists and her little instruction manual to bed with her. Soon after the *accouchement* she fished the manual out from under her pillow and began to plan the dinner that would do full honor to her new son and heir. She read its advice on the reception of the first sacrament. It clearly stated that the christening should take place "as soon as possible after the birth of the infant." However, there should be time for the infant to gain a little poise and maturity, not to say a regular and dependable feeding schedule; there must be no *malheurs,* calamities. Even the newest infant requires a certain *savoir-vivre* in order to survive the event. This waiting period also permits recovery of the mother, whose presence, the manual went on to explain, "is desirable but not necessary." Actually, most of the allowed time was spent in preparations for the feast and in the attempts of *Maman* to get back into her best little dinner dress, by Chanel, of course, the one with the demure décolletage.

There was no question in the minds of Monsieur and Madame in regard to the grandeur of the celebration. Some of the best families of France might be leaning toward afternoon christenings followed by coffee and cake and a reading of suitable Scriptures (and a great departure of guests immediately after the first reading), but not the de la Chesnayes. They were determined to recapture all the splendor of traditional christenings, complete with lace-covered pillow and rivers of Champagne, even though their son's great-grandmother was only the *veuve* of a general and not, regrettably, the *Veuve* of Monsieur Clicquot.

Madame lay in her bed and received her son every four hours, and between feedings she directed the christening plans. She had several interviews with Monseigneur, who came to instruct her liturgically but ended by advising her on vintages and dropping a few hints regarding his own preferences among the birds and fishes which the bountiful *Dieu* had placed upon the earth for the special enjoyment of the French clergy. Between them, and with the occasional assistance of Monsieur, they settled the menus for the adults, for the children's table, and for the infants' table, where the nurses expected the best even though the infants could count on only a slightly richer formula than usual.

AVANT LA CÉRÉMONIE
Les Apéritifs
Les Sandwiches Mélangés

APRÈS LA CÉRÉMONIE
Consommé Zibeline
Homard à l'Archiduc
Filet de Boeuf Fervaal
Soufflé d'Asperges
Poularde Rose Marie
Salade de Champignons et Cresson
Fromages
Coupe Rêve de Bébé
Gâteau de Baptême
Fruits
Dragées

POUR LES ENFANTS
Consommé Christiana
Poulet en Cocotte Bonne Femme
Purée de Céleri
Salade d'Épinards
Mousse aux Fraises
Dragées

POUR LES NOURICES
Potage Pierre-le-Grand
Filet de Sole Casanova
Noix de Veau Prince Orlov
Salade Mimosa
Bombe Don Juan
Petits Fours
Fruits
Dragées

(No menu would be complete without *dragées,* the traditional confections which all the guests take home from French christenings as Americans carry away little boxes of wedding cake. The *dragées*—Jordan almonds in the United States—are usually almonds coated with enamel-like, liqueur-flavored sugar. They are supplied by confectioners, since it is quite impossible to achieve the smooth sugar coating at home. The coating is white for christenings; for other occasions the almonds are usually tinted in pale pastel shades.)

The de la Chesnayes enlisted two friends to act as *marraine* and *parrain,* godmother and godfather. The manual didn't seem to care whether this *pater spiritualis* or, in fact, the real father was present at the ceremony. But it did say the godfather should be over fourteen years of age and that under no circumstances should he marry his godchild if it happened to be a girl. The godparents had to be of opposite sexes, but not married to each other, and they could not be the parents of the infant. Aside from these stipulations, the parents were to feel free to choose anyone. Despite the restrictions, Madame Villard and Monsieur Courtois accepted the honor, which each of them secretly had been counting on. The christening was set for Sunday, after Mass, and the manual suggested scheduling the event after the second feeding when the infant was *tranquille* ("a screaming infant is disturbing during the ceremony . . .").

The parents also settled on a series of names for their son. Tradition demands that a boy be named for his godfather and his father, and for the saint who will watch over him and whose saint's day he will celebrate as others do their own birthdays. A boy must also be named for anyone else where diplomacy and honor require it. He must be given a call name; by the Latin version of this name he will be called into the church at his christening, and by the French version he will be called for the rest of his days. The result of all this was: Auguste Alphonse Émile Jude Thaddeus Rudolphe Jérôme Georges Maria de la Chesnaye. Madame wrote it out for Monseigneur, who had been forgetting infants' names at the moment of baptism for twenty years. The call name was going to be Georges.

The de la Chesnaye guests assembled for an apéritif at their hosts' home and departed for the church *en caravane.* Young Georges was handed to his *marraine* on his lacy pillow, and they were met at the portals of the church by Monseigneur, who said, "Peace be with you, how shall this child be named?" Madame Villard, who had a good memory, recited the names smoothly, the ceremony was under way, and the christening party followed young Georges to the baptistery.

For some reason it is always taken for granted that if a man aims at a target he will hit it with a certain amount of accuracy. Although skilled marksmanship may be an accomplishment of sportsmen, it is usually sadly lacking in the clergy, and the facility seems to diminish as age and rank increase. If a priest is young and of a sporting turn of mind, the best that can be expected is a hit in the eye or on the nose. In addition to these regrettable shortcomings, the baptismal waters are always cold and inevitably chill the infant as they run down the back of his neck. Needless to say, if the infant has been quiet up to this point, he now starts to yell and usually continues at the top of his lungs until he gets home. The christening guests know that the sacrament of baptism exorcises the devil and so they smile tolerantly, although the yowls and yelps echoing through the church sound more as if the devil had just entered.

Madame Villard had been a *marraine* at Monseigneur's baptisms so often that this time, to keep the infant warm and dry, she devised a safeguard which she thought of as *l'invention Villard*. It consisted of a little rubber collar to be worn inside the christening robe in order to catch the cold water as it came trickling down the nape of the infant's neck. It strongly resembled those little rubber rings that are placed around red-wine bottles to catch the drops and save the tablecloths in the type of Parisian home that boasts a clock set into the navel of a gilded Venus de Milo. In more *recherché* homes—where the clock is surmounted by Leda and the Swan—the red wine is allowed to drip, and the most any good hostess does is to sprinkle salt on each spot.

Although Madame Villard came from a home of the first order and would not have been caught dead with a rubber-ringed red-wine bottle, she felt so strongly for her little *filleul* that she slipped the rubber collar to his *nounou* on the way to church. A realist, Madame Villard had also considered a slight sedative for Georges—nothing dangerous, just a little *cachet* to ensure his dreamless sleep. But after looking at his rosy innocence she was reluctant to administer his first barbiturate.

When the guests were assembled around the font, young Georges was still blessedly asleep. The rubber collar gave him a slightly hunchbacked appearance, which perplexed his parents during the entire ceremony. But the fact remained that *l'invention Villard* worked. After administering the salt and oil without mishap, Monseigneur poured, and the cold water ran down over Georges's eyes and, with the unerring pull of gravity, toward the small of his back. However, the collar deflected it, and even Monseigneur was surprised to find that the ceremony was concluded without sounds from the *sujet*. Satan had been renounced with all his works, and the christening was a vast success. Monseigneur was so charmed by the peaceful silence of Georges that he sent him forth into life with an affectionate pat and a final benediction: "Auguste Alphonse Aemili Judas Thaddee Rudolphe Hieronyme Georgi Maria, *vade in pace.*"

Georges never woke up until he reached home. His long lace dress, symbol of his purity, was dry and immaculate. There was no question now of whether Georges possessed *savoir-vivre.*

The florist had installed a sort of bower under which Monsieur, Madame, Georges, and his *nounou* would receive and hold court. They stationed themselves correctly and prepared to receive their guests, who had lingered between church and home just long enough to allow for the changes that even an exorcised infant requires.

A christening *fête* in Paris has no age limits—everyone is included from the oldest relatives to the infant's contemporaries. The doctor who brought him into the world ranks next to the monseigneur who brought him into the church, and the parents' wedding party and the neighbors are always included as well. Infants coo at each other from adjacent laps while children play games and adults conjecture about the repast. When Georges emerged from his bower his matchmaking aunts noted that he showed a marked partiality for a rosy infant who had been christened Félicité the previous week. She was a splendid *parti* since her father manufactured *pneus* while Georges's father produced *bicyclettes* on which the tires could be used. The well-planned match was toasted, a little prematurely, while Georges showed his *joie de vivre* with an energetic rattle and Félicité responded with squeaks that she produced by squeezing a rubber dog.

Madame's manual said that a "room cart" should be brought in and that the infant should remain near the guests, "who are supposed to cast a glance at him at intervals. Later guests can make a little visit to the infant, who is supposed to be asleep, and gifts are presented to him." Christening gifts, according to the manual, are supposed to be of a continuing nature so that the anniversary of the christening can bring another installment. For a girl, this charming custom usually leaves her with many half-completed strings of pearls and not a full necklace to her name, while boys are likely to end up with more sets of coffee spoons than they know what to do with. The ever-wise manual suggested that the donor start with two classics, in leather of course, and add one each year. Next they suggested a geography of France for the christening, and geographies of lesser nations to be given in ensuing years. The next suggestion was a bankbook: "This beautiful gift bears interest each year." Perpetual calendars and a few good securities were also recommended. The parents do not give christening gifts, only the *fête*. The manual warned, finally, that "the christening gift must be a gift to give pleasure for a lifetime, as immediate enjoyment is impossible." (Rattles, toys, and teething rings are a *faux pas.*) With this in mind, Georges's grandfather gave him a golden key to what would someday be his wine cellar.

The christening guests had stood at the font, they had brought gifts, they had admired and complimented—now they were ready to reap their reward. Monseigneur sat between the *mère* and the *marraine* and enjoyed himself enormously. After having long since abandoned all hope for a dry and quiet baptism, he smugly regarded his great success with Georges as the reward for some special virtues, little knowing the part played by the lady on his right.

The guests sat at tables with their proper age groups: The infants with their *nounous* drank their formula, the children ate their spinach salad, and the adults did what they had come to do—they ate and drank all that was set before them. Having made all necessary conversation in the receiving line, they now relaxed and enjoyed the food and wine as only Parisians can. Madame eyed each new course with complacency. She had planned, she had produced, and *voilà*, she would partake. The christening feast was a *repas formidable*, but fortunately the vast number of infants and children among the guests ensured an early departure. The guests carried off cornucopias of *dragées*, and Georges was awakened so that his hand could be waved at each of them.

It was quite clear that the benefits of baptism and Monseigneur's final blessing had affected Georges profoundly. He had, for this one day at least, gone in peace. So had his guests.

CONSOMMÉ ZIBELINE

Beat 1 egg and 2 egg yolks until they are light. Stir in ¾ cup light cream, ⅓ cup very thick chestnut purée, a pinch of sugar, and salt and pepper to taste. Bake the custard in a buttered shallow dish, set in a pan of warm water, in a very slow oven (250°F) for about 20 minutes, or until a knife inserted near the center comes out clean. Cool the custard and cut it into tiny diamond shapes.

Heat 5 cups clear chicken consommé with 1 cup white wine and season with salt and pepper to taste. Garnish each cup of consommé with the custard diamonds and finely shredded orange peel.

HOMARD À L'ARCHIDUC
(*Lobster Archduke*)

Place 6 pounds live lobsters in cold salted water and bring it to the boiling point. Drain the lobsters, split lengthwise, and crack the claws. Lay the halves shell side down in a wide shallow pan and surround them with the claws. Add 2 carrots, 8 sprigs of parsley, 2 bay leaves, a little salt and pepper, and enough liquid, half white wine and half water, to reach to the top of the shells. Place the lobsters in a moderate oven (350°F) and cook for 20 minutes, or until the meat is tender and opaque. Remove and discard the veins and sacs. Slice and reserve the claw and tail meat and reserve the tomalley and the coral, if any. Sauté 5 shallots, finely chopped, in a little butter. Add the lobster pan juices, strained, and reduce the liquid by one half. Add 1 cup heavy cream and the reserved tomalley and coral. Warm the sliced lobster meat in butter, flame it with ½ cup heated brandy, and use it to fill the half-shells. Pour part of the sauce over the filled shells and pass the rest separately.

Filet de Boeuf Fervaal
(Fillet of Beef Fervaal)

Have the butcher trim a large fillet of beef. Tie the thin end back toward the center to make a shorter and thicker roast, and lard the meat at ¾-inch intervals with strips of larding pork. Lay the fillet in a deep earthenware dish and cover it with 2 carrots, 1 large onion, and 1 peeled lemon, all thinly sliced. Add 3 sprigs of parsley, 1 crumbled bay leaf, ½ teaspoon dried thyme, a dash of white pepper, and ½ cup oil. Cover the dish with a cloth and marinate the fillet for 3 hours, turning it six times.

Reduce 4 cups beef bouillon over high heat until it is thick and syrupy. Set this glaze aside.

Remove the meat from the marinade and roast it in a buttered roasting pan in a very hot oven (450°F), basting it occasionally with ½ cup melted butter, to the rare stage. Allow about 12 minutes per pound. During the last 5 or 6 minutes of roasting, brush the meat with the prepared glaze three times. Turn off the oven heat and open the door for 3 minutes. Close the door and let the meat rest in the oven for 12 minutes. Arrange the fillet on a flameproof platter in a ring of duchess potatoes and ham and put the platter under the broiler long enough to brown the potatoes lightly. Garnish the platter with artichoke bottoms sprinkled with chopped herbs.

To make the sauce, add the remaining glaze to the roasting pan with ½ cup Madeira and cook over moderate heat, stirring in all the brown bits. Strain the sauce and add 1 truffle, finely minced and heated for 5 minutes in ¼ cup Madeira. If the sauce is too salty, add a little more Madeira. Pour the sauce into a heated sauceboat and pass separately. Serves 6 to 8.

Duchess Potato and Ham Border

Cook 6 to 8 large potatoes, cut in pieces, in boiling salted water until they are very soft. Drain off the water, cover the pan, and shake it over low heat for 3 to 4 minutes to dry the potatoes well. Rice the potatoes, beat in 5 tablespoons butter and salt to taste, and set them aside to cool. Beat in 4 egg yolks, one at a time, to make the duchess potato mixture.

Make ham balls as follows: Combine 1 cup ground cooked ham with 2 shallots, minced, 2 tablespoons finely chopped blanched almonds, 1 tablespoon each of minced parsley and mayonnaise, and a little salt, if necessary. Shape the mixture into 16 marble-sized balls and chill them well.

Spread a strip of the duchess potatoes, large enough to enclose the fillet, on a flameproof platter. Press the ham balls at even intervals into the strip. Pack the remaining potato mixture into a pastry bag fitted with a large fluted tube and pipe large rosettes over the ham balls. Fill the areas between rosettes with potato swirls. Sprinkle the potatoes with melted butter and brown them under the broiler with the fillet, as above.

Soufflé d'Asperges
(*Asparagus Soufflé*)

Snap the tough ends from 2½ pounds asparagus and steam the green spears in salted water until they are tender. Drain the asparagus and reserve the water. Force the asparagus through a sieve or purée it in a blender to make 1½ cups purée. Melt a generous ¼ cup butter in a heavy saucepan, stir in 6 tablespoons flour, and add gradually ¾ cup milk and ¼ cup of the reserved water. Cook the sauce over low heat, stirring constantly, until it thickens. Add the purée and cool the sauce slightly. Beat in 4 egg yolks, season with salt and pepper to taste, and fold in 6 stiffly beaten egg whites. Pour the mixture into a buttered soufflé dish, set the dish in a pan of water only slightly larger than the dish, and bake the soufflé in a moderately hot oven (375°F) for 45 minutes, or until it is puffed and brown. Arrange rolled-up prosciutto slices around a platter, allowing enough space in the center for the soufflé dish. Brown ¾ cup bread crumbs in 1 cup butter and add 1 teaspoon grated orange rind and salt to taste. Serve the soufflé at once and pass the brown butter sauce.

POULARDE ROSE MARIE
(*Chicken Rose Marie*)

Truss 2 fat pullets as for roasting and parboil them in salted water for 10 minutes. Drain them, cover with fresh cold water, and add 2 onions, 2 carrots, and 2 celery stalks, all thinly sliced. Bring the water to a boil, reduce the heat, and simmer the chickens, covered, for 35 to 45 minutes, or until they are tender. Transfer the cooled birds to a platter, remove the skin, and chill the birds.

Skim the fat from the chicken stock and reduce it over high heat to 4 cups. Gradually stir in 2 lightly beaten egg whites, bring the stock to a rolling boil, and remove it from the heat. Let the stock stand for 10 minutes and strain it through a sieve lined with cheesecloth. Melt 3 tablespoons butter, stir in ¼ cup flour, and cook the roux until it is smooth. Add gradually the strained stock and cook the sauce, stirring constantly, for 10 minutes. Tint the sauce pink with paprika and add salt and pepper to taste. Soften 2 envelopes gelatin in ½ cup dry sherry and dissolve it in the hot sauce. Cool this *chaud-froid* sauce until it is on the point of setting but is still liquid. Trim the chickens and cover them with several coats of the sauce, applying two or three layers with a pastry brush and pouring on the final layer to achieve a smooth surface. Let each layer set before applying another. Decorate the top layer with truffle cutouts and tarragon leaves before it sets. Arrange the chickens on cold rice salad and garnish the platter with chopped aspic. For 6 to 8.

COLD RICE SALAD

In a flameproof casserole brown lightly ⅓ cup minced onion in a generous ¼ cup butter. Add 2½ cups long-grain rice and 2 truffles, peeled and chopped, and stir the rice with a wooden spoon over moderate heat until the grains are glazed and slightly transparent. Slowly stir in with a fork 7 cups boiling chicken stock. Cover the casserole and bake the rice in a moderately hot oven (375°F) for 20 to 25 minutes, or until the rice is tender and the stock is absorbed. Stir in 2 tablespoons each of French dressing and heavy cream and 1 cup chopped mushrooms sautéed for 5 minutes in 3 tablespoons butter. Cool the rice, press it into an oiled shallow round pan, and chill it thoroughly. Unmold the rice onto a chilled platter and use as a base for arranging the chicken Rose Marie.

This rice may also be served as a salad, with French dressing.

SALADE DE CHAMPIGNONS ET CRESSON
(*Watercress and Mushroom Salad*)

Marinate 1 cup thinly sliced mushrooms for 1 hour in a mixture of ½ cup olive oil, ¼ cup wine vinegar beaten with 2 teaspoons heavy cream, ½ teaspoon each of salt and sugar, and ¼ teaspoon freshly ground black pepper. Combine the mushrooms and marinade with 1 onion and 1 peeled and cored tart apple, both thinly sliced, and the leaves from 2 bunches of watercress. Sprinkle the salad with 1 teaspoon each of chopped chervil and chives.

COUPE RÊVE DE BÉBÉ
(*Baby's Dream*)

Hull 1 quart strawberries and pick out 1½ cups large perfect fruit. Steep this fruit in a mixture of ⅓ cup orange juice and 1 tablespoon orange-flavored liqueur sweetened with 1½ tablespoons confectioners' sugar. Force the remaining berries through a sieve and add 1 tablespoon orange-flavored liqueur and confectioners' sugar to taste. Chill a 2-quart glass bowl and half-fill it with 3 cups pineapple sherbet. Cover the sherbet with the strawberry purée and cover the purée with 2 cups raspberry sherbet, rounded in a dome shape. Cover the raspberry sherbet with the whole strawberries and their liquid. Decorate the edges of the bowl with ⅓ cup heavy cream, whipped, sweetened with confectioners' sugar and flavored with 2 teaspoons grated orange rind. Decorate with crystallized violets.

GÂTEAU DE BAPTÊME
(*Baptismal Cake*)

Cream ½ cup butter, gradually add 3 cups sugar, and beat the mixture until it is creamy. Add 12 egg yolks, 2 at a time, beating after each addition. Sift 6 cups flour with 4 teaspoons baking powder and add this to the batter alternately with 2 cups milk. Line the bottom and sides of a buttered 10-inch springform pan with brown paper, allowing it to extend 2 inches above the rim of the pan, and butter the paper. Pour the batter into the pan, smooth the top with a knife, and put the pan on a baking sheet. Bake the cake in a moderately slow oven (325°F) for about 1 hour, or until it tests done. Cool the cake on a rack and set it aside until the following day.

Cut the cake into 4 layers and sprinkle each layer with a little orange-flavored liqueur. Spread with orange butter cream and sandwich the layers together, smoothing and trimming the sides and edges. Glaze the sides with white fondant icing and transfer the cake to a platter. Pack pale yellow royal icing into a pastry bag fitted with a fluted tube and pipe rosettes around the base of the cake. Spread the top with pale yellow fondant icing and pipe a row of pearls of royal icing around the edge of the top where it meets the white icing. The infant's name may be piped around the top in royal icing. An elaborate bouquet of pastel-colored flowers should be piped onto the top of the cake, but this can be done only by someone who has learned cake decorating. Fresh flowers may be laid around the cake.

CONSOMMÉ CHRISTIANA

Bring to a boil ½ cup water, ¼ cup butter, and a pinch of salt. Add ½ cup flour all at once and stir the dough briskly until it forms a ball and cleans the sides of the pan. Cool the dough slightly and beat in 2 eggs, one at a time, beating well after each addition. Shape the dough into tiny rounds with 2 spoons, or press small rounds through a pastry tube onto a buttered baking sheet. Bake the puffs in a very hot oven (450°F) for 5 minutes, reduce the heat to moderate (350°F), and bake them for 15 to 20 minutes, or until they are golden, dry, and crisp. Turn off the heat, open the oven door for 3 minutes, close the door, and let the tiny profiteroles dry in the oven for 30 minutes. Make a small incision in the side of each and fill it with a well-salted chestnut purée.

Simmer 6 cups beef consommé with a generous cup of pitted and drained sweet cherries for 5 minutes. Serve each cup of consommé garnished with some of the cherries and with a few chestnut profiteroles, added at the last minute.

POULET EN COCOTTE BONNE FEMME
(*Chicken in the Pot Bonne Femme*)

Season two 3-pound broiling chickens with salt and pepper and brown the birds on all sides in ½ cup butter in a large earthenware casserole. Add ½ cup chicken consommé and ¼ cup dry white wine and lay the chickens on their sides. Roast the birds in a moderate oven (350°F), basting and turning them frequently, for about 1 hour, or until they are tender. Add more wine and consommé if necessary. Turn the birds breasts up for the last 20 minutes.

Cook 2 cups potatoes, cut into ½-inch cubes, in ⅓ cup butter until they are tender, shaking the pan frequently. Sprinkle the potatoes with 2 tablespoons minced parsley and add salt and pepper to taste. Skim the fat from the broth in the casserole and add the potatoes, 3 table-spoons finely diced pimiento, 3 thick slices of bacon, cut into dice and sautéed until crisp, and 1½ cups button mushrooms, sautéed in the potato butter for 5 minutes. Garnish with watercress and serve the chicken from the casserole.

SALADE D'ÉPINARDS
(*Spinach Salad*)

Wash and pat dry 1 pound spinach, remove all the large stems, and tear the leaves into pieces. Wash and pat dry 1 bunch of watercress and re-move all the stems. Chill the leaves until they are crisp and mix them together in a large bowl.

Combine 1 garlic clove, crushed, ½ teaspoon each of salt and grated lemon rind, ¼ teaspoon each of paprika and pepper, and 2 tablespoons tarragon vinegar. Add gradually ½ cup olive oil, beating constantly, and beat in 2 tablespoons sour cream. Pour the dressing over the greens, toss them well, and crumble 6 slices cooked crisp bacon over the salad.

MOUSSE AUX FRAISES
(*Strawberry Mousse*)

Force 1 quart hulled strawberries through a sieve, or purée them in a blender, and add the juice of ½ lemon and ½ cup confectioners' sugar. Whip 1½ cups heavy cream until it is stiff and fold in 2 egg whites stiffly beaten with ½ cup confectioners' sugar. Add the strawberry purée and a few drops of grenadine. Pour the mixture into an oiled mold, stretch wax paper or plastic wrap over the top, and adjust the lid. Pack the mold in a mixture of 6 parts chopped ice to 1 part rock salt, and freeze the mousse, without stirring, for 4 hours. Or set the mold in the home freezer for 4 hours. Unmold to serve.

POTAGE PIERRE-LE-GRAND
(*Peter the Great Soup*)

In a large saucepan cook 2 cups diced celery, 1 cup sliced carrots, 2 sprigs each of thyme and parsley, and ½ bay leaf in boiling salted water to cover for 35 minutes. In another pan stir 3 tablespoons flour into 2 tablespoons melted butter and add gradually 2 cups scalded milk. Cook the sauce for 5 minutes, stirring constantly. Stir it into the vegetables and simmer the soup for 15 minutes. Force the soup through a sieve or purée it in a blender. Fold 2 beaten egg yolks into 1 cup heavy cream, lightly whipped, add this mixture to the soup, and season with nutmeg, salt, and pepper to taste. Serve with toasted croutons and a garnish of tiny balls of Roquefort rolled in minced parsley.

FILET DE SOLE CASANOVA
(*Fillet of Sole Casanova*)

Arrange 8 fillets of sole in a buttered pan and sprinkle them with salt, white pepper, and 2 tablespoons melted butter. Add ⅔ cup dry white wine and bake the fillets in a moderately hot oven (375°F) for about 15 minutes, basting them every 5 minutes. Poach 16 small oysters in their own liquor until the edges curl. Simmer 1 cup tiny bay scallops in salted water to cover for 5 minutes. Arrange the fillets on a flameproof platter, cover them with the oysters and scallops, well drained, and keep them warm. Add the oyster liquor and scallop water to the pan in which the sole was cooked. Reduce the stock over high heat by two thirds and cool and reserve it.

Melt 1½ tablespoons butter in a heavy saucepan, stir in 3 tablespoons flour, and cook the roux, stirring, over low heat for 3 minutes. Scald 1½ cups milk with 2 thin onion slices and 1 sprig of parsley. Strain the milk into the roux, stirring with a whisk, and cook the sauce, stirring, until it thickens. Reduce the heat and cook the sauce, stirring occasionally, for 10 minutes. Add 2 tablespoons heavy cream and nutmeg, salt, and white pepper to taste. Cool the sauce slightly, beat in 3 egg yolks, and stir it into the reserved fish stock. Reheat the sauce over low heat but do not let it boil. Pour it over the sole and put the platter under a very hot broiler to glaze the sauce. Surround the fillets with triangles of white bread browned in saffron butter and lightly salted.

Noix de Veau Prince Orlov
(*Veal Prince Orlov*)

Season a boneless "nut" of veal with salt and pepper and let it stand at room temperature for 30 minutes. (The "nut" is the tender piece of meat that lies along the inner side of the calf's hind leg. If it is unavailable use a boned rolled leg of veal.) Rub the meat generously with butter and lay it in a casserole on a bed of 2 onions and 2 carrots, all thinly sliced. Braise the meat in a moderate oven (350°F) until it is lightly browned. Add ½ cup melted butter and cook the meat, basting it frequently with the pan juices, for 40 to 50 minutes, or until it is very tender. Transfer the meat to a flameproof platter, reserving the vegetables.

Cook 2 large onions, cut in pieces, in a little boiling salted water until they are soft. Drain the onions and force them through a sieve or purée them in a blender. In a large saucepan sauté 1 shallot, chopped, in 3 tablespoons butter until it is transparent. Add ⅓ pound mushrooms, finely chopped, and cook for 5 minutes. Combine the onion purée, the chopped mushrooms, and 2 cups Mornay sauce. Season the sauce with salt and white pepper.

Slice the cooked veal, dip each slice in the sauce, and reshape the roast. Spread the roast with more of the sauce and keep it warm.

Force the reserved vegetables through a sieve and return them to the casserole. Add ½ cup Madeira and stir the sauce over low heat. Thicken the sauce with 1 teaspoon flour kneaded with 1 teaspoon butter, season with salt and pepper to taste, and strain into a sauceboat.

Sprinkle the veal with ½ cup grated Gruyère, brown the topping under the broiler, and sprinkle with 1 truffle, peeled and finely chopped.

Bombe Don Juan

Line a bombe mold rinsed in cold water with a 1-inch layer of peach ice cream, adjust the lid, and store it in the freezer. Prepare a *pâte-à-bombe:* Boil together ½ cup each of water and sugar until a candy thermometer registers 217°F. Cool the syrup. Beat 4 egg yolks in the top of a double boiler until they are light. Set the pan over simmering water and add the sugar syrup in a thin stream, beating constantly. Cook the *pâte-à-bombe,* stirring slowly, for about 12 minutes, or until it is thick and has doubled in volume. Set the pan in a large pan of ice and beat the *pâte-à-bombe* until it is cold. It will be smooth, pale, and thick. Fold in 1½ cups heavy cream, whipped, ½ cup praline powder, and 2 tablespoons kirsch. Pour this mixture into the hollow center of the bombe mold, cover the cream with wax paper or plastic wrap, and adjust the lid. Freeze the bombe for 6 hours in a home freezer or in a mixture of 3 parts chopped ice to 1 part rock salt. Unmold the bombe and circle the base with candied cherries.

October 1962

HIGH AND DRY

Joseph Wechsberg

We paid a sentimental visit to our friend Raymond Cordier, who retired a couple of years ago as first barman on the S.S. *France*. The day before, the *France* had been taken over by its crew in a desperate attempt to create public sentiment that might save the beautiful ship. She was obstructing the harbor in Le Havre. But the fate of the *France* had been decided, and we knew it. Raymond, one of my all-time favorite barmen, could make a special drink for every conceivable symptom of *mal de mer* and *mal au coeur*. Great barmen are kindhearted, wise men, and Raymond had spent many nights at the Riviera Bar, listening to confessions of his customers. He could have written a fascinating book, but, unlike many characters of our show-off age who can't wait to tell all, Raymond keeps his secrets; he is a gentleman.

He has been lucky. No man likes to stop working at fifty-five, the obligatory retirement age of the French Line's seagoing personnel, and his pension is rather small. One of his loyal customers at the Riviera Bar was James Rothschild. A few months after Raymond left the *France*, he was approached and offered the job of *directeur* of Le Café Français, the top restaurant of the Rothschild-controlled Hotel P.L.M. Saint-Jacques.

We found Raymond, wise and warm and dignified as ever, at his new empire, a successful evocation of the Belle Époque, with marble tables and old-style chairs, red plush banquettes and lace curtains, palm trees and old lamps. Everything looked a little too new for 1900, but Raymond's pride, an old up-right player piano (PLEASE DO NOT TOUCH), conveyed an authentic impression, and so did the lovely old posters of the Paris-Lyon-Méditerranée railroad (also a Rothschild enterprise), offering Wagons-Lits with *"lits-salons et cabinets de toilette,"* *"Menton à 17½ heures de Paris et 11 minutes de Monte Carlo,"* *"L'Hiver à Nice,"* *"Allevard-les-Bains, Billets à Prix Réduits."* Those were the days— and nights.

Now the atmosphere, shortly before lunch, was fittingly nostalgic for our depressed frame of mind. Raymond said he'd hoped that President Giscard d'Estaing might reconsider and save the *France* though it cost the French taxpayers millions of dollars. But the prestige! "They might have turned her into a floating showroom for our *haute couture*. Many industries might have helped. It *could* have been done. . . . I've hired a few youngsters who just finished the French Line's hotel school in Le Havre. I hope the restaurant personnel and the kitchen people will find jobs. They are superbly trained. But there will be severe problems during the transition period." Not everybody has the background of Raymond, who in 1969 was awarded the Diplôme d'Honneur of the Ordre de la Courtoisie Française, under the patronage of the President of the Republic. Another superstar who found a job was Henri Le Huédé, retired *chef de cuisines* of the *France*, who will take over Laurent in Paris after it is completely re-decorated.

Raymond said his landlocked bartenders don't make his nautical specialties such as the "Bullshot" (consommé with lemon juice, a little vodka, a few drops of Worcestershire sauce and Tabasco, salt and pepper), which was the preferred breakfast for passengers who had gone to bed rather late. Instead we had another Raymond specialty, a Fernet Branca with a drop of crème de menthe. The chefs began to arrange the hors d'oeuvres on a large sideboard. The Café Français offers a meal of regional specialties, with "all the wine you can drink," for sixty-five francs, everything included. This time it was the Quercy and Périgord, with *vin de Cahors*. The *prix fixe* menu is enormous. Half a dozen salads, among them *salade de tomates à l'eau-de-vie* (tomato salad with brandy) and a cucumber and green pepper salad. Cold things: *rillettes de dinde* (spiced turkey spread), *pâté de foie de porc* (pork liver pâté), and wonderful *charcuterie*. Hot hors d'oeuvres: *fraise de veau ravigote* (tripe ravigote) and *saucisse et gésier confits aux lentilles* (conserve of sausage and gizzards with lentils). At that point I would quit. But Raymond's sturdy eaters (Germans and Belgians, but also quite a few Frenchmen) now start really going, with a heavy entrée—*confit d'oie aux deux pommes* (preserved goose with potatoes) or *magret de canard* (breast of force-fed duck) or *aiguillette de boeuf lardé et braisé au vin* (braised beef in wine)—and cheese (the fine goat cheese from Rocamadour), and dessert and coffee. Whereupon they continue their business meetings or go to look at the Mona Lisa. It seemed incredible, but perhaps I was like that when I was young.

Raymond said the Rothschilds often come in to keep an eye on their culinary investment. "Monsieur Élie likes to prepare the salads himself. Monsieur Guy will come on Saturday with a small party, and I'll see him this afternoon about the menu. All of them are exacting and gracious—a good mixture. After lunch I'll go home to Le Havre. Usually I go home on Friday afternoons and return Monday mornings, in time to supervise lunch. I have only a tiny apartment here, but I am in Paris only five days, and my wife has become used to my being away. It used to be weeks or months. Now it's only five days." There was a wistful look in his eyes. I asked him whether he missed the *France*.

"Of course I do. We'll always be homesick for the beautiful ship. Some former passengers come here, and inevitably we talk about her. I worked very hard there at the Riviera Bar, but sometimes I wish I were back. Not that I have problems here. I was a steward and a *chef de rang* before I became barman; I learned the restaurant business quite thoroughly."

I said he had been a fine barman, never making a mistake when a dozen orders came at the same time. He would look at you while he mixed your drink, never glancing at his bottles, never spilling a drop. People were ecstatic about his Bloody Mary and his "Mimosa," half a glass of orange juice filled to the brim with Champagne.

"Yes," Raymond said. "It was a wonderful time. And now it's all over. Nothing remains but the memory of the *France*."

We drank to the memory, shook hands, and I walked out.

January 1975

PARISIAN POLICE

Joseph Wechsberg

The Paris police force was created on March 15, 1667, under Louis XIV. It was then called La Lieutenance de Police. In 1800 it was reorganized and has since been known as the Préfecture de Police. Even its bitter enemies in the best criminal circles consider it an exceptionally well-organized force. It publishes a monthly magazine, *Liaisons* (which is not what you think). The Préfecture's formidable archives were often used by Victor Hugo and other novelists, by historians and mystery writers. The Musée de la Préfecture de Police occupies the top floor of the rather sinister building at 36, quai des Orfèvres, exhibiting documents about important crimes and weapons from prominent murder cases. Certain things are not shown because of their "immoral aspects." One can draw one's own conclusions.

The museum is open on Thursday afternoons, and I was surprised to find so many visitors there in spite of the lack of elevator and the many stairs. Most visitors cared little for the historical exhibits and seemed morbidly attracted by the pistols, knives, hammers, pieces of rope, and other tools of murder used by celebrated killers who bumped off wives and lady friends, neighbors and enemies, rich people and politicians. Monsieur Roger Coutarel, the curator who took me through, said regretfully that *la petite salle de criminologie* was the most popular of all. In fact, he said, some visitors complain because the murder weapons have been cleaned and show no bloodstains. M. Coutarel, a slim, nonviolent specimen, seemed ill at ease in the presence of so much cruelty. "Everybody seems deeply interested nowadays in violence and aggression," he said with a sigh.

The museum is arranged chronologically. I found the first two rooms, devoted to the *ancien régime* and the Revolution, the most fascinating. I suppose I too am a nonviolent specimen. I wouldn't mind spending some time in the archives, though. The oldest surviving police documents are dated 1584. They are written in Old French, and I couldn't read them anyway. In the *salle de l'ancien régime* I saw documents about the assassination of "Roy Henry Quatrième" (Henri IV) by François Ravaillac, a fanatic, in 1610. Ravaillac was tortured and quartered, and for a while at least no one felt like assassinating another king. There is a picture of the Marquise de Brinvilliers, who was executed in the Place de Grève. The nice woman had quietly poisoned her father and brothers. Papers document the "affair of the necklace," involving Marie-Antoinette and Cardinal de Rohan. Did I hear, *"Oh la la!"*? Correct. Some engravings show the sad life of the "daughters of joy." One is entitled "La désolation des filles de joie" and dated 1760. The poor call girls never had it easy. The police were always after them.

There is an interesting letter written by the Marquis de Sade on January 3, 1786, from the Bastille, as well as documents about the notorious Cartouche, who (according to M. Coutarel) "kept the police in check for almost ten years before he was caught." Various papers signed by Louis XIV and countersigned by the unpopular Colbert are exhibited along with letters from the same king authorizing the Jesuits to hear confession if the prisoners at the Bastille wanted to go (1691). The displays include a view of the Opéra fire in 1763. There even is an ordinance dated 1725, fixing the prices of meat. Obviously, everything has happened before. The museum shows the history of France, seen through a somewhat darkened looking glass, and illuminates lots of long-forgotten *affaires célèbres.* Who remembers that the Maréchal de Biron was executed in 1602? So was the wife of the Maréchal d'Ancre. Now, what did *she* do? What was *le massacre de Henri le Grand*?

I didn't want to profess my ignorance by asking M. Coutarel. He thought I knew.

Room No. 2 gives a fine (police) insight into the French Revolution. M. Pierre Augustin Caron, better known as Beaumarchais, was arrested—not for the first time—on November 28, 1792. Earlier he had married a rich widow and bought himself a fancy title, Général des Chasses et la Capitainerie de la Varenne du Louvre. That had been in 1763, when a seven-year-old *Wunderkind,* Wolfgang Amadeus Mozart, happened to be in Paris with his father, performing on the harpsichord. Beaumarchais later acted as a double or maybe triple agent for Louis XVI, got involved as corespondent in several adultery cases, and played a part in the American Revolution, but that is past history. We are happy that he wrote *Le Mariage de Figaro,* which Lorenzo Da Ponte and Mozart, no longer a *Wunderkind* but a perfect Wonder, turned into the masterpiece of masterpieces, *Le Nozze di Figaro.* Apropos the American Revolution, there is the decree naming Lafayette Commandant en chef des Gardes nationales de France.

Much space is given to the arrest of Louis XVI and Marie-Antoinette, who were taken to the Temple prison where the king, a super-gourmand, was served three soups, four *entrées,* three roasts, three compotes, a bottle of Champagne, a carafe of Bordeaux, one of Madeira, and four cups of coffee. That was lunch, and dinner was similar. Well, we all know what happened to him and his Queen; let us hope he enjoyed his last supper before going to the guillotine. There is also a picture of Docteur J. I. Guillotin, who introduced the lovely gadget named after him. He is perhaps considered by some a glorious member of the medical profession. The *docteur* was arrested though in 1792; serves him right. Jean-Paul Marat was assassinated by Charlotte Corday on July 13, 1793. She was guillotined four days later. A copy of Marat's newspaper, *L'Ami du Peuple,* is exhibited under glass.

Room No. 3, "La Préfecture," shows portraits of all the Préfets, including the present one, and records of many crimes. A certain Louvel, the assassin of the duc de Berry, is seen walking to the scaffold in 1820. (Criminals seem to have no first names as far as the Paris police is concerned.) A list of jewels of the Queen of Westphalia, stolen by one Maubreuil in 1814, boggles the visitor. A report was written about "L'Affaire Maubreuil" for Talleyrand, who was going to attend the

Congress of Vienna, taking along his celebrated chef, Carême, thereby introducing the diplomacy of the palate. How about reviving it, Dr. Kissinger?

The cholera epidemic in Paris in 1832 is recalled, along with an early infernal machine designed by one Fieschi and a model of the bomb thrown by Orsini against the coach of Their Majesties. Napoleon III and his Empress were not hurt. After this attempt Napoleon commissioned Charles Garnier to build the grandest, most expensive opera house in the world. The Paris Opéra is still there, but no one remembers poor Orsini to whom—in some way—we owe it. Other exhibits include police reports about Messrs. Verlaine and Rimbaud in 1870 and 1873 and the *"crise de jalousie"* between the two poets. (I'm quoting M. Coutarel.) On February 10, 1894, "the poet Verlaine had drunk so many apéritifs at a *banquet littéraire de la plume,* that he had to be taken forcibly back to his domicile," according to the police. Forcibly. The thought of poor Verlaine, a sensitive poet, in the hands of the *flics* is not pleasant.

Some of the most interesting exhibits are the uniforms displayed on mannequins in the various rooms. They show the development of police uniforms, from riches to rags, getting more simple (and comfortable) as the years went by. Of the oldest uniforms only engravings exist: the seventeenth-century Arbalétriers de la Ville, the early Garde de Paris, the Gardes Françaises. After the establishment of the Préfecture a succession of regular uniforms was designed, the latest in 1950. Originally the police wore black. During the nineteenth century their uniforms seemed to reflect the earlier black clothes of the Inquisition. Few uniforms were worn during sieges and revolutions. Prudent people didn't know which way the tide might turn. (After the sadly mishandled Revolution of 1848 in Vienna, many ex-revolutionaries put on top hats to appear solidly bourgeois.) Even the police were careful: Many agents wore dark gray outfits that blended into the dark house walls. Gradually, the official uniforms switched from black to dark blue and finally to the shade of blue that is worn today. The modern uniforms were introduced in 1930 and later made more comfortable. Today the *agents de police* wear blue shirts in summertime. Some wear white jackets, but basically blue remains the color of the police.

Historically, the development of uniforms began with the Gendarmerie Impériale (Napoleon was still around) in 1813, the Garde de Paris in 1814, the Garde Impériale in 1815 (the return of Napoleon), the Gendarmerie Royale in 1816, the Garde Municipale in 1830, and the Garde Civique Parisienne, an auxiliary citizens' force, in 1848. The fateful year 1848 also saw a change in the uniforms of the Garde Républicaine. Apparently one of the first things every new regime in France did—and that goes for monarchists and republicans, reactionaries and revolutionaries—was to call in designers and tailors and order new uniforms for the Paris police. During the siege of 1870 there was the Garde Républicaine, and three years later, with the Third Republic firmly established, there was the Légion de la Garde Républicaine.

Time marches on at the police museum. One sees the pistol that Gorgulov used to fatally shoot President Paul Doumer, who had edited the magazine *Rapide,* as well as a picture of Raoul Villain (*nomen est omen*), who murdered Jean Jaurès on the eve of World War I. A plan of the district, with the rue Montmartre marked by a cross indicating where the assassination occurred, is displayed. (As early as 1895 some fellows tried to blow up the Banque Rothschild.) One is reminded of the terrible fire down in the *métro* in 1902, two years after it began operating, that killed seventy people. Many people said, "I knew it wouldn't work; I told you so." Well, it does work and is a great subway. There is also a model of the oven where Monsieur Bluebeard, alias Landru, burned his ladies—or what remained of them.

And, toward the end, there is a photograph of General von Choltitz as he arrived at the Préfecture de Police on August 25, 1944, after surrendering, ignoring Hitler's paranoiac orders to "burn Paris." No doubt a visit to the museum is instructive and entertaining. It proves, among other things, that human nature never really changes.

April 1974

A NOSE

Joseph Wechsberg

Among the two-thousand-odd French perfumes that were created during the past hundred and fifty years, less than two dozen have been lastingly successful. A great perfume is created only once every ten years or so, and there are fewer than ten men in the world who have the extraordinary sense of smell, as well as the imagination, taste, and olfactory memory, needed to create a good perfume. The French call such an expert *un nez* (a nose). The world's three best-selling perfumes—Chanel's No. 5, Lanvin's Arpège, and Guerlain's Shalimar—are all half a century old. These and other fascinating facts of the fragrant life were given to me by M. Robert Guerlain, the fifth-generation member of the celebrated perfume firm that was founded in 1828 by Pierre François Pascal Guerlain. His picture hangs in the beautiful boardroom of the Guerlain building at 68, avenue des Champs-Élysées. He looks like a twin brother of Giuseppe Verdi, and he was also a genius, in his own way. He came to Paris from Picardy, built a small factory near the Arc de Triomphe (which was then "almost in the countryside"), and opened a small shop in the rue de Rivoli. In 1844 the shop was moved to the rue de la Paix and in 1914 to the Champs-Élysées. The factory is now in Courbevoie. To this day the firm is completely family owned. Fortunately, the Guerlains always produced "a nose." Jacques Guerlain (1874–1963) created Mitsouko (1919) and Shalimar (1925), two great successes. The oldest perfume on the list is Jicky, which was created in 1889. The youngest "nose" is Jean-Paul, thirty-six, who created Chamade (1970), the firm's best seller in France.

I first discovered Guerlain in the summer of 1944, shortly after the Liberation of Paris, when I was on the staff of *Stars and Stripes* in the nearby rue de Berri. (Then some tricky generals sent me for penal servitude to Radio Luxembourg.) Actually it wasn't the perfumes that interested me but the attractive, aromatic young women who sold them. The policy seems to have been changed; today know-how is considered more important than feminine charm. Maybe too many men escorting the women customers looked at the salesladies before paying for the perfumes. This time I went back mainly to look at the beautiful Guerlain building—one of the three or four houses left in the Champs-Élysées that are considered national monuments. Years ago, when the Guerlains wanted to have the façade of their building repainted in a darker color, a high official from the ministry of cultural affairs called them. Nothing must be changed, he said; the same shade of green must be preserved.

Charles Mewès designed the building in 1913 in art nouveau, much ridiculed then and much admired today. The façade of the Guerlain building is very beautiful, with its stucco ornaments, wrought-iron balconies, and brass fixtures; there is a sense of overall harmony in the design, and at night, lighted up, this elegant building is a lovely sight. Unfortunately, the building is flanked by nondescript modern structures; next to it are textile shops, a cinema, a television showroom. That's progress for you. Inside, the building was tastefully decorated by Christian Bérard with white marble and stucco walls, wood paneling, and furniture in the Directoire style. The framed diploma appointing Guerlain Fournisseur de l'Impératrice Eugénie hangs in the corridor of the Beauty Institute. Napoleon III signed it after the firm created Eau de Cologne Impériale, which is still popular. The boardroom below is wood paneled and has a Napoleon III desk. There is a lovely Monet on the premises and not a wrong note in the whole building.

Great perfumes are complicated blends of flower essences, animal matter (taken from the glands), and synthetic (chemical) products. The ingredients are imported from everywhere: jasmine from Morocco, musk from India, cloves from Madagascar, wildflowers from the Ivory Coast, and coriander from Russia. The scents of lilies of the valley, lilacs, and violets are now produced synthetically, but roses, thank goodness, are still roses, although they are very expensive. One kilo of rose essence costs over six hundred dollars, and seventy women are needed to make it. No wonder good perfumes are expensive. Guerlain's Chamade has some fifty ingredients and was perfected after two thousand experiments. The top-secret formulas are known to only two or three members of the family. A great perfume (like a great Champagne) cannot be imitated, even with the help of chemical analysis, because the phenomenon of scent is inexplicable; a scent cannot be "measured." Reproducing a successful perfume year after year is a great problem because the ingredients are never exactly the same. At Guerlain the perfumers are proud of the "roundness" of their finest products—no rough edges—but there is nothing they can do about the changing quality of jasmine from the Atlas Mountains. There are no "vintages" in perfumes, but some are more perishable than others. They should be kept out of light, away from heat, well closed, and preferably in the box. The Guerlain firm still takes the founder's advice: "Make good products, have simple ideas and apply them scrupulously."

January 1973

The Seventh Art

Joseph Wechsberg

Film buffs in France and all over the world revere Henri Langlois, the founder and secretary-general of the French Cinémathèque and of the recently opened Musée du Cinéma. Students of the "seventh art" have called him the most important man in French films. Langlois never wrote, directed, produced, or criticized a film, but his influence on generations of filmmakers has been enormous. He was the first man to realize that films were going to disappear unless somebody collected them. "To show a work of art, it must exist; that is, it must be collected and conserved." No one did this in the early 1930s. There were museums for paintings and sculptures and many other things, but not for films.

"In 1930 the silent film died, and many things were lost. Then Hitler came to power in Germany, and the Nazis burned the great masterpieces of German expressionism by Murnau, Pabst, Fritz Lang. In twenty years no one would have known what *The Cabinet of Dr. Caligari* had been like. I decided to do something about saving this volatile medium."

Langlois—a round man with the face of a sad clown, a soft voice, and a deceivingly quiet manner—has devoted his life to rescuing films from oblivion. He considers cinema "the most significant art of our times." He had no money, no backers, no position; all he had was his idea and the determination to go on in spite of incredible handicaps.

———

The Association de la Cinémathèque Française was created in 1936 to preserve everything concerning films. Among the *présidents d'honneur* are Charlie Chaplin, René Clair, Jean Renoir, and Alain Resnais. All the work was done by Langlois, with the help of admiring acolytes.

Today the Cinémathèque Française is called the National Library of Films. Langlois has collected some sixty thousand films, which are kept at the *"blockhaus"* at Bois-d'Arcy and at the Hôtel de Courcelles. Like all great collectors, he is also an artist who knows the subtle, secret rules. He doesn't just collect; he creates a deeper harmony among his treasures. He wants to preserve the various epochs and schools and watch their interplay. He doesn't talk about his favorites though he admitted, *"Monsieur Chaplin, c'est un très grand monsieur."*

He soon understood that the film collection was only the beginning. He began to look for documents, scripts, scenarios, designs, and letters; he added a laboratory and a large library with thousands of books on the history of the cinema. He began to think about a museum that would be the logical evolution of the Cinémathèque. There were difficulties. French officialdom wasn't impressed by this sloppy genius with the stains on his lapels. Langlois has no patience with petty bureaucrats, snobs, and people who don't share his lifelong fascination. In 1968 he was fired by the government, but his fans raised such a fuss that he got his job back with much more freedom. He is not interested in administrative detail. He likes to visit a retired projectionist or the Flea Market looking for old posters. In Moscow he even managed to get some films from Eisenstein's widow.

After years of hard work he saw his museum opened late in 1972 at the Palais de Chaillot. The City of Paris gave him the space, some two thousand square meters, where he set up sixty small halls with a chronological display of his treasures called "Seventy-five Years of the Cinema of the World." The show is still unfinished, no catalogue exists, and the collections are unlabeled, but the exhibition is fascinating. It starts with the prehistory of the cinema—the sixteenth-century shadow theater in Ceylon, the first *lanterna magica,* an eighteenth-century view-shower, the old panorama box for showing colored slides, the first hand-turned animation machines, giving the illusion of movement, and the early experiments with "decomposing" the movement of flying birds and racing horses. Émile Reynaud's *"jouets d'optique,"* Étienne Marey's first motion picture camera, Edison's experiments, and Max and Emil Skladanowski's Bioskop shown in Berlin in 1895 are represented.

Then came Louis Lumière. One sees the first posters of the Phono-Cinéma-Théâtre with the names of Sarah Bernhardt and Cléo de Mérode; a model of the first studio built by Georges Méliès in the Paris suburb of Montreuil; a model of the first Pathé studio from about 1905; a poster showing Max Linder; the first cartoons; and the start of Gaumont's *actualités*. At this point a sense of déjà vu develops. One seems to walk back into one's youth. (My mother always claimed that I caught pneumonia in 1913 when I was six after sitting through two showings of Victor Hugo's terrifying *Les Misérables*. I had come home in a cold sweat. Could be.)

Walking through Langlois's labyrinth is like hearing an old fairy tale one has almost forgotten. There is the robot one saw in Fritz Lang's *Metropolis,* Buster Keaton's porkpie hat, the caftan Valentino wore in *Son of the Sheik* (remember, ladies?), Greta Garbo's plumed hat from *Queen Christina,* enlargements from D. W. Griffith's *The Birth of a Nation.* The grand epoch of the cinema has begun: Chaplin, Douglas Fairbanks, a uniform worn by Erich von Stroheim, posters showing Clara Bow and Wallace Beery, dresses worn by Mae Murray, Joan Crawford, and Marilyn Monroe. There is much about the great Eisenstein, including a small room filled with exhibits from *Ivan the Terrible.* There are relics of the work of the Italian neorealists: *The Bicycle Thief* and *Miracle in Milan.* There are small screens with slide projections, and there is a replica of a small modern studio, not to mention the red poplin jacket worn by James Dean in *Rebel Without a Cause.* A recent addition is the scenario of Harold Pinter's *The Servant.*

Langlois estimates the value of his exhibits at about five million francs. The French government gave him one and a half million. Where did he get the rest? He gives a tired shrug. "I got it—somehow." He thinks he has more material than anyone else but admits that the Rus-

sians have a lot. ("They were smart; they started collecting very early.")
The Italians, Swedes, and Americans are not far behind. When Langlois wants to buy dresses and other memorabilia, he must compete
with wealthy collectors at public auctions. He gets nothing from the
stars themselves because they don't own the things they wear in their
films. They turn everything back to the studio, "and the studios are
very tough. They don't care about posterity. They want money."

The Cinémathèque's projection room shows five films a day, the
first at three in the afternoon, the last at half past midnight. Some films
date from the early years of the century, and some are much more recent. The day I was there they showed Eisenstein's *Ivan the Terrible*,
Bresson's *Pickpocket*, Mankiewicz's *All About Eve*, Buñuel's *Viridiana*, and
Browning's *The Unholy Three* with Lon Chaney (of *Phantom of the Opera*
fame). Tickets are inexpensive (four francs), and there are always excited people queuing up.

I asked Langlois who comes to see the films he selects.

"Mostly young people and generally people who don't go to the
cinemas on the Grands Boulevards. When we started these showings
thirty years ago I had no idea that Astruc, Resnais, Truffaut, Godard,
Chabrol, and Rivette were regularly in the audience. All of them
admit that their ideas were shaped by these shows. Our Cinémathèque
and the museum are not directed toward the past, as are so many museums, but toward the future. The cinema is a living art, and we must
always be conscious of the future. That's why I am glad that so many
children come here. Museums should be designed primarily for children. The grown-ups come for nostalgia, but the young come for inspiration and excitement, and you never know what may come of it."

July 1973

The Most Intimate Room

Diane Johnson

Many of my best food experiences in France have come at the table of
Colette, who can ski all day and then blithely fix dinner for fourteen
guests from ingredients carried into her Alpine chalet over snowdrifts
several weeks before. For more than twenty years we have joined Colette and her husband, Paul, for ten days of skiing. Colette and Paul
do almost all the cooking for their guests (an English couple, a Swiss
couple, half a dozen French, and us, the token Americans). In the
chalet's *cave* they have stowed hams, cheeses, and wines. Also lettuces,
cabbages, carrots, yogurts by the dozen, cans of tomatoes, smoked
salmon, foie gras, mustard, *cornichons, confitures faites maison,* herrings in
a crock. Legs of lamb and the cubes of veal for *blanquette* are kept
frozen by virtue of being left outside under the snow on a terrace. All
of which makes the atmosphere charmingly approximate that of a
French farmhouse in some earlier century.

The rest of us help scrub vegetables, pare and peel, set the table.
The French guests will take turns preparing some dish or other in ro-
tation, but I, being American, am strangely exempted. We have never
discussed this, but I think it is assumed that, being an American—
even one who has lived in Paris part of the year for many years—
I can't cook. And the worst of it is that when I am there, something

intimidates me, and they are right . . . I can't cook a thing. Nor can I think of a dish I know by heart that is typically American. I might have claimed apple pie, but the Englishwoman, Hilary, has taken that as her specialty—never mind our belief that there is nothing as American (though, to be fair, I suppose it came from England originally). Once, I brought tortillas and chili powder, intending to claim enchiladas as our national dish, but was tactfully waylaid on the grounds that this was the night for Jeanette's cheese fondue.

What our French friends tend to cook *chez eux* is, I've noticed, classic French food right out of Escoffier or Tante Marie: *blanquette, boeuf bourguignon,* and so on—dishes they know well, having cooked them many times before. When you ask about recipes, however, a certain vagueness sets in. Not that they are reluctant to tell you how they do it (as I first suspected), but rather that they often do not exactly know. Whereas, from the time when as a new bride in the '50s I received my first copies of the *Gourmet Cookbook* (volumes 1 and 2), I have yet to be weaned from my dependence on cookbooks, my Paris friends seem never to have had one. Certain French dishes are just made a certain way. True, French magazines offer recipes. My friend Marie-Claude tells me that one such magazine, *Elle à Table,* is really quite good, but Marie-Claude is the exception to my classic-French-dish generalization, having perfected several exotic creations of her own devising. My son-in-law's mother, Josette, tells me: "Some people put tomatoes into a *boeuf bourguignon.* I do so myself. Others do not. It depends." Well, on what? But it's no use asking.

Luckily, the kitchen at Colette's chalet permits me to pry into her cooking secrets, as it has been designed to include guests. This used to be a fairly uncommon arrangement in France, but many an apartment now for sale in Paris boasts of possessing a *cuisine américaine.* Unfortunately, all this usually means is that the kitchen has been put in the living room—a convenient notion for property developers trying to squeeze as many tiny apartments as possible out of formerly grand ones.

In the normal run of things, the guest in a French home does not venture into the kitchen. The first time I tried helpfully to gather the plates at a dinner party, I caught the shocked expression in my hostess's eye. Parisian kitchens can be small, cramped affairs where miracles are produced, but, whatever their size, they contain secrets not to be shared (such as which of the courses was bought at the caterers).

But to return for a moment to *cuisine américaine*. It has always seemed strange to me that a nation so devoted to the idea that American cooking is horrible should be willing to embrace not only its hardware but its name. American cooking is the subject of many a joke. At a recent dinner party where oysters were being served, for instance, someone recounted having seen an American horror film in which the heroine was trustfully dining on oysters with the man who would soon murder her. "Huge, huge oysters. Like that. And she poured ketchup on them." The French guests screamed with mock horror—not for the violence to come but at the idea of ketchup on oysters.

The tradition of tried-and-true, excellent French home cooking by natural-born cooks has expanded over the years, resulting in those comfortable country restaurants that serve what is termed *cuisine bourgeoise*, or *cuisine simple*. And it is simplicity—plus, always in France, great local ingredients—that is its hallmark. There is very little emphasis on "fast" or "easy." Whether cooking in a country inn or at home, the French have a much greater understanding than we Americans do of the fact that certain preparations simply take time. They also rely far more on things that are in season, like certain mushrooms—the sinister *trompette-de-la-mort*, for example. And when asparagus is in season, it is likely, and perfectly acceptable, that you will encounter it at many dinner parties in a row.

But certain more complicated dishes stand out in the repertoires of our friends. Colette's *quiche Lorraine* (she really does live in Lorraine) and her *blanquette de veau*. Hélène's *tarte aux moules*. Josette's *veau à la crème*. We thoroughly relish our friend Gérard's *magrets de canard au poivre vert*, and our son-in-law, Jean-François, makes a delicious *saumon à l'unilatéral* (salmon cooked on salt). All of which takes me back to distant, postwar America and the teacher who said that we had no need to learn the *tu* form as it was unlikely that little Illinois children would ever meet anyone French, let alone go to a French home for dinner.

What the French truly eat in the privacy of a *dîner en famille* must, of course, remain a bit of a mystery. If we could just peer in their windows, maybe we would understand how they stay so much thinner and healthier, and are longer-lived, than Americans. Are they cooking what we think of as "real French food"? Or do they simply snack? Or possibly fast? But whatever it is they are eating, food is a major part of daily discourse. They are always talking about food. And they love to shop. The *métro* allows the determined Parisian cook to go all over town for the best chicken (a man in the Marais), the best cheese place (on the rue de Grenelle), and the best *tarte* (Mulot, on the rue de Seine). Near my last apartment, the owner of the local fish market had a huge oven in which he would bake a big salmon for you at the end of the day and bring it over on a plank in time for dinner. For another secret is that the French cook buys a lot of things ready-made, on the sensible grounds that the specialist—whether *boulanger, épicier,* or *boucher*—simply does it better.

And, finally, a wonderfully practical secret. Many French cooks are helped by a clever little appliance called a *saucière*. This Teflon-coated saucepan rotates on a hot plate, stirring itself and thereby making the hollandaise or béarnaise while you attend to the rest of the dinner. I have to admit that although I have invested in one, I still find it a little daunting, even reproachful. Its very existence seems to suggest that I ought to be concocting a *beurre blanc* or a mayonnaise with every meal. I'll call Jeanette and ask her to dinner. Perhaps she could bring her fondue . . .

SAUMON À L'UNILATÉRAL
(*Salmon Cooked on Salt*)

Serves 4
Active time: 10 min   Start to finish: 20 min
    2 cups coarse sea salt or kosher salt
    1 (1¼-lb) center-cut piece salmon fillet

Spread salt evenly in a dry 10-inch heavy skillet (preferably cast-iron) and heat over moderately high heat until salt is hot to the touch and just beginning to smoke, about 4 minutes.

Pat salmon dry and season flesh with salt and pepper, then put, skin side down, on salt. Cook salmon, covered, without turning, until almost cooked through, 8 to 12 minutes. Remove from heat and let stand, covered, until salmon is just cooked through, 1 to 2 minutes.

Slide a spatula between salmon skin and flesh and transfer salmon to a platter (salmon skin will be too salty to eat).

COQUILLES SAINT-JACQUES WITH BEURRE BLANC

Serves 4

Active time: 30 min   Start to finish: 30 min

- 1½ lb medium sea scallops (24 to 28), tough muscle removed from sides if necessary
- ¼ cup dry vermouth
- 1½ tablespoons minced shallot
- 1½ tablespoons white-wine vinegar
- 1½ tablespoons dry white wine
- 1 tablespoon cold water
- 9 tablespoons cold unsalted butter, cut into tablespoon pieces
- 1½ teaspoons finely chopped fresh tarragon

Marinate scallops in vermouth 15 minutes.

Make beurre blanc:

Simmer shallot in vinegar and wine in a small heavy saucepan until liquid is reduced to about 1 tablespoon. Remove from heat and add water. Reduce heat to low and cook, whisking in 6 tablespoons butter 1 tablespoon at a time, adding each new piece before previous one has melted completely and occasionally lifting pan from heat to cool mixture. (Sauce must not get hot enough to liquefy; it should be the consistency of a thin hollandaise.) Remove from heat and whisk in tarragon and salt and pepper to taste. Keep warm off heat, covered.

Cook scallops:

Drain scallops and pat dry between paper towels. Heat 1½ tablespoons of remaining butter in a 12-inch nonstick skillet over moderately high heat until foam subsides. While butter is heating, season half of scallops with salt and pepper. Sauté scallops, turning once, until just cooked through, about 4 minutes total. Wipe out skillet and sauté remaining scallops in remaining 1½ tablespoons butter in same manner.

Serve scallops with *beurre blanc.*

RHUBARB CHARLOTTE

Serves 6

Active time: 45 min   Start to finish: 1 day

2¼ lb rhubarb, leaves and root ends discarded
1   cup granulated sugar
1½ tablespoons fresh lemon juice
37 (3- by 1-inch) soft ladyfingers
2   tablespoons kirsch
¾   cup chilled heavy cream
3   tablespoons confectioners' sugar

Special equipment: a 6-cup charlotte mold

Cut enough rhubarb into ¼-inch-thick slices to measure 6 cups, reserving remainder for another use. Cook rhubarb, granulated sugar, and lemon juice in a large heavy saucepan over moderately high heat, stirring occasionally, until rhubarb exudes juices. Reduce heat and simmer, stirring occasionally, until rhubarb falls apart and is reduced to about 2 cups, 25 to 30 minutes. Cool to room temperature.

While rhubarb simmers, brush flat side of ladyfingers with kirsch. Lightly oil mold and line with two 24-inch-long crisscrossed sheets of plastic wrap, letting excess hang over side. Line side and bottom of mold with some of the ladyfingers, flat sides facing inward and trimming bottom ones to fit snugly.

Beat together cream and confectioners' sugar until it just holds stiff peaks. Spoon half of rhubarb into mold, smoothing top, and spoon half of cream over it, smoothing top. Cover cream with 1 layer of ladyfingers. Repeat layering with remaining rhubarb, cream, and ladyfingers. Fold plastic wrap to cover charlotte and weight with a flat-bottomed dish filled with a 2-lb weight. Chill charlotte 1 day.

Remove weight and dish. Unfold plastic wrap and invert a platter over mold. Invert charlotte onto platter, using plastic wrap to loosen charlotte.

VEAU À LA CRÈME
(*Veal Tournedos in Cream Sauce*)

Serves 4

Active time: 10 min   Start to finish: 25 min

1 (¾-lb) piece Gruyère, rind discarded
4 slices Canadian bacon
1 veal tenderloin (1¼ lb), trimmed and cut crosswise into 4 equal
   pieces (tournedos)
1 tablespoon unsalted butter
½ cup crème fraîche (4 oz)

Preheat oven to 450°F.

Using a cheese planer or a sharp knife, cut 4 thin slices (4 by 2 inches) from Gruyère. Cook bacon in an ovenproof 10-inch heavy skillet over moderately high heat, turning once, until lightly browned, about 2 minutes total, and transfer to a plate. (Do not clean skillet.)

Pat veal dry and season with salt and pepper. Heat butter in skillet over moderately high heat until foam subsides, then sauté tournedos until browned, about 4 minutes total. (Veal will be only partially cooked.)

Remove skillet from heat and put a slice of bacon, then cheese and crème fraîche, on each tournedos. Roast in middle of oven, uncovered, until cheese begins to melt, 8 to 10 minutes. (Veal should be slightly pink inside.)

Transfer tournedos to plates. Whisk pan juices until blended, season with salt and pepper, then divide among plates.

BLANQUETTE DE VEAU
(*Veal Stew*)

Serves 4 to 6
Active time: 1½ hr   Start to finish: 3 hr

For meat and vegetables
2¾ lb veal breast (bone in)
1 lb boneless veal shoulder, trimmed and cut into 2-inch pieces
2½ qt water
6 fresh parsley sprigs
2 fresh thyme sprigs
1 bay leaf (not California)
4 black peppercorns
2 onions, halved
4 carrots, quartered crosswise
1 leek (white and pale green parts only), halved lengthwise and

cut crosswise into ½-inch pieces
2   tablespoons unsalted butter
½   lb mushrooms, quartered

For sauce
3   tablespoons unsalted butter
3   tablespoons all-purpose flour
2   large egg yolks
2   tablespoons crème fraîche
1½ tablespoons fresh lemon juice

Stew meat and vegetables:

Cut meat away from veal breastbone, reserving bone, and cut meat into 2-inch pieces.

Bring veal breast and shoulder, veal bone, and water to a boil over moderate heat in a 7- to 8-quart heavy pot, skimming froth. While water is heating, wrap parsley, thyme, bay leaf, and peppercorns in a small square of cheesecloth and tie into a bundle to make a bouquet garni. Add bouquet garni and onions to pot and simmer, uncovered, until veal is tender, 1¼ to 1½ hours.

Preheat oven to 300°F.

Transfer veal with a slotted spoon to a heatproof serving dish and keep warm in oven, covered with foil.

Discard veal bone, onions, and bouquet garni, then pour stock through a fine sieve into a large bowl. Return stock to cleaned pot, add carrots and leek, and simmer until tender, 10 to 12 minutes. Transfer vegetables to serving dish. Boil stock until reduced to about 2½ cups, about 10 minutes.

While stock is reducing, heat butter in a 10-inch heavy skillet over moderate heat until foam subsides, then cook mushrooms, stirring, until just tender, 6 to 8 minutes. Transfer to serving dish and season veal and vegetables with salt and pepper. Keep warm in oven.

Make sauce:

Melt butter in a 2- to 3-quart heavy saucepan over moderately low heat, then stir in flour. Cook roux, stirring, 3 minutes (do not let brown). Whisk in reduced stock and simmer, uncovered, whisking occasionally, 15 minutes. Whisk together yolks and crème fraîche in a small bowl, then whisk in 1 cup sauce. Whisk yolk mixture into remaining sauce with lemon juice, then cook over moderately low heat (do not let boil), stirring constantly, until it reaches 160°F on an instant-read thermometer and coats back of a wooden spoon.

Season sauce with salt and pepper and pour over veal and vegetables.

March 2001

PARIS TODAY

GRAND MASTERS

Jonathan Gold

My last lunch in Paris this year was at Les Élysées du Vernet, which
is a staggeringly good restaurant a couple of blocks from the Arc de
Triomphe, at the back of a small hotel favored by minor royalty. You
know all the stuff you've heard about French people deserting their
temples of cuisine for the bargain bistros—packed like hamburger
franchises along a turnpike access road—in the neighborhoods around
the Étoile? Well, something else must be going on here, because Les
Élysées du Vernet, the demesne of chef Alain Solivérès, is crawling
with Frenchmen, natty in that particular kind of fitted blue suit they
all seem to be wearing at the moment with almost identical striped
shirts and plain, post-Regis ties, a room full of bankers and government men draining flutes of Champagne and eyeing the ham trolley with the anticipatory gaze of zoo tigers scoping out a pail of raw
chicken. The ham trolley! Of course!

By the time you get to your table, where a small bowl of olives is already waiting to accompany your apéritif, a uniformed hotel doorman
will have ushered you into the vestibule, where a pretty, well-dressed
woman will have brightened in recognition of your name. A smooth
functionary who is turned out in the somber clothes of a deputy assistant cabinet minister will have checked you off a list and nodded his

approval. Which is to say, in about thirty seconds, the restaurant manages to address the three eternal obsessions of a Frenchman's life—seduction, cuisine, and easy mastery of bureaucracy—without so much as breaking a sweat.

French people, you understand, love reservations, probably because the average restaurant owner takes as much pleasure in telling you that his establishment is *complet* (full) as he does in selling you that 1,500-franc bottle of Côte Rôtie that has been sitting above the stove for years. To be fair, it is very pleasant to be greeted by name and led to a table set up expressly for you. When you have reserved, it is your table; it has always been your table; ever will it remain your table. On such certainties does French civilization rest.

All around you, the ham is being shaved into thin, shockingly pink curls; whole, large fish are separated into fillets and neat mounds of bones, fins, and spent fennel branches.

If you have been wondering why Paris is still considered the capital of world dining, you could do worse than look at Solivérès's scallop appetizer. You've probably had a few great scallops in your day, but this one is extraordinary, toasted to a blackened crunch but still slightly underdone, pully-rare inside, with the texture of fresh taffy, an understated sweetness, and a small but unmistakable fragrance of the sea. As incredible as this bare scallop is, it acts basically as a slate on which play the funky, marvelous flavors of its garnish, the various salty muskinesses of chorizo, *lucques* olives, and hard cheese diced microscopically fine, colliding with and glancing off each other on the tongue like billiard balls on baize. The preparation is simple—you could probably do it yourself given matchless ingredients and a good, sharp knife—but the effect is extraordinarily complex, almost too exhausting to contemplate.

Next, perhaps, a superb *Parmentier de sanglier au panais* (a sort of shepherd's pie of stewed boar blanketed with mashed parsnips), followed by a simple dessert of crackly, thin wafers of sugared pastry, vanilla ice cream, and a sprinkling of roasted autumn fruits. With the dessert, a Beaumes-de-Venise. With the demitasse, a big bowl of sugared almonds and pistachios. On the way out the door, women are given long-stemmed roses; men, bags of those sugared nuts.

One could hardly wish for a better lunch. The gently glowing dining room, with a stunning art nouveau ceiling of vaulted stained glass designed by Gustave Eiffel himself, would be a proud addition to any museum in Europe. The food is perfect. The location is smack in the middle of one of the most heavily touristed precincts in the world. And yet almost nobody I know has even heard of this place, despite its two *Michelin* stars and Solivérès's exalted place in the pantheon of Alain Ducasse's disciples.

Which is to say, if the Paris dining scene, despite all its widely publicized setbacks, is rich enough that a restaurant like Les Élysées du Vernet can get lost in the shuffle, the city must still be a pretty great place to eat.

And it is, even when you least expect it to be—in a smoky brasserie like Le Vaudeville at one o'clock in the morning, perhaps, when the frank deliciousness of a simple frisée salad practically knocks you backward, or when an oyster at a basic Les Halles tourist bistro is brinier, sweeter, than anything you've tasted in San Francisco or New York, or when an anonymous Miromesnil wine bar serves you a plate of heart-stoppingly good garlic sausage. If you frequent such American restaurants as Jean-Georges and Citronelle, you will not be much surprised by anything you find within the stark, leather-lined walls of Guy Savoy, but the next plate of mashed potatoes you run across could change your life.

———

I had come to Paris, I suppose, to check out the newest wave of bargain bistros; the small restaurants, mostly run by refugees from grand-hotel kitchens, whose addresses are currently much coveted by American foodies. This may be the first juncture in recent French history, I might add, where you are more likely to happen upon a fashionable restaurant in the *"Pas Trop Cher"* section in the guidebooks than in the more comprehensive listings of *"Tables Branchées,"* and I had greatly impressed the locals by having had a small meal of grilled fish and sherry at an obscure Biarritz-style cantina whose sole virtue as far as I could tell was its proximity to my hotel. Everybody I met was talking about a chicly grumpy couscous place fitted into an old bistro in the Marais, and a new Thai restaurant that served credible Chiang Mai–

style salads. L'Épi Dupin, L'Ardoise, Bookinistes, and the other bargain bistros I visited were barely better than modest neighborhood cafés in New York, the ones that don't make it into the pages of *Gourmet.*

Grand cuisine, which had descended in an unbroken line from at least Carême to the present, was apparently dead, a museum piece of interest only to tourists and the hopelessly bourgeois.

So while I was not surprised, on the second day of my trip, when I lucked into some hare that may have been the single best thing I have ever eaten, I was a little surprised that I had encountered the dish at Pierre Gagnaire, a card-carrying grand restaurant in another small luxury hotel just off the Champs-Élysées. Gagnaire, after all, is a passionate, non-entrepreneurial chef of the sort that is supposed to be obsolete, and his sedate chambers are about as fashion-forward as a corporate boardroom. Gagnaire is beloved by the Gulfstream V crowd. Gagnaire is where you go for delicate plates of sole with grapefruit and baby fennel, not for anything as earthy as this hare, served in three courses.

Gagnaire can be the greatest restaurant in the world if you hit it right, a gallery of modernist flavors that pop as vividly as anything from early Godard when his images come together—lacquered duck skin with honeyed shiitake mushrooms; smoked black olive gelatin with shallot confit; a tiny spiced pig's-blood pudding steamed in a cabbage leaf—and can leave you shaking your head in bewilderment when they do not. Like Glenn Gould, say, or Kurt Cobain, Gagnaire always seems to be prodding at the limits of his medium, perpetually on the brink of mayhem. It is the possibility of failure in his best dishes, plus the impression of an artist working at the edge of his abilities, that makes his cooking so thrilling. I do not think we will be seeing a bargain bistro from Gagnaire soon.

The excitement in most French cooking seems to involve the nuances of a dish, the many sensations produced by the many different bits of a stewed hen, say, and how the meat reacts over time to its garnishes, to the sauce, to the Chiroubles you happen to be drinking. Gagnaire is all about quick hits instead, startling juxtapositions meant to be absorbed in a moment: thirteen ways of looking at a turnip.

Even by three-star standards, Gagnaire serves a lot of tiny courses before the meal even begins: airy little beignets, perhaps; cunning purées of smoked salmon and avocado wrapped into tight spinach dumplings; tiny onion tarts garnished with nasturtium blossoms. These may be only hors d'oeuvres to the hors d'oeuvres proper, which may include a silver dollar of sweetened haddock, a Bloody Mary sorbet garnished with a chiffonade of fresh horseradish, and a weird, wonderful tartare of mixed, hand-chopped beef and fish, topped with a little seaweed. One has the feeling that one of Gagnaire's grails is to create a seamless link between fish and flesh.

The basic unit of cuisine at Gagnaire is the constantly changing tasting menu of many, many courses . . . say, fish layered between puff pastry with paper-thin slices of dried apples and caramel; grilled scallops balanced on their sides in a pistachio sabayon; or lettuce-wrapped shrimp "dumplings" with tiny bits of ice plant for crunch.

———

Other chefs may attempt unlikely pairings, but Gagnaire outdoes them all with a mind-bending dish of molten foie gras and pressed caviar. Two different kinds of Japanese seaweeds assist in this stunning shotgun wedding of luxury ingredients, a symphony of brininess, crowned with dehydrated cross sections of carrot and a single perfect fried oyster. This may be one of humanity's lifelong dreams fulfilled: to marry these two ultimate foodstuffs without their seeming in the least contrived, the foie gras cooked in such a way as to bring out the sharp livery tones more than the lushness.

Among the tangerine-peel *semifreddo* and the chocolate whatevers on the multicourse tasting dessert was a single prune stuffed with braised licorice root, swathed in burnt sugar and bathed in a richly bitter sauce of caramel and quince: Sharp and mellow, licorice paired with jammy fruit, it was a tiny étude in sensation, and it was powerfully good.

And then there was the hare, served in three courses—first, slices of the grilled saddle; then a sort of savory mush baked into a giant pie whose potent, luscious stink turned every head in the restaurant when the waiter broke the golden crust; and then the incredibly rich *royale* itself, made with reduced blood and various giblets, that may have been the strongest meat I have ever tasted, all of existence compressed into a single, reeking tablespoonful of soft protein. I couldn't wait to eat it again.

The new-style bistro La Régalade, you realize, is an entirely different kind of restaurant, with an aesthetic almost diametrically opposed to that of the austere juxtapositions, the strenuous luxuries presented by the restaurants of grand cuisine. At La Régalade, once you shrug yourself free of your coat, you are brought bread, butter, and a huge terrine that practically sizzles with the flavor of browned pork fat, from which you are invited to scoop out as much as you feel like eating.

If you order *cochonaille* (served family style even if you are the only person at the table who has ordered it), there is a seamless segue into a basket of dried sausage, blood sausage, and spreadable Southwest sausages of which you also eat as much as you want and then perhaps a little more, drowning just a bit in the sea of garlic, pork, and cool Chinon, perhaps digging around in your neighbor's big plate of scallops with basil or a beautiful, earthy soup of puréed lentils and chestnuts ladled over a sort of foie gras mousse that melts in the heat of the broth, adding its own bittersweetness, its wallop of luxurious richness to the purée—a spectacular dish.

Just at the moment you have gorged yourself into rapture, out comes a crisply roasted wood pigeon, bursting with sweet, funky juice; breast red as a fire truck and soft as warmed butter, seasoned simply with pepper and buckshot. I had once eaten a *Parmentier* dish at the Montparnasse bistro L'Assiette, which had a layer of blood sausage where I had expected to find chopped beef, and I have spent nearly a decade looking for a version that was half as good. La Régalade's was even better—buttery mashed potatoes frosted with a thick layer of seasoned blood in the style of Béarn, then topped with more potatoes and run under a salamander for a minute to crisp. I was so happy that I almost wept.

"But where should I eat?" I once asked a newspaperman I knew whose specific advice in Barcelona had once led to two full weeks of great meals, and whose knowledge of Paris restaurants was reputed to be deep. He thought for a minute, and his shoulders finally slumped in defeat.

"Go to the old places," he said. "The old places will do."

It is hard to talk much about food in Paris without plunging deep into the world of metacuisine, the world of cooking well-established in Liebling, Curnonsky, and Elizabeth David, which is to say, the struggle between present-day cooking and its romanticized past.

But in Paris, it is, of course, possible to dine on a certain level as if the last half century never happened. Who doesn't like to fall into an ancient bistro like La Tour de Montlhéry: Chez Denise near the old Les Halles, drink sour Brouilly drawn from a barrel, and gorge yourself silly on lamb with beans, marrow-crowned steaks, and formidable tureens of stewed tripe? Or to wander into an art nouveau brasserie like Bofinger and eat essentially the same meal of *choucroute garnie* and thin Alsatian Riesling that Matisse probably enjoyed?

If you hit À Sousceyrac near the Place d'Aligre market in the right season, you can drink a young Corbières and lunch on divinely gamy grouse mousse, slabs of wonderful foie gras, and a splendid hare *à la royale*, marinated for days, then cooked in a concoction of red wine, puréed innards, and the hare's own blood. To finish, perhaps a slice of pear charlotte and a glass of the plum brandy called *vieille prune*.

———

The meal, one can be fairly safe in assuming, is pretty close to the one you would have eaten in the same restaurant in 1923, which is to say, when the nostalgists were busy eating the old-fashioned dinners they would later claim they couldn't find anymore. (À Sousceyrac was undoubtedly intended to induce deep nostalgia in Parisians the day it opened; its southwestern-inflected menu practically reads like a roster of what Frenchmen like to call The Patrimony.) The present proprietor, the grandson of the original owner, has himself been with the restaurant for forty years. The ruddy dewlaps on the customers have been well nurtured with goose fat and Armagnac. The dark wood is further darkened with nicotine; the wine list may be superficially rudimentary but seems well stocked with the sort of black-toned southern wines that go so well with this food. À Sousceyrac is also in its way, perhaps, perfect.

So is Le Petit Marguery, down near the carrefour des Gobelins, which is centered around a glassed-in diorama portraying a moth-eaten hunting ferret surrounded by giant mushrooms and battered copper pots. The restaurant, which has been run by the Cousin brothers for eighteen years, is also an old-fashioned bistro of plenty, populated with middle-aged locals who have the relaxed, satisfied air of people who have eaten well their entire lives and seem to have been looking forward to the exact details of the meal for weeks—hare, of course, and partridge, and bloody-rare slices of wild duck breast dusted simply with finely ground white pepper and fanned out over a mound of crunchy shredded cabbage moistened with sautéed foie gras.

In the fall, the Cousins serve an awe-inspiring sauté of woodsy wild mushrooms with garlic and a few pine needles for authenticity. The dish has a meaty intensity but is better, more complex, than mere animal flesh, a total breath of autumn in the forest: Crunchy and chewy, soft and stretchy, the different mushrooms parse themselves out in your mouth in a thousand different ways, like smoky, piney autumn air come to life.

There may be even more pleasure at Au Trou Gascon, a bastion of southwestern cooking in an obscure precinct of the Twelfth. Au Trou Gascon was apparently a hot address in the mid-'80s, the recipient of a level of attention not unlike that now being accorded to such reinvented bistros as La Régalade, when everybody crowded into the butter-yellow room with florid art nouveau moldings that seem to creep over half the ceiling to celebrate Alain Dutournier's cooking.

Dutournier has been at his very uptown Carré des Feuillants for a dozen years now, but Au Trou Gascon, which he has maintained, is a dream restaurant, all pheasant and cèpes and fat Chalosse chickens, steaming bowls of cassoulet whose fragrance is enough to drive you mad, succulent confit crisp enough to deafen you, and an encyclopedic selection of Bordeaux and Madirans. The cabbage-wrapped young partridge baked in pastry is almost a miracle of execution, buttery, oozing juice, and flawlessly, utterly crisp.

But the meal I had probably been most looking forward to on this trip was at L'Ami Louis, the battered, relentlessly old-fashioned bistro on a dingy street near the Musée des Arts et Métiers that has been a symbol of old-fashioned good times for Americans at least since James Beard started writing about the place fifty years ago, and whose roast chicken, foie gras, and garlic potato cake are in some circles as big an attraction as the Louvre.

L'Ami Louis probably does have the best snails in the world—sizzling hot, plump, drowned in garlicky butter—and formidable scallops *à la provençale.* And actress Neve Campbell was sitting right behind us, ready for action (though perhaps not for three-pound slabs of steak) in tight, low-cut black leather. But the refrigerator-cold slabs of foie gras, rimmed with yellow fat, were as appetizing as raw lard, and the duck was tough as a biker jacket. The huge *côte de boeuf,* as big a hunk of meat as you have ever seen that wasn't impaled on a meathook, had almost no flavor. And even the famous roast chicken didn't differ appreciably from its unfamous brethren all over town. La Régalade was better in almost every respect.

We all want to experience the Paris of Hemingway, of Picasso, of Baudelaire; we want to dine in Atget photographs, to sup on meals that Alice B. Toklas might have approved of, that Mère Poulard might have cooked. Americans are not alone in these fixations. When I walk out the door of my apartment building in Greenwich Village, the sidewalks are almost always crowded with French tourists bent over their guidebooks, trying to find Hart Crane's house or the bar where Dylan Thomas drank himself to death.

———

A friend recommended Chez Georges, a faded-looking place on a weary street near the newsrooms and wholesale decorator showrooms on the Place des Victoires. Chez Georges looks as if it might have come out of the pages of a Maigret novel: handwritten menu smeary and fading into purple, old mirrors darkening in blotches, leather banquettes, century-old ceiling moldings lumpy and misshapen with a zillion coats of paint. The tables are so close together that when someone needs to leave the banquette, practically everyone on that side of the restaurant stands up to allow her to pass, almost as if it were a row of seats in a movie theater.

I was happy, spooning a well-vinegared salad of *museau* (cattle snout) onto my plate from a big bowl the waitress had plopped on the table, plowing through a delicious plate of chops and fries, draining a bottle of Brouilly, looking hungrily at the great-looking *frisée aux lardons* at the next table, and contemplating the steak with shallots or grilled *andouillettes* I might have the next time I came in—until I glanced up from my plate and noticed that most of the other tables were filled with people who were no more working-class Parisian than me—journalists talking shop, decorators with their clients, a healthy subset of the sort of rich Texans (cowboy boots, big belt buckles, expensively dressed wives) that have been a cliché since at least the time when Mark Twain was an innocent abroad.

Ironically, the best bistro cooking reflects old-fashioned French values—values that the grand restaurants in grand, old-fashioned French spaces are barely permitted to embrace. Which brings us to my dinner at Le Cinq, in the newly renovated George V, an ornate hotel dining room that looks like the one every grand hotel in the United States once tried to copy: high ceilings, serene oil paintings, gilt everywhere, carts, gleaming silver domes, and perfected old-style tag-team service. In other words, everything the new bistro chefs are trying to escape.

———

The George V, of course, is famous as the hotel most beloved by Americans in the golden age of travel. The new owners apparently want to reinvent the place as a benchmark of ultraluxury, and the chef, Philippe Legendre, stolen from Taillevent in a famous raid, is amazingly assured, easily up to *Michelin* three-star level. (He had the stars for around a decade at Taillevent.) Legendre's cooking is modern, although unlike Gagnaire he is working in a recognizable idiom, definitely within the context of the three-star luxury meal. But as with Debussy, even when one of the melodies seems familiar, it's not as if you could leave the place humming the tune.

The first dish was Gagnaire-like, but also somehow not: a large, silver soupspoon containing a single warmed oyster, an incredibly fragrant slice of truffle, and a few grains of caviar. The truffle made the natural muskiness of the oyster blossom with loveliness, and the caviar brought out its deep-sea notes like a violin doubling the melody an octave above. There was a drizzle of foamed *beurre blanc,* which deepened the richness. The oyster had been gently warmed to that magic point where brininess was still the most prominent flavor, but the flesh had firmed just enough to make the internal bits slightly crunchy, like a rare scallop: an oyster amplified in all its components, heightened, but still an oyster. This one spoonful may have contained everything great about French cooking at its best. Under the spoon—a single bite, remember—was a sort of ravioli stuffed with a little more caviar, which functioned almost as a Talmudic commentary on the mouthful that had preceded it.

There was an extraordinary fricassee of Breton lobster, in which the tail, still in its shell, had been briefly sautéed, chopped into three hunks, and lowered into a sort of *beurre blanc,* sweetened with bits of chestnut, that gradually darkened into an intense lobster sauce as you dipped your spoon into it. The shell-on technique seemed fairly amazing, both as a way of getting you to interact with your entrée (sometimes in luxury restaurants it almost feels as if the food has been predigested for you) and as a way of adding to the flesh the special succulence that meat roasted on its bone always seems to have.

The captain cheerfully substituted for the scheduled lamb on the tasting menu the moment I indicated even a slight interest in game. And it was hare (it is always hare): *lièvre à la royale,* served under another bed of mashed potatoes, which was perhaps slightly lighter, more refined than anything you might find at a bistro but delicious in its genteel way. The glorious stink of the hare, almost dissolved into the glorious sauce, was all anyone could have asked for. And at this point, twenty days and maybe fifteen hares into my trip to Paris, I was asking a lot.

CHOCOLATE SOUFFLÉS
(*Adapted from Pierre Gagnaire*)

Serves 4 generously
Active time: 20 min   Start to finish: 40 min

The French, who invented soufflés, understand that the whole point is that everything that rises falls. Soufflés should not be overcooked; they should be slightly creamy in the middle.

- 2 tablespoons superfine granulated sugar plus additional for coating soup plates
- 4 oz Valrhona Caraïbe bittersweet (66%) chocolate, finely chopped
- 6 large egg yolks
- ½ tablespoon Cognac

7   large egg whites
⅛   teaspoon salt
Unsweetened cocoa powder for dusting

Special equipment: 4 (1½- to 2-cup) ovenproof soup plates
Accompaniments: pistachio ice cream, warm chocolate sauce, and
    caramelized nuts

Preheat oven to 400°F.

Butter inside of soup plates, then coat well with some superfine
sugar, knocking out excess. Chill plates.

Melt chocolate in a double boiler or a metal bowl set over a
saucepan of barely simmering water, stirring until smooth. Remove
bowl from pan.

Beat together yolks and Cognac in a large bowl with an electric
mixer at high speed until yolks are thick, pale, and form a ribbon when
beaters are lifted (about 4 minutes with a standing mixer or 7 minutes
with a handheld). Mix in chocolate at low speed.

Beat whites with salt in another large bowl with cleaned beaters at
medium speed until they just hold soft peaks. Gradually add remaining
2 tablespoons sugar, beating at medium speed, then beat at high speed
until whites just hold stiff peaks.

Stir one third of whites into chocolate mixture to lighten, then fold
in remaining whites gently but thoroughly in 2 batches. Divide among
soup plates and put 2 plates on each of 2 large baking sheets. Bake
soufflés in upper and lower thirds of oven until puffed and set, 12 to
14 minutes (soufflés on top rack may finish cooking first).

Lightly dust soufflés with cocoa and serve with accompaniments.

Cooks' note:
The eggs in this recipe may not be fully cooked, which could be of
concern if salmonella is a problem in your area.

PISTACHIO ICE CREAM
(*Pierre Gagnaire*)

Makes about 5 cups
Active time: 30 min   Start to finish: 5 hr

*Because the oil in the pistachio paste separates from the solids, it is necessary to
blend the contents of the entire can of paste in a food processor until it is creamy
and light in texture.*

4   large egg yolks
¼   cup sugar
1½ tablespoons water
2   tablespoons well-blended pistachio paste
1   cup chilled heavy cream

Special equipment: an instant-read thermometer

Beat together yolks, sugar, and water in a metal bowl set over a saucepan of simmering water with a handheld electric mixer at high speed until thick, pale, and registers 140°F on thermometer. Continue beating over simmering water, maintaining 140°F, 3 minutes more. Remove bowl from heat and gradually add pistachio paste, beating until incorporated. Chill until cold, about 15 minutes.

Beat cream with cleaned beaters until it just holds stiff peaks. Stir one third of cream into pistachio base to lighten, then fold in remaining cream gently but thoroughly. Scrape into an airtight container and freeze until firm, about 4 hours.

WARM CHOCOLATE SAUCE
(*Pierre Gagnaire*)

Makes about ¾ cup
Active time: 10 min   Start to finish: 10 min
  2   oz Valrhona Caraïbe bittersweet (66%) chocolate, finely
      chopped
  ½ cup heavy cream

Put chocolate in a bowl. Bring cream to a boil in a small saucepan, then pour over chocolate and whisk until smooth. Keep warm, covered, until ready to serve.

CARAMELIZED NUTS
(*Pierre Gagnaire*)

Makes about 2½ cups
Active time: 20 min   Start to finish: 45 min

The coating on these nuts is wonderfully delicate, and the method couldn't be simpler.

  ½ cup hazelnuts (2 oz)
  ½ cup blanched almonds (2 oz)

½ cup unsalted roasted cashews (2 oz)
½ cup whole pecans (2 oz)
½ cup whole walnuts (2 oz)
Vegetable oil for greasing foil
¼ cup sugar
¼ cup water
1½ tablespoons honey

Preheat oven to 350°F. Toast hazelnuts in a shallow baking pan until fragrant and a shade darker, about 8 minutes.

When hazelnuts are cool enough to handle, wrap in a kitchen towel and rub to remove skins. (Not all skins will come off.) Transfer hazelnuts to a large bowl with almonds, cashews, pecans, and walnuts. Line baking pan with foil and lightly oil.

Bring sugar, water, and honey to a boil in a small saucepan over moderate heat, stirring until sugar is dissolved. Pour over nuts and stir until nuts are well coated. Transfer nuts with a slotted spoon to baking pan (discarding syrup) and roast in 1 layer in middle of oven, stirring and redistributing nuts occasionally, until golden brown, 10 to 12 minutes.

Lightly oil another sheet of foil and put on a work surface. Spread nuts in 1 layer on foil and cool completely. Break apart any nuts that are stuck together.

Cooks' note:
Candied nuts can be made 1 week ahead and kept in an airtight container at room temperature.

March 2001

THE NEW FACE OF PARIS

Paul Goldberger

In Paris, the writer Françoise Sagan once observed, the past was ever present; you could not escape it. For all its beauty, the city could sometimes be stifling, which is why Sagan, like so many Parisians in the 1950s and '60s, looked across the Atlantic for a sense of the new. "The French are the spoiled children of history, and the Americans are its resourceful orphans," she declared.

That was then, and this is now. The days when Paris felt like a Belle Epoque theme park have been over for a while, but today, forty years after Sagan made that remark, Paris is less in the grip of its past than ever before. The Paris that everyone knows, the extraordinary city of old buildings, streets, parks, and monuments that make up the most sensual urban fabric in the world, isn't gone, and it isn't even terribly different. But it is no longer the inhibiting force it once was. What has changed is the way that the Paris we all carry around in our heads no longer makes architects afraid to design new and different things. All of that history that weighed so heavily on creativity now seems to have the opposite effect. There is more of a sense of adventure, more sheer modernist exuberance, in the public architecture of Paris right now than in that of any city in the United States.

It isn't just a matter of great modernist monuments, like the Centre

Pompidou and the pyramid at the Louvre, or the immense and odd Grande Arche de la Défense, a 362-foot-high hollowed-out cube. But they set a tone that has now shown up in things as small as phone booths, bus shelters, and the design of the *métro*, and as large as new and innovative parks along the edges of the city. Most of these places are far off the tourist route (though the phone booths and bus shelters are everywhere), and they don't so much change the fabled image of Paris as coexist beside it. The new architecture and design that have come increasingly to define the public realm in Paris have created a setting for the routines of daily life that is far more connected to the twentieth century—or the twenty-first. Almost no other city in the world can make that claim.

Where else, after all, would you walk your dog past a sleek, white office building housing a television network to enter a park that is designed with abstract structures of concrete and monumental glass houses? Nowhere, I suspect, but in the Fifteenth Arrondissement, in the southwest corner of Paris, where Richard Meier's headquarters for Canal Plus sits beside the entrance to the Parc André-Citroën, the site of a former automobile factory that has been turned into a kind of thirty-five-acre shrine to avant-garde landscape design. You wouldn't see either one of those places in New York, let alone both of them.

So, too, with the glass phone booths, refined little structures that are light, crisp, and simple, or the sleek new traffic lights on the Champs-Élysées, or the freestanding structures of corrugated metal containing public toilets, or the fully automated cars with all-glass fronts on the new Météor line of the *métro*, where station platforms are separated from the tracks by glass walls that silently slide away after a train arrives. There's nothing that radical about any of these things, but they wouldn't get past the bureaucracy almost anywhere else, and when you look at them together, they give you the sense that in Paris the design of public places is taken as seriously as the making of public policy.

———

On one level, that's always been the case. After all, this is the city that once commissioned Hector Guimard to design those extraordinary art nouveau arches—nearly as much a symbol of Paris as the Eiffel

Tower—to serve as entrances to the *métro*, and that was about as avant-garde as you could get at the turn of the last century. Probably those round, green kiosks with the pointy domes, which confer a certain majesty on even the most routine posters and public announcements, were ahead of their time at some point, too. Public places here aren't just highly styled, they're inventive and different.

Parisians, who have always cared what things look like, have always believed in the grandeur of the public realm and in the ability of small, everyday things to affect the quality of life. Tiny details as much as great gestures have defined the look of Paris for more than a century: The street signs on the corners of buildings shape our sense of the city as much as the sweep of the Place de la Concorde; the rattan seats and tiny tables of the cafés work their way into our unconscious as much as the awesome scale of the Arc de Triomphe.

But for a long time—the years between World War II and the 1970s—nostalgia seemed to dominate creative energy, as if Parisians, or at least the architects who worked for them, feared that the cityscape that everyone so loved was too fragile to take on anything new, that it could only be respected by being preserved in aspic. But it was the worst kind of respect, since it implied that the image of the city was too frail to handle any change, a delicate flower that could not be expected to renew itself. And it suggested that the best future for the city was to freeze itself in time.

In some ways, you couldn't blame people for thinking like that. What modernism there was in Paris during those years wasn't the brilliant, cutting-edge work of great architects like Le Corbusier or Jean Prouve, but structures like the Tour Maine-Montparnasse, or the clusters of office buildings at La Défense and Front de Seine, clunky projects that had none of the grace, not to mention the sophisticated urbanism, that makes Paris what it is. When the Maine-Montparnasse skyscraper went up on the Left Bank, it made you wonder if the French, operating out of either cynicism or deviousness, hadn't decided that the best way to show the world what they thought of America was to knock off the very worst of our architecture.

It was the Centre Pompidou, I think, that began to give modernism a good name in Paris. Nothing changed overnight in 1977, when

Renzo Piano and Richard Rogers's extraordinary high-tech cartoon of a building was finished—there would still be that awful underground shopping mall at Les Halles, suggesting that the French hadn't quite finished copying American mistakes—but finally there was a contemporary building people were talking about in Paris that didn't seem to have been put up to destroy the image of the city that everyone loved.

———

Then came Mitterrand's Grands Projets, like I. M. Pei's pyramid at the Louvre, which emerged from the belief that it was possible to create a modern equivalent to the monumental architecture that gives the city its opulent grandeur. Not all the Grands Projets turned out quite as successfully as the pyramid; almost no one, for example, has a good word for the ruthlessly nonfunctional new Bibliothèque Nationale. But at least Dominique Perrault's design, which places books in four glass towers, doesn't look like another refugee from midtown Manhattan. And the message these buildings sent as a group could not have been more clear: The new, the different, and even the experimental were to be encouraged at the very highest levels.

That is surely why the new office structure put up to house Paris municipal employees on the Quai de la Rapée beside the Seine, which was designed by Aymeric Zublena and opened in the early 1990s, doesn't look like a typical office building but rather like a sleeker, even more high-tech version of the Centre Pompidou. Its main feature is an immense glass wall, seven stories high, that slides across the façade to open up the building for business each morning. Not quite as striking, but nearly as refined, is the nearby office building for the *métro* system, a crisp structure of glass and steel that is the perfect headquarters for the kind of subway whose new lines celebrate sleekness.

One of the most ambitious of the Grands Projets, if not one of the most beloved, is Bernard Tschumi's Parc de la Villette, in the northeast corner of Paris, an attempt to create a park that would express the complex realities, not to say the disconnections, of contemporary life. Tschumi eschewed picturesque landscaping in favor of a series of red-painted metal objects he called follies, which are open-framework structures that look vaguely like Cubist sculptures. The park is considered one of the high points of the deconstructivist movement in architecture, and if it came across more like a self-indulgent statement of architectural theory than a park that encouraged relaxation, it led the way to the more successful Parc André-Citroën, designed by landscape artists Alain Provost and Gilles Clément with architects Jean-Paul Viguier, Jean-François Jodry, and Patrick Berger. This time, the French tendency toward intellectualizing landscape design yielded something monumental, strikingly beautiful, and eminently usable, a park that both honors the French tradition of grand, formal open axial vistas (think Versailles) and goes beyond it to create a whole series of different kinds of landscape experiences into which a series of simple modernist structures are set. There is no illusion of rural naturalness here; this park belongs firmly in the French tradition of trying to order the world. As in the best work of Lenôtre, Parc André-Citroën manages to be both rigid in its order and deeply sensual in its form; it is a kind of miniature city of landscapes, utterly urban and yet in no way looking like the city.

Nearly as powerful in the way in which it uses landscape to enlarge the notion of urban experience is another project by Patrick Berger, the Promenade Plantée (also known as the Viaduc des Arts), on the Avenue Daumesnil, an abandoned elevated rail line that has been turned into a lushly planted, elevated walkway that runs through a whole neighborhood at the eastern edge of the city, just beyond the Opéra Bastille, another of the Grands Projets. It is a linear garden, a spectacular example of urban reclamation both on top, where the landscaped promenade gives you a sense that you are hovering over the city, and below, where the arches under the viaduct have been turned into antiques shops and restaurants. To walk on the Promenade Plantée is both to escape the city and to celebrate it.

The best thing about both of these new public places is the way in which they fit so neatly into Paris even as they completely reinvent the notion of the urban park. The newest architecture does the same thing and stands in total contrast to the modern buildings of the pre–Centre Pompidou years, which were entirely indifferent to the old urban fabric. The best new buildings fit in not by imitating the old but by respecting what really matters in Paris—the scale, the rich texture, and the orientation to the street.

A splendid new series of buildings throughout Paris includes neighborhood post offices and on-site housing for the postal employees. One such complex, by Frédéric Borel on the rue Oberkampf, is an intense combination of solids and voids that seems at once like a piece of abstract sculpture and a Cubist essay on the Parisian streetscape. At one of the smaller post offices, on the rue Castex, at the edge of the Marais, just before Place de la Bastille, a wonderful art moderne façade from a 1935 post office was retained and a new building incorporating the housing was built behind it.

All of the ambitions behind the new public architecture of Paris come together in Jean Nouvel's Fondation Cartier, a gallery and headquarters for a cultural foundation on the boulevard Raspail in the Fourteenth Arrondissement. It is a glass box of exceptional elegance and lightness that is fronted by a series of glass walls that stand out at the sidewalk, like transparent fences. Between the walls and the building itself is a lush, somewhat untamed landscape that plays off against the glass. The whole setting is an essay in ambiguity, blurring the distinction between inside and outside, solid and void, material and ethereal. The building is monumental and grand, and yet it appears not to be earthbound at all but to be floating magically, transcendent like Paris itself.

March 2001

The Three Musketeers

Patric Kuh

It was morning in Paris. In the cafés there was the hiss of milk being steamed for *petits crèmes*. By the Sèvres-Babylone *métro* entrance, in the Sixth Arrondissement, a city worker, in green uniform, hosed down the pavement, and two exquisitely dressed school-going children turned to wave to *Maman,* who was standing on the balcony of their apartment. Close by, where the rue d'Assas meets the rue du Cherche-Midi, in the second-floor kitchen of Restaurant Hélène Darroze, three chefs—Ariane Daguin, Anne-Sophie Pic, and Hélène Darroze, the restaurant's owner—gathered to prepare a dinner that would stand as a testament to the two separate major influences on their careers.

The first was the culinary custom of the Mères Cuisinières. In a profoundly late-nineteenth- and early-twentieth-century tradition, women, often working at coal-burning stoves, usually a long way from Paris, introduced a simmered, domestic note into the rigors of French gastronomy. By remaining at the family restaurant for their entire careers, these women came to define the very place in which they labored, just as Mère Blanc did for the tiny hamlet of Vonnas, in the Bresse.

Juxtaposed with this continuity, the trajectories that had brought two of these three chefs and businesswomen to Darroze's kitchen seemed like a study in contrasts. Mère Blanc, after all, never traveled to Paris with three assistants and two huge blue ice chests on the upper deck of the TGV. Mère Brazier never tipped a porter in Newark Airport to carry her seventy-eight-pound Styrofoam container of foie gras. And Mère Adrienne surely never welcomed anyone to her Montmartre restaurant wearing deck shoes and a valentine Swatch, and carrying a red cell phone that played Vivaldi when it rang.

—

The second major influence brought matters closer to home. The three women, ranging in age from thirty-three to forty-four, were all daughters of famed chefs, and the dinner, to which leading gastronomes, selected purveyors, château owners, journalists, and Mère Brazier's granddaughter Jacotte had been invited, was also intended to be a tip of the toque to their fathers. The legacy of the Mères may have been elusive, but this one was concrete. Culinary traditions are passed on from generation to generation, though here there was a twist. Neither André Daguin nor Francis Darroze, who would be guests at the dinner, nor Jacques Pic, who died in 1992, had encouraged their daughters to pursue a career in cooking. But they had. When you're a cook's child, you get restaurants through the pores. You live by the tempo of a kitchen without being in one—the hour you play with your parent is between lunch and dinner, and the grazing good-night kiss that shouldn't wake you comes at midnight. These women had gone out into the world, into different fields of study, only to find that their passion lay, as it had for their fathers, at the professional stove.

So there was both a maternal and a paternal side to the evening. Together, they represented a formidable undertaking. If the three women seemed somewhat sanguine, it may have been that as the daughters, granddaughters, and great-granddaughters of chefs, they understood that, in cooking, the greatest acknowledgment is getting a dish right. The three chefs, together with the assembled *brigade*, were intent on doing just that.

The kitchen itself was set up in the traditional French way, around a stove where cooks have visual contact with each other at all times. Just now, though, they had their backs to it as they worked. A young Greek helped Daguin stuff prunes marinated in Armagnac with foie gras mousse; Keren, from Jerusalem, cleaned gooseneck barnacles; and Sarah, from Poitiers, cut the chorizo made by Pierre Oteiza from free-range pigs that roam the Basque country eating chestnuts. The newest arrival cooked spinach for the staff lunch, nervously lifting it with a spider into a bath of ice water; a much more assured young man, who would soon be leaving for Michel Rostang's restaurant on Anguilla, seared pigeons that had been marinated in olive oil and *piments d'Espelette* on an old freestanding grill.

This magnificent piece of equipment, with twin flues and the manufacturer's name embossed on its shutters, had been brought up from the Darroze restaurant in the Landes when it closed in 1999. "In winter there, it's dead these days," Hélène Darroze said as she tried to explain the closing of a restaurant that had been owned by the same family for generations. With its burning coals, the grill seemed a monument to a France that no longer existed, for it conjured a time when restaurants depended, not on seasonal visits from international gastronomes, but on the itineraries of the traveling salesmen known as VRPs.

These salesmen (*voyageurs représentants placiers*) headed out on Monday morning and returned home on Friday night. The prestige of the restaurants that lined the roads they traveled are proof of the quality they expected. Hostellerie de la Poste, Hôtel de la Côte d'Or, and Lameloise lined Route Nationale 6; Point and Pic took care of Route Nationale 7. As Ariane Daguin spread foie gras mousse over cured duck breast, she recalled the bargains they expected, and how they played one restaurant against the other. "The salesmen would say, 'Hey, the coffee is included chez Daguin,' or 'At Darroze, they *give* you the Armagnac.' "

Those were the days when Daguin's grandmother took over the central courtyard of the Hôtel de France once a year. She would set up pans and cauldrons, and all the local farmers would bring their cèpes. The farmers would sell them, and the grandmother spent the day sautéing and putting them up in Mason jars to use until cèpe season came around again.

As such rituals were left behind, the past in which they had occurred took on a certain luminosity, creating an indefinable, bucolic image of the nation that the French warm to easily. Because the theme of the evening and the names involved brought it into graspable focus, the dinner had garnered a lot of media attention, including a crew from France 3 television.

From one point of view, the unapologetic promotional goals of the evening had already been achieved. But the charged atmosphere constituted the total opposite of what cooking can mean, and that tension seemed particularly acute for Darroze's chef, Jean-Marie Baudic. A veteran of Pierre Gagnaire's restaurant, he was about to open a restaurant of his own in his native Brittany. This was clearly the meal against which whoever succeeded him would be measured. For Baudic, the dinner was a succession of tiny details he carried in his head, and not one of them was going to get lost.

In between herding his blue-aproned corps from one task to the next, he prepared one dish for which he took a special responsibility: poached salt cod that would be served with cockles, the gooseneck barnacles, the chorizo from Basque pigs, and *piquillos* in cast-iron casseroles. His job now was to prepare the poaching oil. In a large copper *sautoir* he heated about three inches of olive oil, enough to brown a few handfuls of garlic slivers. This was simply to perfume. When it had cooled a little, he threw in bay leaves and sprigs of thyme, which would infuse the cooling oil for the rest of the afternoon. The *morue*— lovely thick, white fillets—was from Martín Berasategui, the *Michelin* three-star chef near San Sebastián. "I'll poach it slowly," Baudic said, his hands moving gently, like a conductor leading an orchestra through the most pianissimo of passages. "Just on trays above the stove, until it's all infused and the fish is *à la nacre*."

The term describes the color of mother-of-pearl. It is precisely the color that perfectly cooked salt cod should be, and in using it Baudic touched both on the infinitesimal gradations of temperature on which great cooking depends and on the central paradox of the evening: Nothing may be as timeless as French culture, but nothing is as time-dependent as French cuisine. As a cook, he had his priorities right. Later that night, evoking the eternal glories of poplar-lined roads would be of no use if this beautiful cod wasn't served pearly white.

———

By six P.M., the kitchen was working at a quickened pace, and faces became slightly drawn. The sommeliers had whole cases of various white wines opened on the kitchen counter. They tasted each bottle to see if it was corked, using ice buckets as spittoons. Cooks did what cooks always do before big events—they ran the execution of dishes through their heads and stashed towels. Baudic looked approvingly at a metal tub filled with pigeon blood, made from the liquefied hearts and livers. The deep color would be good for the final sauce. "The pigeons were strangled," he said, playfully testing the limits of a visitor's curiosity. "It means their organs stay filled with blood."

Darroze's parents had arrived. Her mother had been set up in the dining room with an iron and the long white aprons with seven blue stripes (representing the seven provinces of the Basque country) that the cooks would don at the end of the meal. She ironed them while trading salty stories with Daguin. In a suit and tie, Francis Darroze waited in his daughter's cubbyhole office and reminisced a little. He remembered doing the tasting rounds with Frank Schoonmaker, and he remembered, laughing, how his father got ortolans past U.S. customs for Henri Soulé to serve at Le Pavillon. Then he looked at the cooks working. "I don't come into the kitchen often anymore," he said. "One feels powerless." He shrugged, "*Eh bien,* one cooks at home."

But the emotion reached its most affecting point when a portrait was taken. Daguin and Darroze were able to get close against their fathers, and Pic had brought a portrait of her father to be part of the picture. Perhaps it was the proximity—for what cook's child has not smelled the perspiration coming through their parent's vest, sensed the exhaustion when they are brought up onto their laps—but though she tried not to, she stepped away crying. She composed herself. She sat back down and held the portrait. André Daguin reached over, brushing her cheek paternally, and said what one who has kept an inn for seven generations says to one who's the fourth generation of hers. "How was your season?" She knew he was saying, "We're with you." And she smiled, and the shot was taken.

It might be said that when the evening was at its most impossible moment—when the emotions of cooking seemed like something that should never have been touched, that they should never even be spoken about, that one should simply cook and get it right and shut up— it was saved by what threatened to doom it. While the picture was being taken, Baudic had given his troops last-minute instructions.

Some went down to the first-floor dining room to send out the hors d'oeuvres. Among them was *escaoutoun,* a sort of corn gruel that was topped with a slice of sautéed cèpe and served in Chinese soupspoons. The moment those cèpes hit the duck fat in the hot pans, a perfumed link with the past was forged.

What followed was a dinner that never succumbed to mimicry and never became contrived, because each woman was true to her own culinary vision. For Anne-Sophie Pic, it was the laserlike precision with which she laid lozenges of tomato aspic over marinated tuna and roasted off firm, plump langoustines on a *plancha,* coupling them with a chutney of Rhône Valley peaches. For Ariane Daguin, it was her American foie gras. She separated the lobes into dented roasting trays, salted and roasted them off, then plated them sliced with caramelized figs and a *sauce au Jurançon.* Hélène Darroze changed into a pair of Le Coq Sportif white aikido shoes that completed the jai alai look of her white outfit. Her cooking style pushes her native Landes down through Gascony, into the Basque country, and far into Spain, like a spindle that draws thread onto itself.

———

While Darroze expedited, Baudic made sure that the dishes went out as she wanted them to. This was the moment for the salt cod. He ladled the oil over the portioned pieces and watched while they cooked in the trays. Around him, his team moved as one, rocking the casseroles back and forth on the stovetop to open the cockles. Then a piece of cod was placed in among the barnacles, *piquillos,* and chorizo. The last thing Baudic did before closing the lids was to add some of the cooking oil, which was now infused with cod juices. Darroze's other main course was the pigeons, which were finished over the coals of the old grill. At the same time, a small metal funnel with a long handle was heated in the embers, and at the last moment a cook crammed back fat into it so that it sizzled and melted over the pigeons. They were served with a quick-sautéed ragout of *cogollos* (lettuce hearts) and *bellota* ham from southwest Spain, and accompanied by an '82 Lynch-Bages.

There was no stopping now; it was on to the cheeses, Picodons and Basque *brebis,* with a *confiture* of black cherries from Marie Quatrehomme, followed by desserts—a croustade with roasted Mirabelle plums and prune Armagnac ice cream from Daguin, transparent layers of cooked sugar over *fraises des bois* from Pic, and chocolate *café liégeois* in brandy snifters from Darroze, whose father dug deep into the legendary family vaults for a 1936 Armagnac.

Then it was time to honor the cooks. The clean aprons were brought out and placed on the long kitchen counter, and Baudic wanted everyone to also wear a neckerchief in the traditional chef's way. Only a few knew how to tie them, but that didn't matter: The values that had been transmitted in this kitchen tonight went deeper than that. And then Benoît, the pâtissier, remembered the apprentice who was frying the beignets that were served with the coffee and truffles, and he called down on the speakerphone for him to get his butt up there, and Pic found her patent leather shoes. Gathered together, their achievement became clear. They had defied the constraints of the present, run out along the razor's edge of sentiment, and cooked their way to the little France, to what is known as *le pays,* an area that can encompass the distance between two village steeples, a place where an old farmer with a frayed checked shirt buttoned all the way to the top might be called Père, and where a woman who keeps a restaurant might be called Mère. It was twelve-thirty, and Paris was dark. They filed out toward the applause and their aprons were perfectly pressed.

December 2002

It's What's for Dinner

François Simon

Whenever I read an article on my hometown in a foreign periodical, I feel like I'm living in a dream, a beautiful dream, so charming, but, like Peter Mayle's vision of Provence, a frozen time capsule of French life before 1960.

I discover that, like all Parisians, I am supposed to drop by the market every morning before seeking out the flakiest croissants at my favorite *boulangerie,* take pastis before lunch, and then spend three lazy hours over a sumptuous meal attended by a team of waiters whose only concern is my culinary well-being. Perhaps before heading home I'm to run across Paris to find the most sublime cheeses to serve after dinner.

Food is a delicious lie that makes us believe life is heaven. Want the truth? Then follow me to the Marché d'Aligre, just five minutes from my apartment in the Bastille, on a Sunday morning. Unfortunately, the yuppie couple next door won't be coming with us. They hate the market, preferring pizza and takeout from the local *traiteur.* Judging by their trash, they'd rather drink than eat anyway. To make things easier, I've broken Sunday morning down as follows: Twenty-five percent of all Parisians are crazy about good food and are roaming the markets in search of it; another quarter couldn't care less; a further 25 percent are on a perpetual diet; and the remainder are enjoying their *grasse matinée*—a nice late sleep.

Do join me and some of my neighbors, though, as we shop. There's María, who will be grilling sardines for her Portuguese family this afternoon. And Ahmed. He's having friends in for couscous later. All of us are groaning about the mushy apples, the watery tomatoes, and the tired old fish. Yes, there are excellent purveyors here, but we'll have to seek them out—dare I say it?—just as in every other city in the world.

Let's walk a little farther. We'll pass a long line at McDonald's and a sad bachelor walking into Picard Surgelés, a ubiquitous chain of stores dispensing frozen food. Yet even here things aren't what they seem; there are excellent shrimp today, for example, better than those I saw at the *poissonnerie* earlier. And, thank heaven, nearby is À Sousceyrac, a classic old bistro that's filling up fast for Sunday lunch. Let's pop in. A wide selection of the Paris bourgeoisie is already comfortably seated. They start with a *coupe de Champagne*, followed by foie gras, then roast quail and sautéed potatoes, cheese, Grand Marnier soufflé, some *café*, an Armagnac. All the women have apparently gone to the same hairdresser, the men to the same tailor. I once heard that a man was so subdued by his sumptuous meal that he slid slowly off the leather banquette and disappeared forever.

Not long ago, everyone knew where to go for Sunday lunch and the right spot for a special occasion. Like shoes lined up in a closet, you simply picked the appropriate pair. Nothing is that simple anymore; the choices are staggering. Sushi anyone?

Everything changed dramatically in Paris after the student uprisings of May 1968, although the foreign publications may not have noticed. Don't look for the French housewife, slaving over the stove in her kitchen. Madame has gone off to work. Countless French mothers, it seems, have actually forgotten to pass on the recipes that they dutifully learned from their mothers. Oops. Sound familiar?

Right now, Paris has never been so open to new food. And Parisians, especially the young, aren't that interested in long, fussy meals anymore. They aren't even demanding good food. They crave a scene. To accommodate those who would rather hang out than eat well, a new style of restaurant has grown up.

"It's silly to expect a gastronomic demonstration at every Parisian table," says Jean-Louis Costes, who, with his brother, Gilbert, runs some of the hippest restaurants in Paris—Georges, Café Ruc, L'Esplanade. "To eat as a gourmet in Paris these days is considered almost obscene."

In the end, I'm grateful for all of our remaining three-star temples of gastronomy. After a superb dinner recently at one such place, an American friend proclaimed: "Paris is still the gastronomic capital of the world. It must be true."

"It is," I said. Then we clinked our glasses of Champagne.

March 2001

Notes on Contributors

Naomi Barry wrote for the *International Herald Tribune* from Paris and contributed regularly to *Gourmet*.

Hilaire du Berrier was active in the French Intelligence Service during World War II.

George Bijur was a prominent figure in the advertising community in New York City.

Louis Diat popularized French cooking both in *Gourmet* columns and in cookbooks, including *Cooking à la Ritz* and *Gourmet's Basic French Cookbook*.

Don Dresden was a journalist who lived in Paris both before and after World War II.

Jonathan Gold joined *Gourmet* as a restaurant critic and contributing editor in 1999. Prior to that he reviewed restaurants for the *Los Angeles Times*.

Paul Goldberger is the architecture critic for *The New Yorker*. While at *The New York Times*, he won a Pulitzer Prize for criticism.

Diane Johnson's novels *Le Divorce, Le Mariage*, and *L'Affaire* are set in France.

Alaire Johnston was a contributor to *Gourmet* in the 1960s.

JUDITH JONES is an editor at Alfred A. Knopf in New York, where she has published the works of Julia Child, Marion Cunningham, and James Beard. Her late husband, EVAN JONES, was the author of *American Food: The Gastronomic Story* and *The World of Cheese.* The couple collaborated on *The Book of Bread* and *The L. L. Bean Book of New New England Cooking.*

PATRIC KUH is a former restaurant critic and the author of *The Last Days of Haute Cuisine: America's Culinary Revolution.*

IRENE CORBALLY KUHN served as a foreign correspondent for newspapers in Singapore and the Far East during the 1920s.

LILLIAN LANGSETH-CHRISTENSEN was a travel writer and the author of several books, including *How to Present and Serve Food Attractively* and *The Instant Epicure.*

MICHAEL LEWIS lives in Berkeley, California. He is the author of several books, including *Liar's Poker, The New New Thing,* and *Moneyball.*

FRANK J. PRIAL is currently the wine critic for *The New York Times* and is the author of *Decantations: Reflections on Wine by The New York Times Wine Critic.*

FRANÇOIS SIMON specializes in food and travel writing for *Le Figaro* in Paris.

JOSEPH WECHSBERG was a Czechoslovakian-born journalist, a violinist, and the author of a dozen books, including *Blue Trout and Black Truffles.*

ABOUT THE EDITOR

RUTH REICHL, former restaurant critic of *New West* magazine, *California* magazine, the *Los Angeles Times*, and *The New York Times*, is now editor in chief of *Gourmet* magazine. She is also the author of the bestselling memoirs *Tender at the Bone* and *Comfort Me with Apples*. Reichl lives in Manhattan with her husband, her son, and two cats.

A Note on the Type

The principal text of this Modern Library edition
was set in a digitized version of Janson, a typeface that
dates from about 1690 and was cut by Nicholas Kis,
a Hungarian working in Amsterdam. The original matrices have
survived and are held by the Stempel foundry in Germany.
Hermann Zapf redesigned some of the weights and sizes for
Stempel, basing his revisions on the original design.